Agency and Participation in
Childhood and Youth

Also Available From Bloomsbury

Aspirations, Education and Social Justice: Applying Sen and Bourdieu,
Caroline Sarojini Hart
*Justice and Equality in Education: A Capability Perspective on Disability and
Special Educational Needs*, Lorella Terzi
Children as Decision Makers in Education: Sharing Experiences Across Cultures,
Anna Robinson-Pant, Caroline Dyer, Michele Schweisfurth and Sue Cox

Agency and Participation in Childhood and Youth

International Applications of the Capability Approach in Schools and Beyond

Edited by Caroline Sarojini Hart, Mario Biggeri and Bernhard Babic

Bloomsbury Academic
An imprint of Bloomsbury Publishing Plc

B L O O M S B U R Y
LONDON · OXFORD · NEW YORK · NEW DELHI · SYDNEY

Bloomsbury Academic

An imprint of Bloomsbury Publishing Plc

50 Bedford Square	1385 Broadway
London	New York
WC1B 3DP	NY 10018
UK	USA

www.bloomsbury.com

BLOOMSBURY and the Diana logo are trademarks of Bloomsbury Publishing Plc

First published 2014
Paperback edition first published 2015

British Library Cataloguing-in-Publication Data
A catalogue record for this book is available from the British Library.

ISBN: HB: 978-1-4725-1487-5
PB: 978-1-4742-5288-1
ePDF: 978-1-4725-1000-6
ePub: 978-1-4725-1486-8

Library of Congress Cataloging-in-Publication Data
A catalog record for this book is available from the Library of Congress

Typeset by RefineCatch Limited, Bungay, Suffolk

All royalties from the sale of this book will be donated to the international charities Children in Crisis and SOS Children's Villages UK.

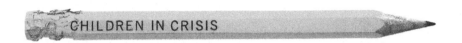

Children in Crisis protects and educates children facing the toughest hardships, in countries affected by conflict or political instability. Through education we improve children's life chances and future earnings, unite communities and build peace. Through adult education and income generation we support families and communities to sustain their children's education. For further information go to www.childrenincrisis.org.

SOS Children's Villages UK is a global charity which provides orphans and vulnerable children with a stable and positive family life. The charity protects and improves the lives of children around the world, working with communities to keep fragmenting families together, and where this is not possible, building new families for children at risk. For further information go to www.soschildren.org and see also www.sos-childrensvillages.org.

Contents

List of Tables and Figures   ix

List of Contributors   xi

Acknowledgements   xvii

Introduction   1
Caroline Sarojini Hart

Part 1   Agency and Participation in Childhood and Youth   15

1   The Capability Approach and Educational Research
     Caroline Sarojini Hart   17
2   Education Policy for Agency and Participation *Mario Biggeri*   44
3   The Capability Approach and Children's Rights *Daniel Stoecklin
     and Jean-Michel Bonvin*   63
4   Agency, Participation and Youth Inequalities *Zoë Clark*   83
5   Child Poverty from a Capability Perspective *Ortrud Leßmann*   101

Part 2   Developing Agency and Capabilities in Schools and Beyond   121

6   Pedagogies to Develop Children's Agency in Schools
     Marina Santi and Diego Di Masi   123
7   Education and the Capabilities of Children with Special Needs
     Cristina Devecchi, Richard Rose and Michael Shevlin   145
8   Evaluating Children's Capabilities Enhancement in Schools
     John Schischka   163
9   Agency, Participation and Transitions Beyond School
     Caroline Sarojini Hart   181
10   School Enrolment and Child Labour *Zina Nimeh and
     Robert Bauchmüller*   204

11 Children's Autonomy in Conflict-affected Countries
    Jérôme Ballet, Claudine Dumbi and Benoît Lallau   225
12 Youth Agency and Participation Outside the Classroom
    Vittorio Iervese and Luisa Tuttolomondo   243

    Concluding Remarks
    Caroline Sarojini Hart, Mario Biggeri and Bernhard Babic   260

Subject Index   265
Author Index   270

List of Tables and Figures

Tables

1.1	Summary of key issues for research using a capability approach	29
1.2	Checklist of key questions for research with children using a capability approach	38
2.1	The human capital and human capabilities models: education elements, policy and outcomes	47
3.1	Young people interviewed according to the types of participatory projects	74
4.1	Distribution of relevant demographic factors	90
6.1	Procedural dimensions of a philosophical enquiry	137
10.1	Jordan's non-enrolment rates for children at compulsory schooling age	210
10.2	Reasons for not enrolling or dropping out of school	211
10.3	Child labour incidence in Jordan	213
10.4	Logistics regression results, 2003	215
12.1	Abbreviations and symbols used for transcription of collected materials	249

Figures

1.1	TASC wheel	35
2.1	Capability approach framework, evolving capabilities and the role of education	48
2.2	Creating capabilities: education for enhancing children's capabilities, agency and participation	54
3.1	The 'actor's system'	71

4.1   Modified 'endless pathways of functionings and capabilities'   87
4.2   Structured youthfulness   92
5.1   Resources, conversion factors and the capability set   108
9.1   Model of aspiration formation and transformation to capability   184

List of Contributors

Bernhard Babic graduated in educational science and started as a scientific assistant at the University of Eichstätt, Germany. From there he left to work as a lecturer and researcher at Ludwig Maximilian's University in Munich, Germany. Thereafter he joined the German Youth Institute as a scientific expert for 'strategies and concepts of external evaluation in child and youth care' within a project sponsored by the German Federal Ministry for Families, Senior Citizens, Women and Youth. Later, as a research adviser and project manager at SOS Children's Villages International, he gained experience in the field of international social development. As a senior project manager and contact person for European Affairs at Caritas in Bamberg, Germany, he expanded his expertise on social work-related aspects of elderly care. Since 2013 he has held a senior lectureship in social work at Salzburg University of Applied Sciences, Austria.

Jérôme Ballet is Senior Lecturer in Economics at the University of Versailles St Quentin en Yvelines and a researcher at the Institut de recherche pour le développement, UMI Resiliences, France. He recently led a research programme on child poverty in Mauritania and Madagascar. He works mainly on child poverty, ethics and economics. He is published widely in journals such as *Children and Youth Services Review, Child Abuse Review, Child Abuse & Neglect* and *Population*, among others. He is also editor of the review *Ethics and Economics*.

Robert Bauchmüller pursued higher and postgraduate education at Maastricht University, the Netherlands, and made several research visits to other academic institutions across Europe. He holds an MSc in Economics and obtained a PhD in Public Policy and Policy Analysis, his dissertation being entitled *Investing in Early Childhood Care and Education: The Impact of Quality on Inequality*. He has attended, and presented his research at, several international conferences and seminars. Since 2011, he has been employed at the Center of Excellence in Finance in Ljubljana, Slovenia, which promotes learning and regional cooperation in public financial management and central banking to countries across south-east Europe.

Mario Biggeri is Associate Professor in Development Economics at the Department of Economics and Management, University of Florence, Italy. He is Fellow of the Human Development and Capability Association (HDCA) and co-director of the Thematic Group on Children's Capabilities. He has worked for other international UN agencies including UNICEF at the Innocenti Research Centre (IRC), Florence, Italy for three years. He is the Scientific Director of ARCO-Action Research for CO-development Lab of the University of Florence, Italy. He has been scientific coordinator of several projects on the applications of the capability approach to children, local development and disability issues. His research interests include local development (clusters of small and medium enterprises and informal activities), child labour and child capabilities, disability issues, international cooperation, rural development, economies of transition, Chinese and South Asian development. He is co-author of three books and co-editor of five. His papers have been published in several international journals.

Jean-Michel Bonvin is Professor of Sociology and Social Policies at the Haute école de travail social et de la santé – éésp – Vaud (University of Applied Sciences Western Switzerland). He is also Lecturer in Public Administration at the University of Geneva, Switzerland. His areas of expertise include social policy (notably in favour of disadvantaged youth), sociology of work and organizations, and theories of justice and the capability approach. His research has been funded, among others, by the European Union (FP6 and FP7) and by the Swiss National Fund.

Zoë Clark is a Research Fellow at the Faculty for Educational Science in the Department for Social Work and Adult Education, Goethe University Frankfurt am Main, Germany. Her main research areas are youth studies, intersectional social inequalities and social justice, social work and welfare policies. She completed her PhD thesis on the capabilities approach in the field of youth research and has been a scholarship holder at the North Rhine-Westphalia (NRW) Research School, Education and Capabilities, Germany, and a research fellow at the Bielefeld Center for Education and Capability Research, Germany.

Cristina Devecchi is a senior lecturer in special education and inclusion, and Deputy Research Leader at the School of Education, University of Northampton,

UK. Since gaining her PhD in 2007, she has been involved in numerous research projects, such as developing mobile technology for young people with autism, transition to further and higher education for young people with disabilities in Ireland, inclusive practices in early years settings in England, and deployment and training of teaching assistants. She is currently involved in the six countries EU-funded project 'Success at School', aiming at supporting young people who disengage from education.

Diego Di Masi has a degree in sociology, a masters in philosophy and a PhD in educational sciences. He is a post-doctorate researcher at the University of Padua's Department of Philosophy, Sociology, Pedagogy and Applied Psychology (FISPPA), Italy. He is an expert on the 'philosophy for children' programme and its implementation in and out of school. His main research topics are children and young people's participation, citizenship education and decision-making processes. He has been an independent expert for the European Commission regarding child poverty and social inclusion. He is currently involved in a national training, intervention and research project that aims to provide support to vulnerable families to prevent children being removed from their homes.

Claudine Dumbi is an agricultural engineer, specializing in rural development at the Institut Supérieur d'Agricultur e de Lille, part of the Université Catholique de Lille, France. She is a Phd student (doctorante agroeconomiste) at Lille University. Her doctoral research looks at market gardening in exurban areas of the Democratic Republic of the Congo, focusing specifically on the towns of Kinshasa and De Mbanza-Ngungu. Claudine is a teacher and researcher at the agro-veterinary Institute of Kimwenza in the Democratic Republic of the Congo where she works mainly on market gardening in Kinshasa.

Caroline Sarojini Hart is Senior Lecturer in Education at Sheffield Hallam University, UK, and Affiliated Lecturer in Education at the University of Cambridge, UK. Caroline holds a PhD from the University of Cambridge and is a social scientist with research interests in education policy, childhood and youth, aspirations, human development and social justice. She was programme leader for the University of Cambridge MPhil in Politics, Democracy and Democratic Education prior to returning to her hometown of Sheffield in 2012. Before moving into higher education Caroline spent 10 years working in secondary schools in England. Beyond the UK she has taught in Malaysia, Italy and France.

Caroline is co-director of the Education and Children's Thematic Groups of the Human Development and Capability Association (HDCA). She has recently published *Aspirations, Education and Social Justice: Applying Sen & Bourdieu* (Bloomsbury 2012). Caroline has worked as an adviser on education and social justice to a range of international organizations including the UNDP and UNESCO.

Vittorio Iervese is currently Researcher of Sociology of Cultural Processes at the University of Modena and Reggio Emilia, Italy, and member of the Department of Studies on Languages and Cultures. His research activity has essentially focused on the following areas: conflict management, intercultural communication, social participation, sociology of children and visual sociology. In particular, his research interests and the related publications have concentrated on child-adult interaction in non-educational contexts. His last book is *Participation, Facilitation, and Mediation: Children and Young People in Their Social Contexts* (Routledge 2012) with C. Baraldi (eds).

Benoît Lallau is a senior lecturer in economics at the University of Lille, and researcher at UMR CNRS Clersé, Lille, France and LERSA, Bangui, Central African Republic. He works mainly on vulnerability and resilience of individuals and households in Central Africa.

Ortrud Leßmann is a senior researcher at the Helmut Schmidt University, Hamburg, Germany. An economist by training, her research interest lies in the overlap of economics, philosophy, philosophy of education and sociology. She has published widely across the disciplines. As the former co-director of the Thematic Group on Education of the HDCA she is currently a member of the executive council. She has just completed a research project on the conception of justice and sustainability on the basis of the capability approach.

Zina Nimeh is an assistant professor in public policy and is the Coordinator, Social Protection Policy Design and Financing Specialization at the UN University-Merit/Maastricht Graduate School of Governance, the Netherlands. Her regional focus is the Middle East. She hold a PhD in Public Policy and Policy Analysis.

Richard Rose is Professor of Inclusive Education and Director of the Centre for Education and Research at the University of Northampton, UK. He has written and researched extensively in the field of special and inclusive education and is currently leading Project IRIS (Inclusive Research in Irish Schools), a longitudinal study of special educational needs provision and practice in Ireland. Richard has worked on research and consultancy in many parts of the world including India, China, Singapore, Georgia and Malaysia. His books include *Confronting Obstacles to Inclusion: International Responses to Developing Inclusive Education*, and *Count Me In: Ideas for Actively Engaging Students in Inclusive Classrooms* (Routledge 2010), written with Michael Shevlin. Richard's research interests are in the areas of inclusive education and the impact of poverty on inclusion and exclusion.

Marina Santi is Full Professor in Teaching Methodologies and Special Education at the University of Padua's Department of Philosophy, Sociology, Pedagogy and Applied Psychology (FISPPA), Italy. Her research looks at the dialogue and argumentation behind knowledge construction processes and investigates social interaction as cognitive potential for learning. She specializes in classroom discussion, both as method and context for the development of higher-order thinking skills and reflective capabilities. She is an expert on 'philosophy for children', a subject into which she has conducted a wide range of empirical research. She is also interested in the improvisational dimension of teaching and learning to improve inclusive contexts and innovative thinking in education.

John Schischka is a lecturer at the MacMillan Brown Centre for Pacific Studies, University of Canterbury, New Zealand. John's research interests are in participatory monitoring and evaluation of development programmes based on the capability approach and in indigenous entrepreneurship. He has written and published in these areas within New Zealand and internationally. Since completing his PhD in 2005 he has developed research links and projects in various parts of the South Pacific, especially New Zealand, Vanuatu, Samoa and Tonga. John works with NGOs to develop participatory evaluation of their projects based on the capability approach. He is a member of the HDCA and is associated with the thematic groups for participatory methods, children's capabilities and indigenous peoples.

Michael Shevlin is a lecturer in inclusive education at the School of Education, Trinity College Dublin, Ireland. Michael has researched and written on policy and provision in the areas of inclusive education, teacher education for inclusion and the role of student voice and agency in developing inclusive learning environments.

Daniel Stoecklin is Associate Professor in Sociology at the University Institute Kurt Bösch in Sion, Switzerland. His areas of research and teaching are the sociology of childhood, children's rights, street children and participation. He is also working with the International Institute for the Rights of the Child (www. childsrights.org) on a teaching programme on children's rights in China. He has worked for several NGOs regarding projects with children in difficult situations, and as an independent expert for the Council of Europe regarding children's participation. He is a member of the European Sociological Association, the International Association of French-Speaking Sociologists, the Swiss Sociological Association and the Swiss Centre of expertise in Human Rights.

Luisa Tuttolomondo graduated in Cultural Planning at the University of Modena and Reggio Emilia, Italy. She is currently a PhD student in territorial planning and public policy at Iuav University of Venice, Italy. She also collaborates with Next – Nuove Energie X il Territorio of Palermo, Italy, where she is responsible for ethnographic research, field research, action research, territorial animation and participative events management. Her main research interests concern participative processes involving youngsters and adults, deliberative processes, evaluation of social interventions and local sustainable development.

Acknowledgements

The conceptualization of this book began in Jordan in 2010 and it represents the culmination of an international collaboration between interdisciplinary scholars over several years. In September 2010, Mario Biggeri and Bernhard Babic organized a workshop for the Children's Thematic Group of the Human Development and Capability Association (HDCA) at the SOS Children's Village in Amman. The SOS Children's Villages aim to provide a loving atmosphere within a family in which children feel respected and secure. We would like to thank all the children and adults we met who were living in the SOS Children's village in Amman, Jordan. We would also like to thank the University of Jordan who hosted the HDCA 2010 conference, as the rich and stimulating dialogues during our time there gave us the opportunity to develop our thinking for this book. The HDCA has been continually supportive of developing links between scholars interested in children and development and so we also thank those who work hard to ensure that each year we have an opportunity to gather in different parts of the world to develop new critically reflexive insights on child and youth agency and participation.[1]

All of the authors would all like to extend their appreciation and thanks to their various host institutions and sponsors. We would also like to thank Clemens Sedmak for help in reviewing early drafts of several of the chapters in the book and for his general support for the project at the outset. The editors are also particularly grateful to five reviewers who generously offered helpful and constructive feedback on the original proposal for this book.

Special thanks go to all the participants who have so generously taken part in the research presented here. We are particularly thankful that individuals have consented to their stories and perspectives being shared with a wider audience in order to stimulate further debate on how children and young people can be supported in leading flourishing lives.

Mario would like to thank his family Elena, Andrea, Pietro Pio, Francesco Maria for their love and understanding during this work. Ortrud Leßmann would like to acknowledge the support of the international research centre in Salzburg where she benefited from their hospitality while writing Chapter 5 of this book. Vittorio Iervese would like to acknowledge the support of Oxfam Italy towards the research in Palestine presented in Chapter 12. Caroline Sarojini Hart would like to thank Sheffield Hallam University for supporting the completion of this book and also the Economic and Social Research Council (ESRC) and Bradford Aimhigher for funding the research reported in Chapter 9. She would like to thank Amartya Sen for helpful insights regarding conceptual issues in Chapter 1 and Justin Rowntree for helpful discussions related to Chapter 9. Caroline would also like to acknowledge the personal assistance of Michelle Maycock and the eternal patience, love and support of Ollie, Jasmine and Martha Hart. Now we can all be 'festival fish'.[2]

Finally we would like to thank our publishers, Bloomsbury, for supporting our work and for their attention to detail. Special thanks go to Rosie Pattinson for calmly prizing the manuscript out of us.

Notes

1   See www.hd-ca.org for more information.
2   It is sometimes hard to explain to your children why you cannot come out to play. Especially when you are writing a book about children's agency and participation. Jasmine, aged 8, coined the term 'festival fish' to describe the perfect playmate.

Introduction

Caroline Sarojini Hart

The 'capability approach' was initially developed by economist and philosopher, Amartya Sen, recipient of the Nobel Prize in 1998 for his contributions to welfare economics and social choice theory. Sen has made particular contributions to understanding poverty and famine and to the nature of human development and the pursuit of social justice. Walker and Unterhalter have described the capability approach as 'a counter-weight to neoliberal human capital' approaches (2007: 152). However, rather than rejecting John Rawls' human capital approach to development, Sen complements and extends that work to draw attention to the inadequacy of economic wealth in explaining the basis of human development and freedom (Sen, 2005). Sen has argued that Rawls' focus on primary social goods is inadequate in taking account of the heterogeneity of human beings and their variable possibilities for converting resources into 'capabilities' (1999a). In this sense, 'primary goods are not constitutive of freedom as such, but they are seen as a means to freedom' (Sen, 1992: 80). Capabilities, on the other hand, are viewed as having an intrinsic value. That is to say, the freedom to achieve ways of being and doing that the individual has reason to value is as important as the 'functionings' themselves. Furthermore, the capability approach offers a framework for the evaluation of social arrangements more broadly (Sen, 1999b). Whilst education arguably offers more than a resource or means to an end, educational qualifications have been commodified and marketized such that the artefacts of education correspond to the notions of commodities and resources. In this sense the opportunity to participate in education may give rise to capabilities that are part of what Hazel Wright (2012) has described as 'capability chains'. That is to say, education within schools forms a link with necessary prior capabilities and also leads on to the potential to generate new capabilities. This is one reason why it is not enough to look only at the experiences of children in educational settings to understand the pertinent issues that enhance and diminish child and youth well-being. It is argued in this book that a holistic development approach is more fruitfully situated around the child rather than within the institutions they frequent. Trani *et al.* (2012) have emphasized the importance of including health and poverty dimensions, alongside education, in the study of child well-being. Other studies of well-being have included a range of measures alongside those linked specifically to education (Bradshaw and Mayhew, 2005; UNICEF, 2007). Much has been written on the capability approach from both Amartya Sen and Martha Nussbaum's perspectives as well as those of others. It is beyond the scope of this volume to go into great depth but there are numerous introductory and advanced sources for further detailed discussion (Comim *et al.*, 2008; Deneulin and Shahani, 2009; Nussbaum, 2000, 2010, 2011; Sen, 1992, 1999a, 1999b, 2006, 2009). Sen (2005: 37) has been keen to foreground that in the quest for a deeper understanding of the role of human capabilities, we need to pay attention to:

- 'their direct relevance to the well-being and freedom of people;
- their indirect role through influencing economic production; and
- their indirect role through influencing social change'.

With particular respect to children and young people, in the ensuing chapters, these three aspects of understanding the role of human capabilities are reviewed and further examined in a variety of social, cultural and environmental contexts.

The capability approach is widening its appeal beyond the economic and development spheres where it was originally developed. There has been a wide spectrum of journal articles and books published on the capability approach and yet the specific concerns of children have been largely overlooked. This book examines the ways that the capability approach may inform how we live our lives and the strategies that societies may choose to develop in order to enhance the quality of the lives of their children and young people. Therefore this book is about the future and how, in a spirit of social justice, we might be able to enhance the capabilities of new generations to lead flourishing lives they have reason to value. We have also strived to connect the work presented in this volume to other key contributions to this growing field. The content is relevant to the disciplines of childhood studies, education, sociology, social policy and development studies. We have aimed to make the book accessible to undergraduates, postgraduates and established academics across these fields. Ultimately, this book has been written for a wide audience including teachers, students, policy analysts, academics and careers advisers.

This introduction aims to set the scene by introducing the capability approach and illuminating the way that this book connects to the existing literature in this field. It also touches on some of the core concepts addressed in the book related to the theorization of childhood and youth, notions of agency and participation, the role of education in society and methods for research, drawing on the capability approach. The latter part of the introduction offers an introduction to the chapters and organization of the book in two main parts.

Education in schools

Education in schools is situated within social, cultural, economic, environmental and technological contexts. International goals for education have tended to centre around issues of access, enrolment and academic achievement (UNESCO, 2000; United Nations, 2010). Gender inequalities have also come under the spotlight due to the continuing trends of more limited educational experiences for girls (Berges, 2007; Raynor, 2007). Although there have been significant developments with regard to these measures of educational progress, the relationship between schooling and well-being has been problematized as far from a straightforward one (Kelly, 2007). Unterhalter and Brighouse (2007: 68) posed the question, 'how will we know whether we have social justice in education?'. This turns out to be a critical question. It depends on the construction of the notion of social justice and also on the units of evaluation selected as indicators of movement toward greater justice (Sen, 1992). There is certainly some debate about whether or not we should be seeking to identify age-specific capabilities in our pursuit of social justice, as has been advocated by Sadlowski (2011). Supposing capabilities were identified as part of a list, in a specific context there is significant debate about who should be responsible for developing an individual's capabilities. For example, Bates (2007) has argued that the responsibility for the development of capabilities is both a curricular and pedagogical one. This position seems to place the responsibility firmly with educational settings such as schools. However, in considering the agency and participation of children and young people it becomes less clear where the responsibility lies.

In 2003, Saito commented in an article that the relationship between education and the capability approach was under-theorized. Since then there has been a plethora of research and publications in this area and so it is clear that this is now a rich area of enquiry yielding important data that is helping to illuminate knowledge and understanding of the potential merits of applying the capability approach in the field of education. Over the last decade there have been several books and special journal issues that have considered the capability approach in relation to education, schooling (Hart, 2012a, 2012b; Terzi, 2007; Walker, 2006; Walker and Unterhalter, 2007) and the development of children and young people (Biggeri *et al.*, 2011; Leβmann *et al.*, 2011).[1]

In writing this book the authors are motivated to explore the relationship between education and young people, not only within formal educational settings but also in the wider public and private spheres. It is argued that the places and spaces in which education occurs are not limited by policy and institutional boundaries but rather overflow into all areas of life. Children and young people interact with their social and physical environments in ways that constantly fuel their educational experiences both with and without the scaffolding of adult interpreters and instructors. Understanding these processes of connection between the individual and their environment, as well as with fellow human beings of all ages, helps to inform understandings of child and youth agency, well-being and participation in society. Children may associate with their environments in ways that are unconventional to the adult. Some of these are readily apparent, such as the impulsive desire of many children to climb trees or jump in puddles. However, other associations are hidden, subtle and complex, and are rendered obscure to the observations of adults.

Schooling and society

UNESCO (2012a) has estimated that there are around 57 million primary-aged children and a further 67 million lower secondary-aged children without access to schools. Some countries are more significantly affected than others, with the highest rates of out-of-school children mainly being concentrated in sub-Saharan Africa. Aggregate figures on these indicators obscure gender and socioeconomic differences. Although gender disparities have reduced there are still more girls (53 per cent) out of school compared to boys and in poor rural areas the gender disparities are multiplied many times over (UNESCO, 2011: 1). The average number of days in school, the length of the school day and the age of enrolment in different countries vary significantly. Similarly there are ongoing challenges related to the training and retention of teachers, with additional challenges linked to high levels of staff absence in many countries. The estimates on the number children failing to complete their primary education are startling, and in 2011 it was estimated that 19 per cent of out-of-school primary aged children had left education (UNESCO, 2011: 4). Once this figure is disaggregated we can see that in Central Asia, whilst only 5 per cent of out-of-school primary aged children have left education, 76 per cent of out-of-school children in this region are expected to never enter education in the first place. By contrast, in North America and Western Europe, although 41 per cent of out-of-school primary aged children have left school, only 1 in 10 children among the out-of-school children is expected to never attend school in this region (UNESCO, 2011). Some nations have greatly reduced the number of out-of-school children over recent years, such as India where the statistic for out-of-school children has fallen from 20.3 million in 2003 to 2.3 million in 2010. However, by contrast, in Nigeria over the same period, the numbers of out-of-school children have risen from 6.9 million to 10.5 million (UNESCO 2012b: 62). These statistics highlight the often limited and variable role of school-based education provision in many children's lives. Education may be taking place outside of formal school environments and therefore families, communities and businesses have crucial roles to play. Indeed, Ballet *et al.* (2011) have reported that a child's relationship with school may not remain intact or consistent despite initial enrolment in primary schooling. They conclude that educational efforts need to extend beyond school through outreach work on the street. UNESCO defines street children as, 'girls and boys for whom the street has become their home and/or source of livelihood and who are inadequately protected or supervised by responsible adults. They are temporarily, partially or totally estranged from their families and society' (2006). Children's relationships with school may be intertwined with their relationship with the street and the breakdown of relationships with family members, whether through conflict, illness and mortality, or for other significant reasons. Where relationships break down with school, children can find themselves on the street, whether as orphans, abandoned children or simply working there by day (Ballet *et al.* 2011).

This research further supports the need to understand how schools are socially situated within the wider physical environment and also the role that social networks and communities may have to play. In another example of the fuzzy boundaries between school, home and the community in which a child lives it is interesting to consider statistics on UK road traffic accidents. According to the AA Motoring Trust (2003:6) , 'an 11-year-old is twice as likely as a 10-year-old to be killed or seriously injured in a road accident on the school journey' as they begin to travel independently to secondary school. The implication is that safeguarding and encouraging young people's capabilities in schools has a reach that extends beyond the school gate. Indeed, as internet access and mobile digital technologies become more widely available, there are new connections being made between the physical school environment and the wider community. Children in the UK are encouraged to undertake homework tasks online from the first stages of primary school. Whilst safeguards may be put in place, with varying success in schools, it is much more difficult to operate safeguards on internet use among children and young people as a whole. Growing challenges for children are related to the consequences of excessive 'screen time' and the increase in 'cyber-bullying', particularly via online social networking sites and mobile technology. Issues that may have been played out in the school playground or classroom now reach more readily into life outside the school.

The nature of childhood

There is already a substantial body of work that questions what is inferred by the concept of 'childhood'. In the light of the plurality of conceptions of childhood, in this book we are following in the tradition of James *et al.* (2012) and Biggeri *et al.* (2011), in constructing children and young people as active social actors. Comim *et al.* (2011) have argued that children can be competent in social interactions and in attaching social meanings to their world. They can have agency, sometimes via these interactions, but not always. Therefore, whilst promoting interaction, and hence participation, there is also a need to protect children (Babic *et al.*, 2010). Indeed, James *et al.* (2012) underscore the distinction between, on the one hand, changing adult perspectives on the role of childhood in a given society, and, on the other hand, the experience of childhood from the perspective of the child. It is clear that different societies have variable perspectives on the role of childhood, and the childhoods of different children, even within the same state, are perceived differently by a range of adults. It is also increasingly apparent that children themselves vary in their own interpretations of what childhood means to them. Therefore, in writing a book of this kind the aim is not to suggest that there is a 'right way' of viewing and experiencing childhood but rather to explore the capability approach as a means by which to understand, orientate and perhaps rethink those interpretations and perspectives. For example, James *et al.* (2012: 37) comment, 'we might suggest that children either occupy designated spaces, that is they are placed, as in nurseries or schools, or they are conspicuous by their inappropriate or precocious invasion of adult territory'. Children may be associated with particular places and spaces and may seem out of place in other settings. The capability approach helps to broaden this view and to take greater interest in what the child may have reason to value irrespective of whether this strays from previously held expectations and norms.

Thus, *Agency and Participation in Childhood and Youth* presents a new critical engagement in conceptualizing the roles of youth agency and participation in education, development and the pursuit of social justice.

The wider context

In beginning a book of this kind we are compelled to reflect for a moment on the sociopolitical context in which it has evolved. We are living in an international climate of austerity which is impacting globally and disrupting the lives of individuals at all levels of the various socioeconomic structures around the world. Moreover, welfare reforms in many countries are struggling to address the care needs of an ageing population, whereas elsewhere life expectancy remains disturbingly low. In the USA, the UK and elsewhere, the role of citizen participation is under scrutiny in changing societies and a discourse of 'new civics' is emerging. However, for many countries, the daily struggle for survival overwhelms more comprehensive citizenship objectives for either national policy or local-level community action. For example, more than half of the populations of Senegal, Mali, Nigeria, Cameroon, Cote D'Ivoire and Burkina Faso are under the age of 18 years. Average life expectancy in these countries is also significantly lower than other countries, averaging around 45 years (WHO, 2012). There are widespread disparities in child mortality across nations, with some areas severely affected. In the Democratic Republic of the Congo (DRC) the child mortality rate for under 5s was 168 in 2011. Overall the World Health Organization (WHO) has estimated that globally around 7 million children under the age of 5 die each year.

Civil conflict affects many children around the world and in fragile and conflict-affected states children are significantly less likely to enrol in school, more likely to drop out and more likely to die before their counterparts in similar countries elsewhere. Conflicts tend to endure over a number of years, causing severe disruption to whole generations of children. This has led Children in Crisis to estimate that by 2015 there will be around 150 million illiterate 15–24-year-olds. The Department for International Development (2010) has found a correlation between educational achievement and lifetime earnings as well as increased gross domestic product. In addition, despite the targets set by the Millennium Development Goals and 'health for all' strategies, infant and child health remain a cause for international concern and action. The Global Partnership for Education (2011: 29) has estimated that 'Over 40 per cent of the more than 60 million children worldwide who are not attending primary school live in countries that are characterized by weak institutional capacity and governance, political instability, and, in many cases, persistent violence'. There are generally very limited opportunities for children, and particularly those in fragile states, to be part of decision-making processes and to raise their 'voices' as advocates for themselves. This limited participation creates injustice and is related to constrained agency formation and the lack of spaces for dialogue, leading to an age-bias in society.

Aims and organization of the book

There are five principal aims of this edited volume. First of all, the book aims to explore constructions of agency and participation and to identify key challenges in promoting these core concepts in relation to children and young people. These concepts in turn raise questions about further related concepts, such as 'inclusion', about which Hedge and MacKenzie (2012) have argued there is no meaningful consensus, and 'engagement', a term prevalent in the 'new civics' discourse. Second, the book aims to position schooling within the wider landscape of children's lives, for example with regard to poverty, labour, health and democratic participation in society. The third principal aim of the book is to endeavour to illuminate the factors in wider society that affect individuals' capabilities to participate in schooling in ways that promote their human flourishing. The fourth aim is to explore the places and spaces where education takes place and to examine responsibilities, duties and obligations towards children and young people at individual, local, national and international levels. The fifth aim is to draw upon empirical data from a number of international case studies to facilitate the conceptual discussions and also to offer examples of the application of the capability approach to research with young people in schools and beyond.

These aims are responded to from diverse international perspectives as contributors to the individual chapters draw upon conceptual work and empirical findings from a variety of settings. Some of these settings are traditional school- or college-based spaces where formal education takes place and others relate to broader facets of young people's lives, enlivening the debate about the nature of interconnections between different environments. Individual authors have expressed complementary and contrasting views and we hope this will stimulate further debate. Chapters are cross-referenced in order to direct readers to connecting issues.

Part 1

This book has been divided into two parts. Part 1, 'Agency and Participation in Childhood and Youth' contains five chapters addressing broad theoretical and conceptual issues. Part 2, 'Developing Agency and Capabilities in Schools and Beyond', contains seven chapters, drawing on international case studies to consider how children and young people's agency and capabilities can flourish.

The exponential increase in research applications and theoretical development of the capability approach with regard to education has been mapped in recent literature (Comim *et al.*, 2008; Hart, 2012a, 2012b). Therefore, within the landscape of the capability approach, Chapter 1 introduces some of the key challenges to successfully applying the capability approach to empirical research. Caroline Sarojini Hart explores how research may be undertaken, drawing on the capability approach to inform the evaluative framework used to measure and understand matters of justice for children and young people, inside and outside of schools. Drawing on her earlier work (2012a), Hart suggests a framework of questions that can help to guide the development of capability-based research with children and young people.

In Chapter 2, Mario Biggeri observes that children and young people are often excluded from decision-making processes leading to an age-bias. In particular, Sen has argued that democracy is contingent on individuals' active participation in public deliberation, and here Biggeri considers the implications for participation by children and young people in such processes. He further argues that the process of acquiring communicative competences and 'complex thinking', including dialogical attitudes and argumentative practice, becomes central. Fostering participation is central to the process of children evolving capabilities as it takes into account their priorities, values and aspirations.

Chapter 3, by Daniel Stoecklin and Jean-Michel Bonvin, explores issues which are central to understanding children's rights from the capability perspective. In particular these authors note how participation rights, contained in the *United Nations Convention on the Rights of the Child*, challenge some longstanding conceptions of childhood. The chapter foregrounds children's constructions of reality based on a systemic theory of the social actor. Stoecklin and Bonvin draw on empirical data from Switzerland, Finland, Slovakia, Moldova and France and grapple with how to overcome the theoretical dichotomy between the agent and structure.

Chapter 4, by Zoë Clark, offers a close examination of the relationship between functionings and capabilities in order to illuminate the way in which the capability approach might provide a metric for assessing the standard of living of children and young people. Structural equation modelling (SEM) is used in order to explore measures for opportunities and barriers in relation to the development of capabilities.

Ortrud Leßmann presents the final chapter in Part 1 and in doing so she considers the application of the capability approach to understanding and exploring the nature of child poverty. She critiques indirect poverty measures that utilize equivalence scales which may overestimate the economies of scale enjoyed by large households. Issues are also raised related to the low command over household income that children tend to experience compared to adult members (albeit that gender and other differences also prevail among adults). A more direct poverty measure is suggested in order to overcome the weakness of the indirect method, however, the challenge of identifying child-relevant poverty dimensions emerges and new directions for further research are suggested.

Part 2

Part 2 begins with Marina Santi and Diego di Masi's chapter which explores pedagogies to develop children's agency in schools. In particular they explore the effectiveness of philosophical activity in promoting child agency inside and outside school. Contrasting theorizations of citizenship are drawn upon which locate the capability approach in relation to other agency-based perspectives and practices.

Chapter 7, by Cristina Devecchi, Richard Rose and Michael Shevlin, addresses the relationship between education and the development of the capabilities of children identified as having special educational needs. In particular, these authors focus on the notion of 'voice' in relation to expanding capabilities and its necessity as a 'prerequisite for the social, psychological and intellectual development of children'.

Chapter 8, by John Schischka, presents findings from an empirical study of a New Zealand educational programme to support pupils experiencing social, economic and environmental barriers to achieving their potential in school. Schischka explores the extent to which the capability approach can inform the development of programmes such as the New Zealand 'StandTall' initiative in order to convert individuals' life goals into capabilities. The importance of being able to monitor and evaluate these kinds of initiatives is highlighted along with the importance of a continual process of qualitative evaluation of children's perspectives.

In Chapter 9, Caroline Sarojini Hart offers a new conceptualization of the nature of aspirations and psychosocial transition processes in relation to secondary schooling and young people's journeys beyond and outside formal education. Empirical data are reported from the UK from two studies in Yorkshire. It is argued that mechanisms of conversion factors are linked to processes of 'transition', enhancing and constraining individuals' capabilities to aspire and to transform capabilities into functions. The implications for developing policies and practices to support young people's transition experiences are discussed and suggestions are made for further reflection.

Moving on to Chapter 10, Zina Nimeh and Robert Bauchmüller consider the disparities in school enrolment and labour among children in Jordan by mapping the socioeconomic and demographic structure of households to which those children belong. The findings presented indicate substantial variation among different household types and reveal the complex interrelationships between school participation and child labour. Nimeh concludes with recommendations for the development of holistic social protection policies which may help to support the most vulnerable children in Jordan and which offer insights in addressing these issues elsewhere.

In Chapter 11, Jérôme Ballet, Claudine Dumbi and Benoît Lallau draw upon findings from research in the DRC in order to explore children's autonomy in conflict-affected countries. They observe how social norms in DRC have affected children's capabilities and agency. Deeply embedded cultural practices and perspectives both work for and against children's well-being in a setting where many children are considered sorcerers. These individuals can become the victims of accusations and violence in situations where they have little opportunity to act in ways that would avoid these outcomes. The discussion leads to a consideration of the role of resilience in developing children's capabilities in this context.

In the final chapter, Vittorio Iervese and Luisa Tuttolomondo, explore the nature of youth participation outside the classroom. The chapter presents findings from an evaluation of a Palestinian project developed by the Italian non-governmental organization (NGO) Ucodep. The aim of the project was to promote social participation and to raise awareness of children's rights among Palestinian children and young people. The analysis draws on the capability approach as well as wider literature on childhood studies. Alongside the substantive findings of this study there are useful insights regarding the development of methodological instruments for the analysis of agency and capability in children and young people.

Finally, the book closes with some concluding remarks from the editors which reflect on the pertinent issues going forward in thinking about child and youth participation and agency. Although the book offers many important insights into these issues, many new questions are raised and further challenges emerge.

Note

1   For special journal issues on the capability approach and education see (a) Hart, C.S. (ed.) (2012c) The capability approach and education, *Cambridge Journal of Education*, 42(3); (b) Hinchliffe, G. (ed.) (2007) Capability approach and education, *Prospero, A Journal of New Thinking in Philosophy for Education*, 13(3); (c) Hinchliffe, G. and Terzi, L. (eds) (2009) Capability approach and education, *Studies in Philosophy and Education*, 28(5); (d) Walker, M. (ed.) (2012) Education and capabilities, *The Journal of Human Development and Capabilities*, 13(3). For higher education see Walker (2006) and Boni and Walker (2013).

References

AA Motoring Trust (2003) *The Facts About Road Accidents and Children*, www.theaa.org.

Babic, B., Graf, G., Germes Castro, O. (2010) The Capability Approach as a framework for evaluation of child and youth care, in *European Journal of Social Work*, 13(3), pp. 409–413.

Ballet, J., Bhukuth, A. & Radja, K. (2011) Rethinking access to education through the capability approach: The case of street children, in Biggeri, M., Ballet, J. & Comim, F. (eds) *Children and the Capability Approach* (Basingstoke, Palgrave Macmillan).

Bates, R. (2007) Developing capabilities and the management of trust, in Walker, M. & Unterhalter, E. (eds) *Amartya Sen's Capability Approach and Social Justice in Education* (Basingstoke, Palgrave Macmillan).

Berges, S. (2007) Why the capability approach is justified, *Journal of Applied Philosophy*, 24(1), pp. 16–25.

Biggeri, M., Ballet, J. & Comim, F. (eds) (2011) *Children and the Capability Approach* (Basingstoke, Palgrave Macmillan).

Boni, A. & Walker, M. (eds) (2013) *Human Development and Capabilities: Re-imagining the University of the Twenty-first Century* (London, Routledge).

Bradshaw, J. & Mayhew, E. (eds) (2005) *The Well-being of Children in the UK*, second edition (London, Save the Children).

Comim, C., Ballet, J., Biggeri, M. & Iervese, V. (2011) Introduction: theoretical foundations and the book's roadmap, in Biggeri, M. Ballet, J. & Comim, F. (eds) *Children and the Capability Approach* (Basingstoke, Palgrave Macmillan).

Comim, F., Qizilbash, M. & Alkire, S. (eds) (2008) *The Capability Approach: Concepts, Measures and Applications* (Cambridge, Cambridge University Press).

Deneulin, S. & Shahani, L. (2009) *An Introduction to the Human Development and Capability Approach: Freedom and Agency* (London, Earthscan).

Department for International Development (2010) *Learning for All: DfIDs Educational Strategy 2010–2015* (London, DfID).

Global Partnership for Education (2011) *All Children Learning Report 2011*, www.globalpartnership.org.

Hart, C.S. (2012a) *Aspirations, Education and Social Justice: Applying Sen and Bourdieu* (London, Bloomsbury).

Hart, C.S. (2012b) Editorial: The capability approach and education, *Cambridge Journal of Education*, 42(3), pp. 275–282.

Hart, C.S. (ed) (2012c) The capability approach and education, *Cambridge Journal of Education*, 42(3).

Hedge, N. & MacKenzie, A. (2012) Putting Nussbaum's capability approach to work: re-visiting inclusion, *Cambridge Journal of Education*, 42(3), pp. 327–344.

Hinchliffe, G. (ed.) (2007) Capability approach and education, *Prospero, A Journal of New Thinking in Philosophy for Education*, 13(3).

Hinchliffe, G. & Terzi, L. (eds) (2009) Capability approach and education, *Studies in Philosophy for Education*, 28(5).

James, A., Jenks, C. & Prout, A. (2012) *Theorizing Childhood* (Cambridge, Polity Press).

Kelly, A. (2007) *School Choice and Student Well-Being. Opportunity and Capability in Education* (Basingstoke, Palgrave).

Leßmann, O., Otto, H. & Zielger, H. (eds) (2011) *Closing the Capabilities Gap: Renegotiating Social Justice for the Young* (Opladen, Barbara Budrich).

Nussbaum, M.C. (2000) *Women and Human Development: The Capabilities Approach* (Cambridge, Cambridge University Press).

Nussbaum, M.C. (2010) *Not for Profit* (Princeton, Princeton University Press).

Nussbaum, M.C. (2011) *Creating Capabilities: The Human Development Approach* (London, Harvard University Press).

Raynor, J. (2007) Education and capabilities in Bangladesh, in Walker, M. & Unterhalter, E. (eds) *Amartya Sen's Capability Approach and Social Justice in Education* (Basingstoke, Palgrave).

Sadlowski, I, (2011) A capability approach fit for children, in Lessmann, O., Otto, H. & Zielger, H. (eds) (2011) *Closing the Capabilities Gap: Renegotiating Social Justice for the Young* (Opladen, Barbara Budrich).

Saito, M. (2003) Amartya Sen's capability approach to education: a critical exploration, *Journal of Philosophy of Education*, 37(1), pp. 17–31.

Sen, A. (1992) *Inequality Re-examined* (Oxford, Clarendon Press).

Sen, A. (1999a) *Commodities and Capabilities* (Oxford, Oxford University Press).

Sen, A. (1999b) *Development as Freedom* (Oxford, Oxford University Press).

Sen, A. (2005) Human capital and human capability, in S. Fukuda-Parr & A.K. Kumar (eds) *Readings in Human Development* (Oxford, Oxford University Press).

Sen, A. (2006) Capability and well-being, in Nussbaum, M.C. & Sen, A. (eds) *The Quality of Life* (Oxford, Oxford University Press).

Sen, A. (2009) *The Idea of Justice* (London, Penguin).

Terzi, L. (2007) The capability to be educated, in Walker, M. & Unterhalter. E. (eds) *Amartya Sen's Capability Approach and Social Justice in Education* (Basingstoke, Palgrave).

Trani, F., Bakshi, P. & Nandipati, A. (2012) Delivering' education; maintaining inequality: the case of children with disabilities in Afghanistan, *Cambridge Journal of Education*, 42(3), pp. 345–366.

UNESCO (2000) *The Dakar Framework for Action: Meeting our Collective Commitment* (Paris, Unesco), www.unesco.org.

UNESCO (2011) *Out-of-school Children: New Data Reveal Persistent Challenges.* UIS Fact sheet, June, No.12 (Paris, Unesco Institute for Statistics).

UNESCO (2012a) *Global Initiative on Out-of-school Children. Finishing School* (Paris, UNESCO Institute for Statistics).

UNESCO (2012b) *Global Monitoring Report 2012: Putting Education to Work* (Paris, UNESCO).

UNICEF (2007) *Child Poverty in Perspective: An Overview of Child Well-Being in Rich Countries.* Report Card 7 (Florence, UNICEF Innocenti Research Centre).

United Nations (2010) *The Millennium Development Goals Development Report 2010*, www.un.org, retrieved 29 May 2012.

Unterhalter, E., & Brighouse, H. (2007) Distribution of what for social justice in education? The case of Education for All by 2015, in M. Walker & E. Unterhalter (eds) *Amartya Sen's Capability Approach and Social Justice in Education* (Basingstoke, Palgrave Macmillan).

Walker, M. (2006) *Higher Education Pedagogies* (Maidenhead, Open University Press).

Walker, M. (ed.) (2012) Education and capabilities, *The Journal of Human Development and Capabilities*, 13(3).

Walker, M. & Unterhalter, E. (eds) (2007) *Amartya Sen's Capability Approach and Social Justice in Education* (Basingstoke, Palgrave).

WHO (World Health Organization) (2012) *Global Health Observatory*, www.who.int/gho.

Wright, H.R. (2012) Childcare, children and capability, *Cambridge Journal of Education*, 42(3), pp. 409–24.

Part 1

Agency and Participation in Childhood and Youth

The Capability Approach and Educational Research

Caroline Sarojini Hart

Introduction

In the pursuit of social justice and human development there is exciting potential to bring together new insights into research for, with and by children in synergy with the capability approach. Towards this endeavour, this opening chapter has four key strands. The chapter aims to map the interwoven landscapes of the capability approach, changing perceptions of childhood and youth, the role of education in society and educational research.[1] Amartya Sen's capability approach is underpinned by a drive to pursue human development in a context of social justice. As Dreze and Sen have observed, 'the focus on capability helps to clarify the purpose of public action in different fields' (Dreze and Sen, 1995: 13). In recent decades children have been positioned in international discourses with greater agency than ever before, albeit that the reality does not meet the aspirations of global declarations, policy and legislative frameworks. Education has a pivotal role in developing children's agency and participation in society in schools and beyond. Educational research can contribute powerfully to this agenda by interpreting, informing, stimulating and innovating theory and practice.

The landscape of capabilities

Capabilities

Sen has argued that human capabilities are important for at least three distinct reasons. First, for the direct benefits that accrue to the individual, second for the indirect social benefits that can be derived as a consequence of individuals' capabilities and third, the benefits to society in terms of economic development

(Sen, 2005). These three areas can be divided into individual-level benefits and collective level benefits.

The capability approach highlights the variable abilities of different individuals to convert resources into capabilities – that is, ways of being and doing the individual has reason to value. In relation to other perspectives:

> Although it has been suggested that the capability approach is an alternative to rights-based and utilitarian approaches, Sen is keen to note that the capability approach extends and broadens the human capital approach in an 'additional and cumulative' rather than 'alternative' way (Sen, 2005: 36). Whilst human capital approaches have focused on the individual as a contributor to the means of production, the capability approach foregrounds the development of individual well-being and freedom and indirect effects on social changes in addition to the indirect effects on economic production (Sen, 2005: 37).
>
> Hart, 2013: 11–12

Capabilities and rights

There has been a steady development in the discourse around children's rights and in recent decades this has led to both national and international policy and legislative developments – for example, *No Child Left Behind* (USA), *Every Child Matters* (UK) and the *United Nations Convention on the Rights of the Child* (UNCRC). The capability approach is not intended to displace the rights-based approach and indeed Robeyns (2006) notes that rights are a strategic tool in securing capabilities. Thus the capability approach may be seen as complementing and extending this work.

The capability approach goes beyond securing individuals' rights to consider what will enable different human beings to activate and enact those rights in ways they have reason to value. Sen comments, 'the two concepts – human rights and capabilities – go well with each other, so long as we do not try to subsume either category within the territory of the other' (Sen, 2005: 151). Indeed, rights may reflect ways of being, doing and having that are valued by the dominant cultural group within a society, but which are not valued by a particular individual within that society: 'Capabilities seem to move in a different direction from rights. The latter can be seen to focus on legally and morally pre-determined entitlements for life which the individual then may or may not choose to take advantage of' (Hart, 2010: 25). In contrast, capabilities are valued ways of being and doing that relate to specific individuals and which may or may not have their foundations in hegemonic, moral and legal frameworks. Thus, whilst some capabilities are recognized in rights, others are not.

Well-being freedom and well-being achievement

Within an individual's benefits from the development of capabilities, four areas can be observed related to 'well-being freedom', 'well-being achievement', 'agency freedom' and 'agency achievement'. Sen describes, 'well-being freedom' as 'one's freedom to achieve those things that are constitutive of one's well-being' (Sen, 1992: 57). This is distinct from the concept of 'well-being achievement' which is constituted by the combination of functionings they actually achieve:

> A functioning is an achievement of a person: what he or she manages to do or be. It reflects, as it were, a part of the 'state' of that person. It has to be distinguished from the commodities which are used to achieve those functionings. For example, bicycling has to be distinguished from possessing a bike. It has to also be distinguished from the happiness generated by the functioning.
>
> Sen, 1999: 7

A person's well-being freedom is constituted by a 'capabilities set', that is the full range of ways of being and doing the individual has reason to value, that are real opportunities for them (Hart, 2009). A person's capabilities are reflected by 'the various alternative functioning bundles he or she can achieve through choice' (Sen, 1999: 18). Capabilities are more than rights or aspirations, they are actually realizable goals for that individual in the circumstances in which they live: 'Capabilities represent the freedoms an individual has to achieve beings and doings they have reason to value although only some of them will become realized as functionings' (Hart, 2012a: 29).

Agency freedom and agency achievement

'Agency freedom', from Sen's perspective, is described as 'one's freedom to bring about achievements one values and attempts to produce' (Sen, 1992: 57). This includes freedoms related to one's own well-being but also extends to freedoms to influence others, with both positive and negative consequences. In other words, an individual's agency freedom is not necessarily founded upon dominant views of morality and virtue. For example, most children's superheroes have a nemesis with considerable agency freedom. The concept of 'agency achievement' is a further distinct concept defined as the 'realization of goals one has reason to pursue' but which '... need not be guided by her own well-being (Sen, 1992: 56). For this reason an individual's agency freedom may be used to achieve goals (agency achievement) that could enhance but which could also diminish their own well-being achievement. Examples to illustrate this include the situation where a Good Samaritan steps into danger to help someone in distress, risking their own safety, or in another case, a protester who goes on hunger strike, compromising their (health) well-being achievement to further a political campaign.

While the individual may have the agency freedom to act in ways that benefit society, it is possible to argue that the sum of social benefits may be greater than the individual parts (albeit that this may have negative as well as positive impacts). That is to say, a number of individuals exercising their agency freedoms may achieve more for the development (or detriment) of society than simply the aggregate of the individual endeavours. So, for example, if a number of individuals in a given community participate in democratic deliberative discussion by converting their capabilities to advocate and express their thoughts and opinions into functionings, then the quality and rigour of those discussions may be enhanced. This in turn may facilitate more complex, subtle and meaningful exploration of ideas for the benefit of a wider community than any one contribution could make by itself. The dialogue has life because there is more than one. Two individuals may derive the intrinsic benefits associated with participation in political processes, but their interaction yields some additional value for others. Thus there is an argument that expanding individual capabilities has the potential to give rise to both individual and social benefits.

Linking capabilities and functionings

Nussbaum has argued for a list of 'Central Human Functional Capabilities' (2000: 78–79) and argues that a threshold for each capability is crucial, stating, 'we say that beneath a certain level of capability, in each area, a person has not been enabled to live in a truly human way' (2000: 74).[2] She further argues that reaching the minimum level of capability is not the same as achieving justice in society as there will be differences between those just over the threshold and those significantly above this level.

Furthermore a number of claims have been made for 'foundational' or 'meta-capabilities'. For example, Hart has argued that the 'capability to aspire' is a meta-capability (Hart, 2010, 2012a, 2012c). In relation to education, Terzi argues that 'the capability to be educated' is 'a fundamental capability and foundational to other capabilities' (2007: 31). In relation to health, Venkatapuram (2011: 143)[3] argues, the capability to be healthy (CH) is a person's ability to achieve or exercise a cluster of basic capabilities and functionings, and each at a level that constitutes a life worthy of equal human dignity in the modern world. Making use of Nussbaum's theory of central human capabilities (CHCs), the CH can usefully be understood as a 'meta-capability' to achieve or exercise ten CHCs. These ten CHCs together make up a minimal conception of a fully human life, and provide the bases for determining the decent social minimum of entitlements in the relevant parts of an individual's life (Nussbaum, 2000, p. 75).

These perspectives on those capabilities which are necessary in order to achieve other capabilities are thought-provoking in thinking about the focus of capability-based educational research. Underlying questions relate to the appropriateness of identifying 'lists' of capabilities, thresholds and the weighting of capabilities in educational (or other) contexts. Further questions concern whether the focus on capabilities can be augmented by research on other issues, and indeed the research process itself. Debate on the kinds of capabilities that are important for individuals to be able to lead autonomous, empowered, agentic lives in a context of social justice is ongoing. Having briefly landscaped some of the key concepts and ideas of Sen's capability approach we now turn to consider the landscape of childhood and youth as a second strand in building a picture of how to position educational research within the capability approach.[4]

Perceptions of childhood and youth

The social status of children and the political, economic, civic and cultural roles of children in society have been the subject of competing discourses across cultures and through time. In considering the prospect of research that involves children in some way, it is pertinent to review some of these changing perspectives. A dominant view of childhood for a long time suggested that children were in a process of becoming adults and that young people gradually accumulated skills, experiences and dispositions that shifted them out of childhood and towards adulthood. This move ostensibly involved leaving 'childish' activities behind and engaging with new adult ways of being and doing. This thinking generated a socially constructed dichotomy between childhood and adulthood. This led Aries (1962), cited in Christensen and James (2008: 87), to observe that modern western childhood 'quarantines' children from the world of adults in a social context where childish and adult activities are separated.

James *et al.* (2012) are widely credited with shaping contemporary thinking on perspectives on childhood and their seminal text is still essential reading in this field. They considered childhood from sociological and anthropological perspectives, situating childhood, for example, in terms of space, time and the spheres of work and play. They moved away from thinking only in terms of the chronological maturation of children and rejected the idea that children were not yet fully-formed adults. Rather, children and young people were viewed as socially competent agentic actors in their own right. 'Youth' is a term that may be used to signify a life-stage perceived as a territory between childhood and adulthood. This space seems to have expanded in recent western discourses and yet it is poorly defined. In some parts of the world it could be argued that youth as a status has collapsed, with traditional views of childhood merging with adulthood as children take on 'adult' roles, for example, as heads of households in countries with high parent mortality from HIV and AIDS-related illness. Certainly there are no universal views of the concepts of childhood, youth and adulthood. Definitions shift across time, culture and geopolitical contexts. There are some frames of reference in terms of shared legal rights and social stata related to locally defined 'children' and 'adults'. However, children have widely varying roles in different societies. What is acceptable, permitted or tolerated in one country may be very different from another. Similarly, this applies to political and cultural views on the spaces children should legitimately inhabit, whether as rights-holders or duty-bearers, and this has changed hugely over time. For example, there are significant differences in terms of the likelihood of being engaged in employment, enrolled in school, being head of a household, being the main economic provider or a child soldier. In general, children have different entitlements and privileges compared to adults with regard to the law, they are more likely to be dependent on adults as caregivers, physically and emotionally immature and, particularly in the early years, socialized by interactions with the significant others they encounter.

In recent years increased, although by no means universal, consensus has been reached on the fundamental rights of the child, culminating in the UNCRC (this is discussed in several chapters throughout this book). Article 12 of the UNCRC (as discussed in depth in Chapters 3 and 7) states, that 'state Parties shall assure to the child who is capable of forming his or her own views the right to express those views in all matters affecting the child'. This right can help to inform the kind of approach that might be taken in research processes with children. In order for children to be able to enact this right in research contexts, there is an onus on designing methods, tools and contexts that facilitate this process. In other words, the research context can help to support and develop an individual's capabilities, and not only their participatory right to express themselves in relation to issues that affect their lives.

The capability approach is aligned well with James *et al.*'s positioning of the child as a social actor and it offers the potential to take the rights enshrined in the UNCRC to a more powerful dimension in terms of highlighting the conversion factors involved in transforming children's rights into capabilities. Debate has been ongoing within the capability approach as to whether certain capabilities apply more readily to children than adults and whether families, schools and society more widely have a duty in developing particular capabilities among children. This overview of some key divergences in views on childhood serves to illustrate that in proceeding with educational research involving individuals regarded variously as children, youths, young people or young adults, researchers must come to an understanding and rationale for their own positions with regard to their constructions of childhood and youth. The discussion now moves on to review constructions of the role of education in society.

The role of education in society

Education, in its deepest sense and at whatever age it takes place, concerns the opening of identities – exploring new ways of being that lie beyond our current state. Whereas training aims to create an inbound trajectory targeted at competence in a specific practice, education must strive to open new dimensions for the negotiation of the self. It places students on an outbound trajectory toward a broad field of possible identities. Education is not merely formative – it is transformative.

Wenger, 2008: 263

Education is often viewed as the panacea for overcoming many of the challenges related to poverty, development and the eradication of different forms of inequalities in society. International agendas for education, such as 'Education for All' and the 'Millennium Development Goals', in recent years have focused on access (UNESCO, 2000; United Nations, 2010) and the reduction of gender inequalities in access and experience (Berges, 2007; Raynor, 2007; Unterhalter, 2003).

There is a plurality of perspectives in terms of the role of education, for example, Bourdieu and Passeron (2000) theorized about the role of education in social reproduction, particularly in relation to social class. Freire (1972) argued against the oppressive role of certain forms of education, noting, by contrast, that certain pedagogical styles could be emancipatory and transformative. Becker (1975) wrote about the instrumental economic role of education in terms of developing human capital, whereas Neill (1974) preferred to emphasize intrinsic and non-instrumental roles of education. Tagore (1999), on the other hand, constructed the role of education as a trinity of spiritual, physical and emotional development.

The roles of schools, colleges and universities have similarly been the subject of contrasting conceptualizations. Nussbaum (1997) has written extensively about the notion of 'cultivating humanity' and more recently has drawn attention to what she perceives as a 'crisis' in education (2010: 1). This is related to reductions in the financing of liberal arts programmes in higher education in the USA. Nussbaum argues that the loss of the liberal arts in higher education will reduce students' 'future abilities to become active citizens in democracies' (2010: 2). Thus the role of education in developing active citizens who can participate in democratic society is implied. Furthermore, in Chapter 4 of this book, Clark argues that education may be seen as having a role in social and cultural formation and the development of self.

Education and the capability approach

Both Sen and Nussbaum have been criticized for under-specifying the role of education within a capability approach (Brighouse and Unterhalter, 2011; Terzi, 2007; Walker, 1997). However, others have made a variety of attempts to establish the aims and purposes of education in relation to nurturing particular capabilities. Theorization about the role of education from a capability perspective has led to a pluralistic understanding of the role of education which can be related to Sen's evaluative framework. Ingrid Robeyns (2006) has outlined distinctions between rights-based human capital and capability-based perceptions of the role of education and these have been discussed in other work (Hart, 2007, 2012a). Schooling is viewed as distinct from education itself which may take place in a wide range of settings – for example, in institutions, local communities and virtual environments. Not all education that is done in the name of education is good, and Kelly (2012) problematizes the relationship between schooling and well-being. For example, some children experience separation anxiety when left at school, pupil assessments can be stressful and pupils may be harassed or bullied in school.

Research fostering a capability approach has led to several attempts to identify lists of capabilities which might be expanded through schooling and education to support human flourishing. Perceptions of the roles of schools play into discussions of the kinds of capabilities that might be included in such lists. Robeyns suggested a five-step procedural approach that involved drawing up an ideal-theoretical list in the first instance. This is intended to form the basis of deliberative democratic discussion and the formulation of an actual agreed list for the specific purpose in question. Although a number of writers have identified ideal lists, the transformation to the final stage of Robeyns' procedure remains elusive. For example, Terzi (2007: 37) suggests an ideal list of capabilities for educational functionings. These are related to literacy, numeracy, sociability and participation without shame, learning dispositions, physical activities, science, technology and practical reason. Similarly, Walker (1997: 189) offers an ideal-theoretical list of educational capabilities for the development of gender equality in education in South Africa. These are centred around developing autonomy, knowledge, social relations, respect and recognition, aspiration, voice, bodily integrity and health, and emotions and emotional integrity. According to Walker, the aims of education should relate to developing agency, empowerment and autonomy (Walker, 1997: 179). Regarding tertiary education, Nussbaum (1997) has proposed three central human capabilities for higher education including critical self-examination, the ideal of the world citizen and the development of a narrative imagination.

Certain capabilities have been identified with particular relevance for children. Biggeri (2007) has identified a number of points specifically related to children's capabilities and these are pertinent to highlight. He observes that certain capabilities might be more or less relevant at different points in a child's life. For example, a 1-year-old may not benefit from the freedom to move freely in the outdoors as this may cause fatal injury. There is a philosophical issue here, since capabilities are defined as reflecting ways of being and doing that the individual has reason to value. If others determine which 'capabilities' should be developed we might question whether these are actually capabilities, since they are not identified by the individual child in the first instance. One justification that has been given is that certain capabilities, such as the capability for practical reason, are necessary in order for the individual to reflect on their life and determine what it is they have reason to value (Nussbaum, 2000).

Schools and colleges have key roles in facilitating discussion and reflection on what is of value to individual pupils. For example, in the UK, 'marketing' higher education as the preferred choice for able students potentially influences students' values and hence what they perceive to be valued ways of being and doing. So there is a sort of double-bind in education. Our current processes of schooling are constantly bombarding young people with preferred values in terms of behaviour, morals, career trajectories and so on. Thus can we say that schools offer neutral territory on which to undertake democratic public deliberation on the domains of capabilities that they should support? Can schools afford to be neutral, or is some level of bias necessary to fulfil the wider economic and social needs that are perceived by others in positions of power and leadership?

Furthermore, with regard to securing education justice, Unterhalter and Brighouse (2007) suggest an idealized list of factors to be measured. The factors include transparency in forms of educational governance, opportunities to publicly discuss educational form and content, opportunities to implement recommendations based on such public discussion, multi-dimensional measures of inequality and measures of the resources required to achieve public discussion, political and economic participation. Brighouse and Unterhalter note that 'obviously not all of these factors are readily measurable, but others are, and all are pertinent to justice' (2011: 212). Having reviewed the role of education in society, in general and from a capability perspective, we now turn to consider applying a capability approach to educational research. This begins with a consideration of children and young people's roles in educational research.

Applying a capability framework to educational research

Research has the potential to increase our knowledge and understanding of a subject. Moreover, research can constitute an intervention as well as an investigation – in other words, it may not leave the research environment exactly as it was found due to the interactions and activities that take place during the research process. Furthermore, the questions that researchers ask, and the spotlights they shine on hitherto neglected areas may contribute towards agenda-setting and paradigm-shifting that could be transformative and even emancipatory. Thus research is not a passive and neutral activity but rather a mine of agentic possibilities for both researchers and researched. The topics researchers choose to investigate and the means by which the research is undertaken will be influenced, at least to a certain extent, by the researchers' own values, assumptions and cultural norms. In other words, our views of the world will influence the questions we are motivated to explore and the means we see as optimal for those endeavours.

We need to establish, 'the basic belief system or worldview that guides the investigator' (Guba and Lincoln, 1994: 105). Indeed, Pring argues that 'meanings are "negotiated" between researcher and researched' (Pring, 2000: 40). There has been longstanding debate over the use of qualitative and quantitative methods in educational research. After a period of tending toward a dualistic view of quantitative versus qualitative research, more recent thinking suggests that different research paradigms may draw fruitfully on both qualitative and quantitative methods. Similarly, there is often a binary division between the nature of ontological and epistemological concerns in doing research, whereas from some paradigmatic viewpoints there is less distinction and the boundaries are at best fuzzy. For example, a positivist might be able to draw an effective distinction between the nature of reality (ontology) and the means necessary to understand it (epistemology). However, a constructivist would need to consider multiple socially-constructed realities where meaning-making is interwoven with the creation of multiple lived realities. Thus ontology and epistemology are seen to merge, with unclear moments of differentiation. The way that individuals interact with their environment may lead to new understandings, insights, meanings and relationships. Indeed, it has been argued, 'human behavior . . . cannot be understood without reference to the meanings and purposes attached by human actors to their activities' (Guba and Lincoln, 1994: 106).

Prout suggests that any boundary between research with children and research with adults is 'artificial' and therefore 'special techniques' are not required. Rather he suggests that what we need is 'simply a rigorous application of a general methodological requirement, applicable whether studying adults or children, and that the techniques used in a study should reflect the concrete particularities of the children being studied' (Prout, 2007: Foreword). Hence in the ensuing discussion, whilst the challenges of operationalizing the capability approach in research are largely applicable to all individuals and social groups, specific consideration is given to the nature of the concrete particularities concerning children in different contexts. More general issues around the relationship of the capability approach and the potential for educational research are discussed elsewhere (Hart, 2009).

The informational focus

In terms of capabilities, Biggeri and Mehrotra have discussed a number of methods for selecting domains of well-being involving public scrutiny, consensus and participation by children and other stakeholders (2011: 80). Burchardt and Unterhalter (2011) consider functionings as well as treatment of the individual and level of autonomy in their examination of equality and human rights in Britain. Their methodology represents an attempt to overcome the dilemma of how to take account of the notion of 'capability' as well as 'functioning' in assessing human development issues. In thinking about how their work might inform educational research in schools we might consider further the roles of pupil autonomy and pupil perceptions of how they are treated in school, college or higher education environments. In this case our understandings of 'autonomy' and 'treatment' would need to be made transparent and then operationalized to facilitate the research, since these notions are problematic and subject to plural interpretations (Hand, 2006; Chapter 11 in this book). Table 1.1 outlines some key questions and issues to consider in determining the informational focus for research formulated using the perspective of the capability approach.

Developing children's capabilities for research

In relation to the UNCRC, Alderson highlights three areas of emphasis in the involvement of children in research. These relate to stages of research, levels of children's participation and the methods that are used to 'increase children's informed involvement in research' (2001: 1). Aside from rights-based reasons for including children in research about them, Alderson also notes that it can have efficiency benefits and help to spread the balance of power. The UNCRC highlights the onus on seeking children's views about matters that affect them and also facilitating, and being open to, multiple forms of expression through a range of media (e.g. 'songs, dreams, by models, drawings or maps' – Alderson 2001: 6). Also, working together with children as research partners gives adults more time to get to know the children and can help to overcome power differences, although this is not guaranteed (Alderson, 2001). Key stages of research include the research focus, research methods, fieldwork, coding and analysis of data, and the writing-up and dissemination of findings. The vocabulary used to describe children involved in educational research has evolved over time. In recent years children have been generally repositioned as participants or consultants rather than respondents or informants, recognizing that individuals do not simply give out information but that processes of social interaction, engagement and interpretation in research are complex and dynamic. The levels of participation, in relation to agency, shift from

Table 1.1 Summary of key issues for research using a capability approach

Research issue	Points to consider
1. What is the purpose of the inequality evaluation? (Sen, 1992)	This question can help to identify what kind of equality is of interest
2. What is the choice of informational focus? (Sen, 1992)	Is the individual or a group the unit of evaluation? Sen identifies four possible points of informational focus relating to well-being freedom, well-being achievement, agency freedom and agency achievement
3. Should there be a threshold for any specified capabilities?	Sen and Nussbaum have divergent views Threshold minimum may have an instrumental value in helping to inform policy and practice
4. Are functionings to be measured?	Which functionings? How will they be measured (thresholds, individual episodes, over time, repetition, combinations)? What are the limitations?[5]
5. Are capabilities to be measured?	Consider evaluating the capability to aspire (CTA) and the capability to realize (CTR) aspirations as starting points for evaluating an individual's full capability set Consider language and mode of communication of concepts to research participants
6. Is functioning an adequate proxy for capability?	Functionings do not reflect the individual's full capability set and the intrinsic freedom to choose
7. Are rights adequate proxies for capabilities, or functionings?	Having a right does not mean having the capability to do/be and may not represent a valued way of being/doing for the individual Having a right does not mean that functioning will follow
8. Are aspirations adequate proxies for capabilities, or functionings?	Having an aspiration is not the same as having the real opportunity to achieve the aspiration.[6] It should not be assumed that aspiration will lead to further functioning
9. Is a list of context-specific capabilities to be generated?	Possibly follow Robeyns' (2005) procedural approach Create opportunity for democratic deliberation of suggested capabilities facilitating a strong voice for all stakeholders
10. Are capabilities to be weighted?	How can the differential weighting of capabilities be justified?

Source: An extension of earlier work by Hart (2012a: 68)

child informants through to child participants, children as co-researchers and ultimately independent child researchers.

Indeed, Kellett (2010) suggests that children have the greatest agency potentially when they initiate and undertake their own research. She has spent many years developing children's research skills and promoting research led by the children themselves.[7] The Centre for Studies in Childhood and Youth (Sheffield, UK), where Allison James is co-director, also specializes in research methods for involving children in research at all stages.[8]

In what might be described as a 'digital world', more and more social networking, learning and identity formation takes place online, virtually, even anonymously. In addition to wide-ranging ethical reasons, in this sense, children's high-level participation in all stages of the research process about matters that concern them is further foregrounded. Effectively children are the gatekeepers to their virtual worlds. Adults may need permission to enter. In Chapter 11, Ballet *et al.* report on the role of child sorcerers in the Democratic Republic of the Congo (DCR). In this case the sorcerer's imaginary becomes an additional sphere alongside more widely recognized spheres of public and private, social and economic. Here again, the children are gatekeepers to the sorcerer's imaginary and any exploration necessitates their participation.

Attention now turns to the ways we can engage children and young people in research that concerns their lives, particularly with regard to their education in schools. There is a growing body of work considering participatory methods for collecting data in ways that include children as subjects rather than objects, drawing on work by James *et al.* (2012: 5). This is important, but the influence of the capability approach on research begins much earlier in thinking about the focus of the research itself and the skills children may need in order to increase their agency in research. The nature of the research questions themselves will help to indicate the way in which children are positioned as human capital, automatons or free-thinking autonomous empowered individuals.

For example, Reznitskaya has observed that 'students rarely experience dialogic teaching throughout their schooling' (2012: 449), which means that many individuals lack the capability to critically reflect, to apply practical reason or to develop a narrative imagination. Having said this, for many years, some subject areas in schools (e.g. social studies) have sought to encourage young people to develop their own research projects. I taught sociology in secondary schools for many years, working with children aged 13–18. They routinely learned about how to do social research and they planned and undertook their own research projects based on self-initiated ideas. Young children can develop many of these research skills and there are some creative and innovative pedagogical approaches that may support such development.

Woodhead and Faulkner (2008) highlight the characterization of children as subjects, objects or participants in research whilst others have considered children as respondents (Scott, 2008). These different terms help to illustrate the different power dynamics that might emerge as research is undertaken. In particular, the degree of trust, power and agency experienced by children may vary significantly depending on how their position is determined or negotiated by adult enquirers. Indeed, the norms, values and cultures of many societies readily imbue the adult-child dyad with power-laden meanings and signifiers. In identifying a human as either adult or child, certain expectations, rights, obligations and commitments might be culturally inferred, putting the adult in charge, responsible, or with a duty to protect and control. The role of adolescent, youth or young person may denote an in-between stage in the transition from child- to adulthood which is unclear, shifting and idiosyncratic. In capability-oriented research there is an opportunity to interact and engage with children and young people in ways that strive to redress the balance of power and agency in ways that are empowering and potentially capability-enhancing.

The process of working with children in developing research ideas before, during and after entering the 'field' may help to build 'reciprocal stata'. That is to say, the children may become involved in activities that are usually unfamiliar in their fields of action and similarly the adult researchers may also become involved in new activities and practices as they experience the settings where children are situated in the research fieldwork (school, home, youth centre or otherwise).

Habermas' (1984) notion of communicative action draws attention to the way in which some communication between individuals appears to take place relatively unproblematically, with both parties making meanings in a similar vein and behaving, responding, communicating accordingly. Where the meaning is unclear, individuals may enter into a discourse in order to resolve the true meaning and intention of the communicative action, whether verbal, gestural and so on. The process of discourse is both challenging and complex and it is possible that in a research situation a child may not enter into discourse despite disharmony in the communicative action. So we cannot guarantee that 'authentic' voices will be heard in research with children. Along a similar line, in Chapter 7, Devecchi *et al.* cite the observation of Arnot and Reay (2007) reporting that children may use different voices in response to their knowledge and understanding of the discourses, 'adults use and value' (see p. 151). Furthermore, Corsaro and Molinari

(2008: 92) note the importance of context for children – for example, they may adopt different attitudes or be more relaxed at home, school or in particular environments. Thus as researchers striving to understand the young person's valued ways of being and doing we need to be particularly alert to the limitations of the possible meanings we are making from the research encounters.

In ethnographic studies, 'entering the field and developing a participant status' is seen as important in developing membership status and an insider perspective (Corsaro and Molinari, 2008: 241). Corsaro and Molinari recount a series of 'transitory rituals' that adult researchers may need to go through in order 'to be accepted into the peer world of young children' (2008: 244). It has been observed that 'a balance of entertainment and intimacy is typical of the communication in groups of adolescents and is the most attractive form of communication for adolescents' (Baraldi and Rossi, cited by Iervese, Chapter 12, this book). Furthermore, Roberts (2008) has emphasized the importance of listening to children and actually *hearing* them rather than imposing value judgements and assumptions. Although much research with children will not take an ethnographic stance, in order to build rapport with children it may be helpful to consider how young people communicate among themselves and how researchers hear them.

Participatory techniques

Many different research techniques have been used to engage children in research of various kinds and different methods will suit different purposes. For example, O'Kane (2008) has written about how participatory techniques might help to facilitate children's views about decisions which affect them. There are numerous studies that have used visual methods to stimulate discussion and to generate data with children and young people (e.g. Anich *et al.*, 2011; Kellock and Lawthom, 2011). Christensen and James (2008) have illustrated a 'graphical research technique' that showed that, 'it was the technique itself which enabled children to become reflexive interpreters' (2008: 7). Along similar lines, Stoecklin and Bonvin (see Chapter 3 of this book) note that in order to allow children ample opportunity to express their views, different media, such as drawings, photographs, oral and written communication may be used. Interestingly, these authors propose an 'activity system' to help children to develop their thinking around different aspects of their lives. There are other possibilities for developing children's thinking skills and capabilities for critical reflection in relation to research participation, and in this chapter the potential of 'Philosophy for Children' will briefly be discussed. There is also a significant potential to develop children's research skills to support their capabilities to act as co-researchers and indeed to lead their own research into issues that are of relevance to them. Thinking Actively in a Social Context (TASC) will be discussed later in this chapter in this context.

Research participation and Philosophy for Children

I would like to propose here that pedagogical and enquiry-based practices such as 'Philosophy for Phildren' (P4C) may help to develop children's and young people's capabilities to participate in research (Lipman, 2010). Essentially P4C is a practice which encourages philosophical and dialogical enquiry among children and can be introduced from a very early age. This process of enquiry can be usefully applied to capability-oriented research with children. I think that this is particularly the case when, for example, unravelling children's values, issues of identity and personhood as well as broader moral issues.

Through participation in 'communities of enquiry' children develop skills and practices that help them to be critical and reflexive thinkers (Lipman, 2010). Hymer and Sutcliffe (2012: 18) observe that some of the qualities P4C aims to promote are 'intellectual humility', 'respect for persons' and 'breadth of mind', and they define the 'community of enquiry', central to P4C as follows (p. 10):

> A community of enquiry is achieved when a group of people engage in a cooperative search for understanding through dialogue . . . The onus of these COE is to provide thoughtful and caring environments where children exercise reason, listen to one another and reflect on what is said. Thinking time and 'small group dialogue' lead to a process of question-making, question-airing and question-choosing. The process of enquiry offers the opportunity for group participants to collaborate, 'to develop understanding of and through the question' through a process of critical reasoning.

Fisher proposes that the relationship between individuals and the community of enquiry should be 'reciprocal and organic' and 'communities should develop through adapting to the needs of [their] members' through a process of 'reasoned argument' (2013: 43). Importantly, 'a community of enquiry[9] attempts to follow the enquiry where it leads rather than be penned in by the boundaries of existing disciplines' (Lipman, 2010: 20). This latter point has particular relevance for the development of children's agency in relation to research about them.

My own experience of communities of enquiry is that they develop a space for thinking and a sense of community and cooperation. Such communities develop skills, vocabulary and a state of mind or disposition where individuals are stimulated to build on the thoughts of others in a critical and reasoned manner. Profound insights are often revealed and many individuals change their thoughts on a question as a consequence of participation in the enquiry. The skills suit Sen's notion of democratic processes of deliberation well and help to nurture in children the capability to be active agents in such processes. It helps to develop creative thinking and 'good judgement' (Lipman, 2010).

Thus the kind of educational practices we engage in with children during their schooling are vitally important in helping to develop their capabilities *per se* as well as for participation and the initiation of research. There is evidence that children can be critical reflexive thinkers from an early age (Biggeri, 2007). Indeed, I was recently at a P4C conference where one of the children (boy, aged 8) was asked by an adult, 'at what age do you think children become philosophical?' The boy answered, 'I think it starts the first time you ask your parents, "why?"' This then sparked further dialogue where an adult said they were reading about philosophy for babies and queried whether individuals can think philosophically even at the pre-verbal stages of development. In my own experience of participation in 'communities of enquiry' with children, I have observed deep, critical and reflexive thinking in children as young as 4 years of age.

In Chapter 2, Biggeri acknowledges that P4C, 'can constitute a suitable pedagogical approach for developing critical thinking and democratic citizenship among children and youths' and goes on to outline some of the key aspects of P4C as introduced by its inceptor, Matthew Lipman. Santi and Di Masi (Chapter 6) discuss P4C as a pedagogy for developing children's agency in schools. Hence readers are encouraged to relate the potential for P4C in research, with and by children, to Biggeri, Santi and Di Masi's broader discussions.

Thinking actively in a social context

Earlier in this chapter Mary Kellett's (2010) work on developing children's research skills was introduced. There is increasing support for the idea that even young children can be effective co-researchers and also lead researchers. Kellett argues that children have the highest level of agency when they are responsible for their own research and has developed a programme for developing research skills among children. I would like to propose that Belle Wallace's thinking skills framework, Thinking Actively in a Social Context (TASC) is a powerful way of supporting children in working together, and can be fruitfully applied to the realms of research with and by children (Wallace, 2000). Figure 1.1 shows Wallace's TASC wheel which is used by children, usually in small groups, to aid problem-solving and project work in a growing number of primary and secondary schools.

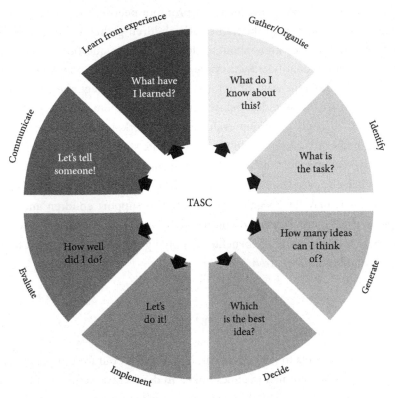

Copyright © Belle Wallace 2000

Figure 1.1 TASC Wheel

Source: Wallace (2000)

The framework aims to facilitate inclusive and differentiated learning experiences to enable as many children as possible to contribute to their full potential.[10] Moreover, by working effectively together the process of working in a social context aims to be intrinsically rewarding and the combined efforts of individuals help to create a greater whole than the sum of the parts. From a capability perspective the TASC framework can be seen to support the development of an individual's well-being and agency freedoms. Wallace *et al.* (2012: 60) argue that

> All children can think, but thinking can be enhanced and developed through appropriate practice, in the same way as a gymnast trains and perfects complex movements so that he or she becomes automatic and controlled but also highly flexible and creative.

Wallace has found that TASC helps to promote peer-learning and problem-solving. In the first stage of the framework, children 'gather and organize' ideas about what they already know about the topic or issue in question. In the second stage participants 'identify' what they are going to do and then in the third stage they 'generate' different ways of doing it. At the fourth stage the group has to 'decide' which are the best ideas before 'implementing' them in terms of action at stage five. At stage six the group 'evaluates' their work, looking at strengths and areas for further development. In the penultimate stage children 'communicate' what they have learned. Finally, at the eighth stage, the TASC group reflects on what has been learned from the process. TASC is described as a problem-solving process and it may have significant potential to support children and young people in participating in and doing research. In a sense learning is research.[11] Thus there are parallels in the benefits of applying the TASC framework to both research and learning-centred issues.

Ethics and research

There are many facets to the ethical nature of research but for our purposes the discussion here it is limited to ethics linked to democratic values and the ethos of the capability approach, with specific reference to children and young people. Section 16 of the British Educational Research Association (BERA, 2011) *Ethical Guidelines for Educational Research* state:

> The Association requires researchers to comply with Articles 3 and 12 of the United Nations Convention on the Rights of the Child. Article 3 requires that in all actions concerning children, the best interests of the child must be the primary consideration. Article 12 requires that children who are capable of forming their own views should be granted the right to express their views freely in all matters affecting them, commensurate with their age and maturity. Children should therefore be facilitated to give fully informed consent.

The BERA guidelines also emphasize the need for voluntary informed consent and the right to withdraw from research 'for any or no reason, and at any time' (Section 15). Alderson and Morrow (2011) highlight the need for *ongoing* informed consent not only from parents but also from the young people themselves. If data are to be used in reports then further consent may need to be sought. It is important to think about what to do if a child research participant changes their mind later. The extent to which research participants can be offered anonymity and their data kept confidential should be discussed at the outset of any project. However, this needs to take account of duties around disclosure (Section 29) and the BERA guidelines note that, 'if the behaviour is likely to be harmful to the participants or to others, the researchers must consider disclosure'. Other ethical issues relate to identifying the potential harms and benefits of all aspects of the research process. For example, consideration is needed regarding the physical and emotional safety of child participants during and after the research process, especially where children are vulnerable (e.g on the street, neglectful home, areas of conflict and so on).

Particularly with regard to research in international contexts, there is an onus on researchers to minimize the risk of cultural imperialism. This may relate, for example, to the possibility of going into different cultural settings and intentionally or unintentionally, imposing particular ideas about democracy, participation, autonomy and ways of being and doing that the individual researcher may have reason to value. This requires critical reflection and the development of self-knowledge to understand the values that underpin our own thinking. For example, Iervese and Tuttolomondo, in Chapter 12, reflect on an example of where the adults attempted to steer the research activity to gain responses in relation to particular criteria. In doing so they effectively missed the contributions that the young people were making and with this the opportunity to support participation at a deeper level. In other words, as Iervese puts it, there are 'expectations of adjustment of the children to the social worker's requests' (see p. 253). Researchers can be perceived as being in a position of power in relation to potential research participants and it is important, ethically, to set clear boundaries with anyone who engages in the research process about the harms and benefits of participation. As researchers our power to improve living conditions, for example, may be limited but we may face very difficult situations and expectations from research participants. There may be some tension between the boundaries of our humanity, agency freedom and our professional responsibilities. It is pertinent to reflect on the extent to which researchers are duty-bearers with regard to the children and young people they connect with during the research process.

Concluding remarks

A core strength of the capability approach lies in adding and complementing existing work. Our perspectives on childhood, schooling and education are informed by our values and positionality. The capability approach encourages us to think in a particular way that places an onus on expanding individual capabilities, that is the ways of being and doing that the individual learner has reason to value. There may be difference, even dissonance, with the aspirations of parents, teachers and the state in determining the kinds of qualities, skills and attributes that ought to be developed in children and young people through schooling, whether or not a capability approach is pursued. This is illustrated by the ideal-theoretical lists and the fact that children may be resistant to learning certain things at set points in time and in particular ways.

This chapter has attempted to highlight some of the important developments that have taken place in childhood studies and research with and by children. In doing so, the aim has been to conceptualize how the capability approach links to and extends existing work in relation to researching childhood and youth for and with young people. Educational research has a crucial role to play in understanding the dynamics and challenges of the educational contexts in which children and young people find themselves, and in contributing to exploring socially just ways of expanding capabilities in meaningful, empowering and emancipatory ways. By applying the capability approach to research with children there is the potential to support a shifting of policy and pedagogical agendas to take account of capabilities as well as rights. The ways in which we might think about the possibilities for engaging children in research will be influenced by the way we think about children. This includes whether their age, perceived maturity and

Table 1.2 Checklist of key questions for research with children using a capability approach

1.	How will the research design be influenced by capability-based views of the world and how it might be understood?
2.	Is it important, or appropriate, for children to be integral to the research at all stages of the process, from inception to dissemination?
3.	What methods can be developed that will include children and young people in ethical and respectful ways?
4.	What approaches will enable adults to develop partnerships with children as 'consultants', co-researchers and even encourage children to initiate their own research into matters that are of value to them?
5.	When the coding and analysis of data is taking place, in what ways might the capability approach inform thinking on these processes and the ways in which data are coded and interpreted?
6.	In discussing the findings from research with children, and disseminating research to wider audiences, how might the capability approach inform thinking on the ways these stages evolve?

competences make a difference to adults' perceptions of what children might be able to contribute. References have been made to a variety of empirical studies related to children and young people where attempts have been made to apply the capability approach, and several of these are presented in ensuing chapters of this book. To conclude this chapter, Table 1.2 provides a checklist of key questions to reflect upon in planning research with children, drawing upon the capability approach.

Notes

1 For further discussion see Hart 2012b; Walker 2012.
2 Nussbaum has different views from Sen on the distinction between agency and well-being freedom (see Nussbaum, 2011: 201 for further discussion).
3 Sridhar Venkatapuram has written a very insightful book on health justice, from which this extract is drawn. It has significant relevance for the development of education policy and practice and is recommended reading for those interested in this area.
4 For further discussion see Hart, 2009.
5 Hart (2012a) observes that 'the challenge of identifying functioning n-tuples as compared to individual functionings is very complex and presents a challenge for operationalizing the approach'.
6 In Chapter 9 the 'capability to aspire' is described as a meta-capability. Aspiring is defined as a functioning. The capability to aspire is viewed as a precursor to many other capabilities.
7 See http://childrens-research-centre.open.ac.uk for further information about children as researchers.
8 For further details see www.cscy.group.shef.ac.uk
9 'Inquiry' and 'enquiry' and the two different terms used by different writers on this subject. 'Inquiry' tends to be the common US term and 'enquiry' is more commonly used in English texts although both refer to a process of questioning in the quest for knowledge and understanding.
10 For further discussion on the use of the TASC Wheel, see Wallace, et al. 2004, 2008 and 2009.
11 This point was made to me by my daughter (aged 8). She regularly uses the TASC framework to solve problems and work on projects with peers.

References

Alderson, P. (2001) Research by children: rights and methods, *International Journal of Social Research Methodology: Theory and Practice*, 4(2), pp. 139–153.

Alderson, P. & Morrow, V. (2011) *The Ethics of Research with Children and Young People: A Practical Handbook*, second edition (London, Sage).

Anich, R., Biggeri, M., Libanora, R. & Mariani, S. (2011) Street children in Kampala and NGO's action: understanding capabilities deprivation and expansion, in Biggeri, M., Ballet, J. & Comim, F. (eds) *Children and the Capability Approach*, second edition (Basingstoke, Palgrave).

Arnot, M. & Reay, D. (2007) A sociology of pedagogic voice: power, inequality and pupils' consultation, *Discourse Studies in the Culture Politics of Education*, 28(3), pp. 311–25.

Baraldi, C. & Rossi (2002) La prevenzione delle azioni giovanili a rischio. Angeli, Milano.

Becker, G.S. (1975) *Human Capital: A Theoretical and Empirical Analysis* (Chicago, University of Chicago Press).

BERA (British Educational Research Association) (2011) *Ethical Guidelines for Educational Research*, www.bera.ac.uk.

Berges, S. (2007) Why the capability approach is justified, *Journal of Applied Philosophy*, 24(1), pp.16–25.

Biggeri, M. (2007) Children's valued capabilities in Walker, M. & Unterhalter, E. (eds) *Amartya Sen's Capability Approach and Social Justice in Education* (Basingstoke, Palgrave).

Biggeri, M. & Mehrotra, S. (2011) Child poverty as capability deprivation: how to choose domains of child well-being and poverty, in Biggeri, M., Ballet, J. & Comim, F. (eds) *Children and the Capability Approach*, second edition (Basingstoke, Palgrave).

Bourdieu, P. & Passeron, J-C. (2000) *Reproduction in Education, Society & Culture*, second edition. (London, Sage).

Brighouse, H. & Unterhalter, E. (2011) Education for primary goods or for capabilities? in, Brighouse, H. & Robeyns, I. (eds) (2011) *Measuring Justice: Primary Goods and Capabilities* (Cambridge, Cambridge University Press).

Burchardt, T. & Unterhalter, E. (2011) Operationalizing the capability approach as a basis for equality and human rights monitoring in twenty-first-century Britain, *Journal of Human Development and Capabilities*, 12(1), pp. 91–119.

Christensen, P. & James, A. (eds) (2008) *Research with Children: Perspectives and Practices*, second edition (London, Routledge).

Corsaro, W.A. & Molinari, L. (2008) Entering and observing in children's worlds: a reflection on a longitudinal ethnography of early education in Italy, in Christensen, P. & James, A. (eds) *Research with Children, Perspectives and Practices*, second edition (London, Routledge).

Dreze, J. & Sen, A. (1995) *India: Economic Development and Social Opportunity* (Oxford, Oxford University Press).

Fisher, R. (2013) *Teaching Thinking: Philosophical Enquiry in the Classroom*, third edition (London, Bloomsbury).

Freire, P. (1972) *Pedagogy of the Oppressed* (London, Penguin).

Guba, E.G. & Lincoln, Y.S. (1994) Competing paradigms in qualitative research, in Denzin, N.K. & Lincoln, Y.S. (eds) *Handbook of Qualitative Research* (Thousand Oaks, CA, Sage).

Habermas, J. (1984) *The Theory of Communicative Action, Volume I, Reason and the Rationalization of Society* (Boston, MA, Beacon Press).

Hand, M. (2006) Against autonomy as an educational aim, *Oxford Review of Education*, 32(4), pp. 535–550.

Hart, C.S. (2007) The capability approach as an evaluative and developmental framework for education policy: the example of widening participation in higher education in England, *Prospero*, 13, pp. 34–50 (special issue on the capability approach).

Hart, C.S. (2009) Quo vadis? The capability space and new directions for the philosophy of educational research, *Studies in Philosophy & Education*, 28(5), pp. 391–402 (special Issue on the capability approach).

Hart, C.S. (2010) *Aspirations Re-examined: A Capability Approach to Widening Participation in Higher Education*, PhD thesis, University of Cambridge.

Hart, C.S. (2012a) *Aspirations, Education and Social Justice: Applying Sen and Bourdieu* (London, Bloomsbury).

Hart, C.S. (2012b) The capability approach and education, *Cambridge Journal of Education*, 42(3), pp. 275–282.

Hart, C.S. (2012c) Aspirations, Education and Social Justice: Applying Sen and Bourdieu, *BERA Research Intelligence*, Spring, pp. 34–5.

Hart, C.S. (2013) *Education and policies on the aspirations of young people*, background paper for the 2013 UNDP Panama Human Development Report.

Hymer, B. & Sutcliffe, R. (2012) *P4C Pocketbook* (Alresford, Teachers Pocketbooks).

James, A., Jenks, C. & Prout, A. (2012) *Theorizing Childhood* (Cambridge, Polity Press).

Kellett, M. (2010) *Rethinking Children and Research: Attitudes in Contemporary Society* (London, Continuum).

Kellock, A. & Lawthom, R. (2011) Sen's capability approach: Children and well-being explored through the use of photography, in Biggeri, M., Ballet, J. & Comim, F. (eds) *Children and the Capability Approach*, second edition (Basingstoke, Palgrave).

Kelly, A. (2012) Sen and the art of educational maintenance: evidencing a capability, as opposed to an effectiveness, approach to schooling, *Cambridge Journal of Education*, 42(3), pp. 283–296.

Lipman, M. (2010) *Thinking in Education*, second edition (Cambridge, Cambridge University Press).

Neill, A.S. (1974) *Summerhill* (London, Penguin).

Nussbaum, M.C. (1997) *Cultivating Humanity: A Classical Defense of Reform in Liberal Education* (London, Harvard University Press).

Nussbaum, M.C. (2000) *Women and Human Development: The Capabilities Approach* (Cambridge, Cambridge University Press).

Nussbaum, M.C. (2010) *Not for Profit: Why Democracy Needs the Humanities* (Princeton, NJ, Princeton University Press).

Nussbaum, M.C. (2011) *Creating Capabilities: The Human Development Approach* (Cambridge, MA, Harvard University Press).

O'Kane, C. (2008) The development of participatory techniques: facilitating children's views about decisions which affect them, in Christensen, P. & James, A. (eds) *Research with Children: Perspectives and Practices*, second edition (London, Routledge).

Pring, R. (2000) *Philosophy of Educational Research* (London, Continuum).

Prout, A. (2007) Foreword to the second edition, in Christensen, P. & James, A. (eds) (2008) *Research with Children: Perspectives and Practices*, second edition (London, Routledge).

Raynor, J. (2007) Education and capabilities in Bangladesh, in Walker, M. & Unterhalter, E. (eds) *Amartya Sen's Capability Approach and Social Justice in Education* (Basingstoke, Palgrave).

Reznitskaya, A. (2012) Dialogic teaching: rethinking language use during literature discussions, *The Reading Teacher*, 65(7), pp. 446–456.

Roberts, H. (2008) Listening to children: and hearing them, in Christensen, P. & James, A. (eds) *Research with Children: Perspectives and Practices*, second edition (London, Routledge).

Robeyns, I. (2005) The capability approach: a theoretical survey, *Journal of Human Development*, 6(1), pp. 93–114.

Robeyns, I. (2006) Three models of education: rights, capabilities and human capital, *Theory and Research in Education*, 4(1), pp. 69–84.

Scott, J. (2008) Children as respondents: the challenge for quantitative methods, in Christensen, P. & James. A. (eds) *Research with Children: Perspectives and Practices*, second edition (London, Routledge).

Sen, A. (1992) *Inequality Re-Examined* (Oxford, Clarendon Press).

Sen, A. (1999) *Commodities and Capabilities* (Oxford, Oxford University Press).

Sen, A. (2005) Human capital and human capability, in Fukuda-Parr. S. & Kumar, A.K. (eds) *Readings in Human Development* (Oxford, Oxford University Press).

Tagore, R. (1999) *The English Writings of Rabindranath Tagore*, edited by S.K. Das, Part III, Essay on my school, pp. 399–419 (New Delhi, Sagar).

Terzi, L. (2007) The capability to be educated, in Walker. M. & Unterhalter, E. (eds) *Amartya Sen's Capability Approach and Social Justice in Education* (Basingstoke, Palgrave).

UNESCO (2000) *The Dakar Framework for Action: Meeting our Collective Commitment* (Paris, Unesco), www.unesco.org

United Nations (2010) *The Millennium Development Goals Development Report* 2010, www.un.org, retrieved 29 May 2012.

Unterhalter, E. (2003) The capability approach and gendered education: an examination of South African complexities, *Theory and Research in Education*, 1 (1), pp. 7–22.

Unterhalter, E. & Brighouse, H. (2007) Distribution of what for social justice in education? The case of education for all by 2015, in Walker, M. & Unterhalter, E. (eds) *Amartya Sen's Capability Approach and Social Justice in Education* (Basingstoke, Palgrave).

Venkatapuram, S. (2011) *Health Justice. An Argument from the Capabilities Approach* (Cambridge, Polity Press).

Wallace, B. (2000) *Thinking Actively in a Social Context, TASC Wheel*, www.tascwheel.com.

Wallace, B., Maker, J., Cave, D. & Chandler, S. (2004) Thinking Skills and Problem-Solving: An Inclusive Approach. London: Taylor and Francis, Routledge.

Wallace, B., Cave, D. & Berry, A. (2008) Teaching Problem-Solving and Thinking Skills through Science. London: Taylor and Francis, Routledge.

Wallace, B. (Editor) (Guest Editors: June Maker and Bob Zimmerman) (2009) TASC International: Thinking Actively in a Social Context: Theory and Practice.

Wallace, B., Bernardelli, A., Molyneux, C. & Farrell, C. (2012) TASC: thinking actively in a social context. a universal problem-solving process: a powerful tool to promote differentiated learning experiences, *Gifted Education International*, 28(1), pp. 58–83.

Wenger, E. (2008) *Communities of Practice: Learning, Meaning and Identity* (Cambridge, Cambridge University Press).

Woodhead, M. & Faulkner, D. (2008) Subjects, objects or participants? Dilemmas of psychological research with children, in Christensen. P. & James, A. (eds) *Research with Children: Perspectives and Practices*, second edition (London, Routledge).

Walker, M. (1997) Selecting capabilities for gender equality in education, in Walker M. & Unterhalter, E. (eds) *Amartya Sen's Capability Approach and Social Justice in Education* (Basingstoke, Palgrave Macmillan).

Walker, M. (ed.) (2012) *Journal of Human Development and Capabilities*, special issue, 'Education and Capabilities', 13(3).

2

Education Policy for Agency and Participation

Mario Biggeri

Introduction

Children and young people are too often excluded, in a sort of *age-bias*, from participation processes and collective deliberative choices. In this chapter, the capability approach is applied to rethink education in order to increase children's agency[1] and participation[2] in individual and collective decision-making processes.

The capability approach, exemplifying the intellectual foundation for the Sustainable Human Development (SHD) paradigm,[3] considers human well-being, participation and freedom to be central objectives of economic and social policies (Sen, 1999). Indeed, the capability approach 'focuses on the ability of human beings to lead lives they have reason to value and to enhance the substantive choices they have' (Sen, 1997: 1959). Furthermore, according to Sen, education can foster public debate and dialogue about social and political arrangements in a democratic society (Sen, 1992).

These few initial elements already reveal the idea of education for freedom such that 'education is thus central to human flourishing' (Nussbaum, 2006). 'It not only opens the mind to further horizons, it also opens the way to acquire other valuable capabilities' (Unterhalter, 2009: 208) both for the individual and for society. Indeed, not only scholars consider education as 'the driving force of change in the world ... Education (which is not always the same as schooling) brings empowerment' (Unterhalter, 2009: 208),[4] but also *children themselves value education as one of the most important instrumental capabilities for change* (Biggeri *et al.*, 2006, 2011a; Biggeri, 2007).

In addition, the capability approach perspective considers children not simply as recipients of freedoms, but rather as active social actors and agents in their communities (Biggeri *et al.*, 2011a). This conceptualization is not neutral in education and social policies and it requires children and young adults to have the agency capability and the opportunities to participate[5] to express their own priorities, strategies and aspirations (Hart, 2009, 2012; Biggeri and Santi, 2012) and to promote them in the decision-making processes. Indeed, can we really think about the empowerment of adults without thinking about the empowerment of children? Can individuals learn to participate if they are not given any space and opportunity to exercise their agency since childhood? In this regard, according to academic studies, it is relevant to note that there is no reason to treat even young children as incapable or passive sufferers without recognizing that they can be part of the solution for achieving a better life with dignity (see, for instance, Lansdown, 2001, 2005; Feeny and Boyden, 2004; Baraldi, 2009; Ballet *et al.*, 2011). In particular, sociology has recently placed emphasis on children's self-realization (Prout, 2000) and on children's agency (James *et al.*, 1998; Hallett and Prout, 2003). Therefore, these new cultural presuppositions lead to the promotion of children's active participation, i.e. children's self-expression (Baraldi, 2009) and children's self-determination (Vygostky, 1962; Rogoff, 1990; Murray and Hallett, 2000). In addition, promoting children's active participation means socializing children towards an 'understanding of their own competencies' (Matthews, 2003: 274), i.e. to a sense of responsibility and skills in planning, designing, monitoring and managing social contexts (Prout, 2000). In other words, this view disagrees with the idea of the incapability of children to participate in decision-making processes based on the necessary condition of an adequate degree of cognitive development and appraisal, confirming instead the strict connection between participation, differentiated competencies and personal autonomy. Hence, as Landsdown (2001) points out, there are many issues that even very small children are capable of understanding and on which they can provide thoughtful opinions: 'there is no lower age limit imposed on the exercise of the right to participate. It extends therefore to any child who has a view on a matter of concern to them' (Landsdown, 2001: 2).[6]

This chapter is divided into five sections. In the second section the role of education and the relationship between education, agency and participation are discussed from a capability perspective. In the third section the relationship between the capability approach and education is further explored, while in the following section the central policy implications for education are presented. In the last section the main conclusions are reported.

Development visions and education policy: A capability approach perspective

Recent economic evidence shows that the rate of return of investing in children and especially in early childhood development is substantial, and neurological and biological studies document the malleability of the brain in early child development (Heckman *et al.*, 2012). In addition, evaluations indicate that the benefits of a well-designed programme in early childhood development go far beyond economic outcomes (Heckman *et al.*, 2012). Hence, the central question is different: education for what? In other words, it is not by chance that the starting point of several capability approach scholars has been the evaluation of different educational approaches according to their philosophical meanings and practical outcomes (see, for instance, Nussbaum, 1997, 2011; UNESCO, 2003: 32–33; Robeyns, 2006; Walker and Unterhalter, 2007; Unterhalter, 2009; Brighouse and Unterhalter, 2010; Walker, 2010). Indeed, these scholars start by acknowledging that the variety of education systems and curricula adopted around the world is developed in accordance with different theoretical perspectives and visions of development.

According to Walker (2012), for instance, three main educational models can be identified: the human capital model, the utilitarian model, and the human development and capability approach model. In Table 2.1 the main characteristics of the human capital model approaches and the human development and capability approaches are summarized and implications for education policy, change and outcomes are delineated. In brief, on the one side, education policies are largely shaped by the underlying vision of development (see Alkire, 2002; Clark, 2002; Robeyns, 2006; Nussbaum, 2011; Walker, 2012) and, on the other side, the outcomes of an education system are in part responsible for the present and future outcomes of the development processes (see, among others, Nussbaum, 2006, 2011; Walker and Unterhalter, 2007; Unterhalter, 2009; Walker, 2012). It is thus clear that different visions of development bring different pedagogical means, outcomes and measurements of the education system. Embracing the SHD paradigm pillars,[7] the human capabilities model is central, as the processes of acquiring communicative competences (Habermas, 1981) and 'complex thinking' (Lipman, 2003), including dialogical attitudes and argumentative practice, become fundamental. The idea of capable agents, introduced by Bonvin and Galster (2010) among others (for example, Andresen *et al.*, 2011; Bellanca *et al.*, 2011; Biggeri *et al.*, 2011a; Leßmann *et al.*, 2011; Nussbaum, 2011) is thus central in the process of children's evolving capabilities.

Table 2.1 The human capital and human capabilities models: education elements, policy and outcomes

	Human capital model and outcomes	**Human development and capability approach**
On being human	Individual economic producer and consumer	Full human flourishing and dignity to choose a good life
Children as . . .	Future economic actors	Capable agents who shape and are shaped by their environment
Policy value	Human capital, income and efficiency drives education and economic policy	Human development, human capabilities to foster opportunity, process freedoms and reduce inequality
Implementation: pedagogical activity	Cost-efficient market facing pedagogies; training-focused	Mixed pedagogical approaches to form sustainable functionings for young people; fostering voice; public reasoning alongside education
Type of intervention	Fostering instrumental skills	Holistic, multi-sectorial and integrated; tailored on specific conditions; participatory
Outcomes	Productivity; employability; economic growth	Current well-being; capabilities expansion and future employability; agency freedom; democratic citizens

Source: our elaborations on Walker (2012)

Ballet *et al.* (2011)[8] try to capture the dynamics among three components that trigger the evolving capabilities process: the capacity/ability concept, the opportunity concept and the agency concept (see Figure 2.1). Starting with the initial achieved functionings of a child at time *t*, the process of resource conversion into children's capacities and opportunities is enabled and constrained by different institutions, norms and cultures. Here therefore the child or youth is placed at the centre of the development process, interacting with other agents, i.e. peers, teachers, family and community members, and drawing on his or her entitlements, whose availability is mediated through their families, schools, communities and regional/national entities. In other words, the child's 'capability set' (i.e. the range of 'possible functionings') and their ability to convert resources into capabilities and functionings are crucially influenced both by their personal capacities and individual conversion factors, as well as by the social and physical environments they live and are embedded in (Sen, 1985, 2009). Here therefore

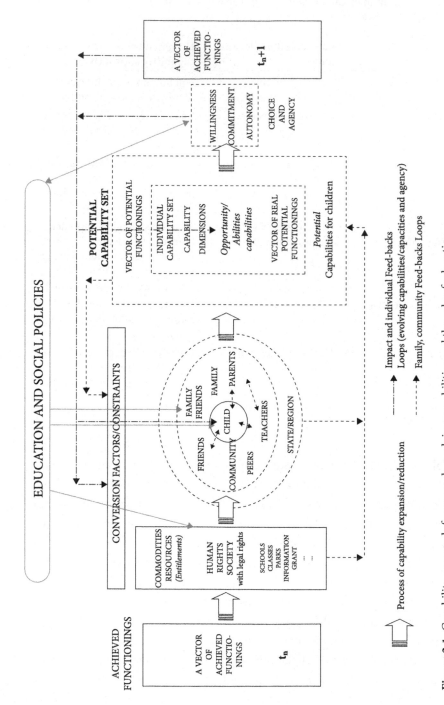

Figure 2.1 Capability approach framework, evolving capabilities and the role of education

Source: our elaborations on Trani *et al.* 2011; Ballet *et al.* 2011; Biggeri and Santi 2012 and Biggeri *et al.* 2009

the education system (Otto and Ziegler, 2006) and parents' and/or teachers' capabilities and actions (Comim, 2011) play a central role in the evolving capabilities. Indeed, the capabilities of children and teenagers are formed through social interaction and receptiveness within the household and broader environments, and constitute to a large extent the foundation of a human being's development.

Then, the functioning vector achieved in the following time period, $t+1$ will be determined by the choices within the available capability set, emphasizing the dynamic core of the evolving capabilities process where feedback loops re-shape the potential capability set of the child and enhance or reduce agency at each time period (Biggeri and Santi, 2012). Indeed, as Sen has pointed out, both regarding children and adults, 'while exercising your own choices may be important enough for some types of freedoms, there are a great many other freedoms that depend on the assistance and actions of others and the nature of social arrangements' (Sen, 2007: 9). Therefore, as we can see from Figure 2.1, educational policies can have a different direct or indirect effect on inter-temporal individual as well as social well-being, through feedback loops (see also Walker, 2012).

In other words, embracing the capability approach perspective, it is not enough that children have rights to be well educated, healthy, adequately housed and clothed, and well integrated into the community. It is also crucial to ensure their right to be part of the process of freedom itself, in line with Articles 5 (on evolving capacity) and 12 (on participation) of the UN Convention on the Rights of the Child (UNCRC). This argument gives, therefore, further salience and quality substance to the enhancement of these rights in the education field, indicating priorities for policy-makers. These include the development of children's capacity for critical thinking and the capability to aspire (Hart, 2010, 2012) alongside the development of spaces for dialogue and the participation within the education system, with a tailored approach suitable for different ages and maturity. In addition, it also underlines the importance of letting children exercise their agency and participation according to the age and maturity of the child, as well as rethinking development democracy mechanisms in order to ensure wider citizenship rights and public deliberation involvement for children, in line with Sen (1999, 2009; see also Crocker, 2007; Freire, 1985). Therefore, in order to accomplish this condition, if participation is assumed to be at the base of the deliberative process of SHD, it is fundamental not only 'to produce' or rather 'to have' capable agents and communities, but also to create wider and more inclusive spaces for dialogue and participation (Evans, 2002; Iervese and Rossi, 2009).

Education and capabilities for agency and participation

Within a human and sustainable development perspective, it is by being capable agents that people (including children and youth) can contribute to the environment in which they are educated, loved and cared for, can speak freely, are able to participate in the community life and decision-making processes and have freedom of expression and association (amongst many other capabilities and basic functionings). In other words people have the opportunity to be agents of change. As Ballet *et al.* (2011) point out, Sen's approach embraces the importance of self-determination and agency freedom (Sen, 1985, 1992, 2009), which implies a person's capacity to exercise their own free will (Sen, 1999). Biggeri and Santi (2012: 179) indeed argue that 'agency is essential in order to exert one's participation and to regulate his/her own behaviour by defining a series of operations, which enable him/her to reach a potential desired condition'. However, the relationship between the role of education and agency is complex. Following Brighouse and Unterhalter (2010) it is possible to discern the value of education within three fields which generate well-being freedom and agency-freedom.

The first field concerns the instrumental role of education. For instance, enhancing human capital to work in a specific job, thus connecting education and training (through certifications) with the labour market. However, education can also have a broader role for children's flourishing. In this regard, Sen (1992) highlights the empowering role for education: an instrumental process role, which enables individuals to take part in decision-making processes at household, community or national level. The second overlapping field involves the intrinsic value of education, i.e. not merely instrumental but given by the education process and outcomes in itself. The third field looks at the positional value of education, related to the individual's success at school. In addition, the positional value of education is experienced in relation to class-based educational opportunities and, vice-versa, the educational opportunities open new class opportunities and influence social mobility (Sen, 1992).

> At the heart of the three overlapping fields is the concern in the capability approach with well-being and agency freedom (Sen 1985). These freedoms relate to the social conditions to secure instrumental, intrinsic, and positional values through education ... With regard to children the freedoms entailed concern freedom from interference with the welfare rights of children and the protection of their potential to develop agency freedom through attending school.
>
> Brighouse and Unterhalter, 2010: 209

For children therefore, in their life cycle, the relevance of agency freedom is central to the discourse of participation, since education is instrumental in expanding freedoms over a lifetime. Sen (1992), however, remarks mainly on the distributive role of education, enabling marginalized groups to gain access to centres of power and to make a case for redistribution. Moreover, both Sen (1987, 1992, 1997, 1999) and Nussbaum (2006, 2011) also acknowledge the social role of education in emphasizing its intrinsic and instrumental value for human flourishing. Education can have an interpersonal effect, because people are able to use the benefits of education to help others as well as themselves and can therefore contribute to democratic freedoms and to the good of society as a whole (Walker and Unterhalter, 2007; Unterhalter, 2009; Walker, 2010). In other words, as stated by Biggeri and Santi (2012: 374), 'the development of a democratic society implies the promotion of critical, creative and caring thinking in its citizens. This will enhance their autonomy and, at the same time, open their minds to confrontation with different perspectives and points of view' (Santi, 2007; Nussbaum, 2011). Promoting children's active participation also means socializing them towards an 'understanding of their own competencies', i.e. towards a sense of responsibility and skills in planning, designing, monitoring and managing social contexts (Matthews, 2003) and thus participating in change (Prout, 2005), thereby affecting children's evolving capabilities (Biggeri *et al.*, 2011a).

In more detail, Nussbaum (2006) points out that it is essential for democratic citizenship (i.e. 'education for freedom') to develop at least three education capabilities which are strongly connected to agency and participation: critical examination (or critical thinking), cosmopolitan ability and narrative imagination.[9] However, these three capabilities are not the result of spontaneous development, but rather emerge from the interaction of personal talents with contextual enabling factors, such as education, leading Nussbaum (2006: 385) to consider public education of good quality as 'crucial to the health of democracy'.

Within a human development and capability approach perspective, education therefore should not be confined to learning mathematics or developing literature skills. Placing principal emphases on life skills and on teaching children how to be autonomous, how to cooperate and collaborate, and how to interact with others and with the world (World Health Organization, 1997; Radja *et al.* 2003; Dubois and Trabelsi, 2007; Walker and Unterhalter, 2007) thus represents the crucial contribution the educational system can provide in expanding children's real opportunities (i.e. capabilities) for present and future functioning.

For instance, focusing on agency as the ability to pursue goals that one values and has reason to value (Hart, 2009), the degree of individual children's autonomy[10] is relevant in the process of choice. Indeed, together with the opportunity for learning, children can be formed as capable agents if provided with voices in their own learning processes, participating in the elaboration and deliberation of decision rules concerning themselves and acquiring instruments, awareness and responsibilities essential to making the choices they value (Biggeri and Santi, 2012). Moreover, this process also contributes to expanding the potentially valuable opportunity to make a difference in the society each agent is embedded in, which may be a fundamental component of a flourishing life.

The latter capability is also strictly related to the freedom to aspire, which entails examining the process behind aspirations (Hart, 2010, 2012). Indeed, as Biggeri *et al.* (2011b: 341–342) argue,

> it is not just a question of opening up multiple opportunities, even if this can
> be the starting point in case of deprivations, but seeing to it that, amongst a
> set of limited and achievable choices, children may develop a capability to
> aspire through their involvement in the decision making process.

Here again, in the context of the capability to aspire, connected to reflective thinking in which imagination, anticipation and evaluation of alternatives are involved, flourishing-oriented education proposals aimed at fostering the development of this evolving can entail a substantial contribution for both individual and social well-being (see Chapter 9). Consequently, alternative or complementary education systems are necessary to foster individual and collective empowerment in terms of the expansion of students', groups' and communities' capabilities as potentialities and choice opportunities in which agency and participation are employed.

Policy implications for education

The previous arguments clearly imply a rethinking of the traditional teaching-centred educational perspective towards a learning-centred approach in which children are considered the active, aware and responsible builders of their own understanding, knowing and growing (Brown and Campione, 1994; Biggeri and Santi, 2012). First of all therefore, it is possible to identify a wider range of faculties for children and youths which can be primarily fostered and promoted by the education system, even more than the family environment, also considering the different maturity stages of the pupils: listening to others, expressing one's own mind, resolving differences, evaluating alternatives, advancing proposals, welcoming challenges, avoiding reasoning mistakes and learning from experiential errors (Biggeri and Santi, 2012).

These capacities are also directly involved in the previously mentioned educational capabilities advanced by Nussbaum (2006): (a) *critical thinking*, which includes a range of capacities from logical reasoning and consistency testing to dealing with differences and disagreements of opinion and taking responsibility for our own arguments; (b) *cosmopolitan ability*, which implies the facility to understand both those differences and shared interests between groups and nations underlying the bridging opportunities among different communities of agents; (c) *narrative imagination*, referring to the ability to understand the emotions, wishes and desires of someone else, as well as 'think what it might be like to be in the shoes of somebody different' (Nussbaum, 2006: 390–1).

With regard to these crucial educational capabilities and the evolving process, whose expansion can be promoted also by pedagogy and other participatory activities where children can learn to engage in flourishing that promotes well-being and well-becoming (Biggeri and Santi, 2012), the potential role of education can be represented as in Figure 2.2. Here it is the combination of the given context of learning on the one hand, and the resources and conversion factors on the other hand, which enable people to flourish and become capable agents.

Within the capability perspective (see Figure 2.2), achievement-based educational systems, curricula and contexts (such as classrooms) are relevant in enhancing learning but are not sufficient: they have to be considered as the empirical starting point which does not fulfil the main elements of the capability approach. Indeed, we have to accept that functionings emerge as achievements – the only directly observable component of individual capability sets (Sen, 1992: 52).

In policy terms, the wide variety of educational models and methodologies within the western tradition (Nussbaum, 2010) provides interesting opportunities for innovative and transformative proposals consistent with the capability approach. For instance, Philosophy for Children (P4C), an educational movement developed in the 1970s, can constitute a suitable pedagogical approach[11] for developing critical thinking and democratic citizenship among children and youths, therefore connecting education to the 'world beyond the classroom' and fostering the authentic expression of child and youth agency in an enlarged community. The cultivation of *complex thinking* (Lipman, 2003), involving students in philosophizing and dialogical activity, is thus promoted by the P4C

Empowerment, inclusion and processes

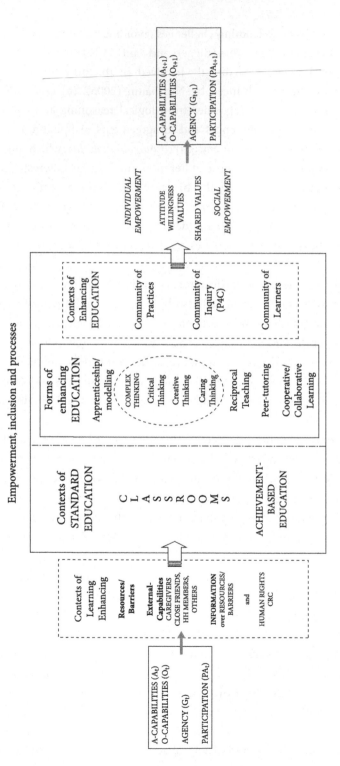

Figure 2.2 Creating capabilities: education for enhancing children's capabilities, agency and participation

Adapted from Biggeri and Santi (2012).

educational proposal through the development of the capacity of 'good judgement', composed by: a *critical* component, based on assessing and evaluating the reasons and evidence on which conclusions are based; a *creative* component, related to the capacity of imagining new ways of seeing and connecting the experience's elements; and a *caring* component, based on the affective, emotional, motivational dimensions of thinking during the practice of reasoning, argumentation, and reflection on authentic problems (Biggeri and Santi, 2012, Chapter 6 by Santi and Di Masi). However, as noted by Biggeri and Santi (2012: 377),

> P4C shares the same tradition as Socratic Dialogue, Montessori's pedagogy of play, Pestalozzi reform of education based on "head, hands, and hearth", Don Milani "school of the people", and the need to embed education in experience toward the establishment of a better living and society. Moreover the learning environment "community of inquiry" shares the dialogical and inter-subjective hallmark with other current educational settings such as "community of learners", "community of practice", while the style of discourse promoted in CoI compares with other interactive communication devices, such as "Reciprocal Teaching", "Cooperative Learning", "Peer Tutoring", and 'Cognitive Apprenticeship'.

Furthermore, social participation is a visible action in public contexts and a clear manifestation of citizenship, intended as inclusion in a society, with full rights and opportunities also for children and youths. In other words, within this perspective, the responsibility of policy-makers is to create an environment – by including children themselves in the process – which facilitates the ability of teachers and, definitely, the ability of children to pursue worthwhile and flourishing lives.

Hence, thinking in terms of 'beings' and 'doings' leads us to consider not only what governments should do to promote children's freedoms, but also what each of us can do in our daily lives to promote fair conditions that help children live with dignity and enable their flourishing as capable agents. Indeed, policies and actions for children's equal opportunities can be part both of governments' strategies and of our daily practices as teachers, parents, academics, doctors, entrepreneurs and so on (Biggeri *et al.* 2011b).

Finally, as emphasized by Biggeri *et al.* (2011b), promoting children's active participation also means socializing children towards an 'understanding of their own competencies' – i.e. a sense of responsibility and skills in planning, designing, monitoring and managing social contexts (Matthews, 2003) and thus participating in changing factors affecting children's evolving capabilities (Prout,

2005). Indeed, all around the world there are some significant and reasonably successful examples of Municipal Councils of Children (see Chapter 6), as well as several other instruments adopted by local administrations to promote children's participation.[12] *Therefore, it appears clear how all over the globe children and youth movements are pressing for change.*

Conclusions

If we place emphasis on children's and youths' ability to be capable agents and social actors, it appears clear that the rethinking of educational systems (Walker and Unterhalter, 2007) – entailing both a cultural and institutional shift, as well as an operative and organizational change – needs to be urgently promoted and enhanced by policy-makers, citizens and pupils themselves. UNICEF has already underlined this point, advocating a radical shift in adult thinking and behaviour, from an exclusionary to an inclusionary focus on children and their capabilities, and from a world which is defined solely by adults to one in which children contribute to building the kind of world they want to live in (UNICEF, 2002: 5).

Promoting a view of children as active, aware and responsible builders of their own understanding (Brown and Campione, 1994), knowing and growing and placing a new focus on the democratic citizenship functionings (Biggeri and Santi, 2012) would thus contribute not only to an external recognition of children as authentic agents and participants in society, but even more fundamentally to their evolving processes of capabilities expansion regarding the personally chosen *doings* and *beings*, as well as social participation in public deliberation and decision-making.

A learning-centred education system focused on critical and complex thinking, cosmopolitan ability and narrative imagination, as well as blending the promotion of the critical, creative and caring component of the ability of 'good judgement' would therefore crucially contribute to the collective construction of values, knowledge and opportunities for flourishing within actual and future communities and societies.

However, the substantial influence of both external and contextual conditions – ranging from access to information and the availability of appropriate training to sociocultural, economic and political characteristics of society – on children's evolving capabilities calls for a broad child-oriented approach in social policy, which, rather than simply focusing on universal access to education, should encourage the proactive behaviour of children in decision-making processes (Biggeri and Santi, 2012, see Chapter 6). Taking into account the priorities, values and aspirations of children, it is the comprehensive enhancement of those 'communities of inquiry' where children and youths might think about (and decide) what they want to be and become which would provide those diffused opportunities for children and youths to act and manifest themselves as full citizens within evolving complex societies.

Acknowledgements

This chapter is the fruit of an ongoing debate with several scholars. During a quite long period I have been privileged to receive very useful comments from a large number of people. In particular, I would like to thank: Caterina Arciprete, Jerome Ballet, Nicolò Bellanca, Sara Bonfanti, Sandra Boni, Jean-Michel Bonvin, Enrica Chiappero-Martinetti, Federico Ciani, David A. Clark, Flavio Comim, Michela Da Rodda, Francesca D'Erasmo, Cristina Devecchi, Diego Di Masi, Maria Laura Di Tommaso, Jean-Luc Dubois, Claudio Fedi, Andrea Ferrannini, Alex A. Frediani, Des Gasper, Sara Guilliano, Ravi Karkara, Vittorio Iervese, Leonardo Menchini, Ayacx Mercedes, Giuliana Parodi, Altair Rodriguez, Marina Santi, Santosh Mehrotra, Daniel Stoecklin, Lorella Terzi, Jean-Francois Trani, Elaine Unterhalter, Polly Vizard and Melanie Walker. Furthermore, I am very grateful to Caroline Sarojini Hart and Bernhard Babic for their contribution in fostering the debate among scholars of the Thematic Group on Children Capabilities of the Human Development and Capability Association (HDCA), and in particular Caroline for the organization of the International Conference at the University of Cambridge, UK (Faculty of Education, April 2011) and Bernhard for the International Workshop organized at Amman (SOS Children's Village, September 2010, Jordan). Finally, I would like to acknowledge and thank the *Journal of Human Development and Capabilities* for the reproduction of Figure 2.2.

Notes

1 Agency is here framed in line with Sen's view of process freedom as 'what a person is free to do and achieve in pursuit of whatever goals or values he or she regards as important' (Sen, 1985: 203).

2 Different scales of participation can be imagined (Hart, 1997; Lansdown, 2001).

3 The vision of development shaped by the SHD paradigm has four main pillars: – equality, productivity, sustainability and participation – which should work together to build up a better society (UNDP, 1990; Sen, 2000). The capacity to take into account these four elements at individual, collective, national and global levels is at the base of social policies for real freedom (i.e. capabilities) expansion.

4 Following Ibrahim and Alkire (2007), empowerment can be conceived as the expansion of individual agency (individual empowerment) and collective agency (social empowerment).

5 If we seriously consider children's participation in decision-making processes regarding their well-being and well-becoming, then participation must take different forms according to their age and maturity.

6 Indeed, as White (2002: 1101) argues, 'there is no problem with the idea that (outsider) adults should be able to determine the best interest of (insider) children. In practice, however, there are often difficulties in the assumptions of superior understanding on the part of self-styled benefactors'.

7 Please see the previous notes.

8 See also Lansdown (2005).

9 'From a cognitive point of view, critical thinking, cosmopolitan ability and narrative imagination would be considered as logical, moral, and creative components of the higher-order faculties involved in democratic thinking and judgment' (Biggeri and Santi, 2012: 375)

10 Note that autonomy and agency do not mean independence and isolation, but interdependence and reciprocity, i.e. socialization.

11 The inquiry activity of P4C focuses on discussion but is sustained also by reasoning exercises. It takes place in a circle, with the teacher/facilitator intervening to push the thinking to a deeper level but aspiring to allow the discussion to follow the emerging interests of the group (Biggeri and Santi, 2012: 376; see also Pardales and Girod, 2006).

12 *Also, the EU Charter of Fundamental Rights* (proclamation at Parliament in Strasbourg, 12 December 2007) is pushing in this direction.

References

Alkire, S. (2002) *Valuing Freedoms: Sen's Capability Approach and Poverty Reduction*, (New York: Oxford University Press).

Andresen, S., Diehm, I., Sander, U. & Ziegler, H. (eds) (2011) Children and the good life: new challenges for research on children, *Children's Well-Being: Indicators and Research*, 4.

Ballet, J., Biggeri, M. & Comim, F. (2011) Children's agency and the capability approach: a conceptual framework, in M. Biggeri, J. Ballet, F. Comim (eds) *Children and the Capability Approach*, (New York: Palgrave Macmillan).

Baraldi, C. (2009) *Dialogue in Intercultural Communities*, (Amsterdam: John Benjamins).

Bellanca, N., Biggeri, M. & Marchetta F. (2011) An extension of the capability approach: towards a theory of dis-capability, *ALTER, European Journal of Disability Research*, 5: 158–176.

Biggeri, M. (2007) Children's valued capabilities, in M. Walker and E. Unterhalter (eds) *Amartya Sen's Capability Approach and Social Justice in Education*, Chapter 10, 197–214, (New York: Palgrave).

Biggeri, M. & Santi, M. (2012) Missing dimensions of children's well-being and well-becoming in education systems: capabilities and philosophy for children, *Journal of Human Development and Capabilities*, 13(3): 373–95.

Biggeri, M., Trani, J.F. & Bakhshi, P. (2009) Le teorie della disabilità: una reinterpretazione attraverso l'approccio delle capability di Amartya Sen, *Studi e Discussioni*, WP, DSE, Università di Firenze, Florence.

Biggeri, M., Ballet, J. & Comim, F. (eds) (2011a) *Children and the Capability Approach*, (New York: Palgrave Macmillan).

Biggeri, M., Ballet, J. & Comim, F. (2011b), Final remarks and conclusions: the promotion of children's active participation, in M. Biggeri, J. Ballet, F. Comim (eds) *Children and the Capability Approach*, (New York: Palgrave Macmillan).

Biggeri, M., Libanora, R., Mariani, S. & Menchini, L. (2006) Children conceptualizing their capabilities: results of the survey during the First Children's World Congress on Child Labour, *Journal of Human Development*, 7(1): 59–83.

Bonvin, J.M. & Galster, D. (2010) Making them employable or capable: social integration policy at the crossroads, in H.U. Otto, H. Ziegler (eds) *Education, Welfare and the Capabilities Approach*, (Opladen: Barbara Budrich Publishers), 71–84.

Brighouse, H. & Unterhalter, E. (2010) Education for primary goods or for capabilities? in H. Brighouse, I. Robeyns (eds) *Measuring Justice: Primary Goods and Capabilities*, (Cambridge, MA: Cambridge University Press).

Brown, A. & Campione, J. (1994) Guided discovery in a community of learners, in K. McGilly (ed.) *Classroom Lessons: Integrating Cognitive Theory and Classroom Practice*, (Cambridge MA: MIT Press/Bradford Books), 229–270.

Clark, D.A. (2002) *Visions of Development: A Study of Human Values*, (Cheltenham: Edward Elgar).

Comim, F. (2011) *Developing Children's Capabilities: The Role of Emotions and Parenting Style*, in Biggeri, M., Ballet, J., Comim, F. (eds) *Children and the Capability Approach*, (Basingstoke: Palgrave Macmillan).

Crocker, D.A. (2007) Deliberative participation in local development, *Journal of Human Development*, 8(3): 431–455.

Dubois, J.L. & Trabelsi, M. (2007) Education in pre- and post-conflict contexts: relating capability and life-skills approaches, *International Journal of Social Economics*, 34(1/2): 53–65.

Evans, K. (2002) Taking control of their lives? Agency in young adult transitions in England and the New Germany, *Journal of Youth Studies*, 5(3): 245–269.

Feeny, T. & Boyden, J. (2004) *Acting in Adversity – Rethinking the Causes, Experiences and Effects of Child Poverty in Contemporary Literature*, Working Paper Series, WP 116, Oxford: QEH.

Freire, P. (1985) *The Politics of Education: Culture, Power, Aad Liberation*, (South Hadley, MA: Bergin & Garvey).

Habermas, J. (1981) *The Theory of Communicative Action, Vol. 1: Reason and the Rationalization of Society*, (Boston, MA: Beacon Press).

Hallett, C. & Prout, A. (eds) (2003) *Hearing the Voices of Children: Social Policy for a New Century*, (London: RoutledgeFalmer).

Hart, C.S. (2009) *Quo vadis? The capability space and new directions for the philosophy of educational research*, Studies in Philosophy & Education, 28(5): 391–402.

Hart, C.S. (2010) *Aspirations Re-Examined: A Capability Approach to Widening Participation in Higher Education*, doctoral thesis, University of Cambridge.

Hart, C.S. (2012) *Aspirations, Education and Social Justice: Applying Sen and Bourdieu*, (London: Bloomsbury).

Hart, R. (1997) *Children's Participation: The Theory and Practice of Involving Young Citizens in Community Development and Environmental Care*, (New York: UNICEF).

Heckman, J.J., Pinto, R. & Savelyev, P.A. (2012) *Understanding the Mechanisms Through Which an Influential Early Childhood Program Boosted Adult Outcomes*, IZA Discussion Papers 7040, Institute for the Study of Labor (IZA).

Ibrahim S. & Alkire, S. (2007) *Agency & Empowerment: A Proposal for Internationally Comparable Indicators*, OPHI Working Papers 005, Queen Elizabeth House, University of Oxford.

Iervese, V. & Rossi, E. (2009) Conflict management, in C. Baraldi (ed.) *Dialogue in Intercultural Communities*, (Amsterdam: John Benjamins), 29–74.

James, A., Jenks, A. & Prout, A. (1998) *Theorizing Childhood*, (Cambridge: Polity Press).

Lansdown, G. (2001) *Promoting Children's Participation in Democratic Decision-Making*, (Florence: Innocenti Insight, UNICEF Innocenti Research Centre).

Lansdown, G. (2005) *The Evolving Capacities of the Child*, (Florence: Innocenti Insight, Save the Children/UNICEF Innocenti Research Centre).

Leßmann, O., Otto, H.-U. & Ziegler, H. (eds) (2011) *Closing the Capability Gap – Renegotiating Social Justice for the Young*, Leverkusen: (Barbara Budrich).

Lipman, M. (2003) *Thinking in Education*, second edition, (Cambridge, MA: Cambridge University Press).

Matthews, H. (2003) children and regeneration: setting an agenda for community participation and integration, *Children & Society*, 17: 264–276.

Nussbaum, M. (1997) *Cultivating Humanity: A Classical Defence of Reform in Liberal Education*, (Cambridge, MA: Harvard University Press).

Nussbaum, M. (2006) Education and democratic citizenship: capabilities and quality education, *Journal of Human Development*, 7(3): 385–98.

Nussbaum, M. (2010) *Not for Profit: Why Democracy Needs the Humanities*, (Princeton, NJ: Princeton University Press).

Nussbaum, M. (2011) *Creating Capabilities: The Human Development Approach*, (Cambridge, MA: Harvard University Press).

Otto, H.-U. & Ziegler, H. (2006) Capabilities and education, *Social Work and Society International Online Journal*, 4(2).

Pardales, M.J. & Girod, M. (2006) Community of inquiry: its past and present future, *Educational Philosophy and Theory*, 38(6): 229–309.

Prout, A. (2000) Children's participation: control and self-realisation in British late modernity, *Children & Society*, 14: 304–315.

Prout, A. (2005) *The Future of Childhood*, (London: Routledge).

Radja, K., Hoffman, A.M. & Bakhshi, P. (2003) Education and the capabilities approach: life skills education as a bridge to human capabilities, paper presented at the 3rd Conference on the Capability Approach, Pavia, September.

Robeyns, I. (2006) Three model of education, *Theory and Research in Education*, 4(1): 69–84

Santi, M. (2007) Democracy and inquiry: the internalization of collaborative rules in a community of philosophical discourse, in D. Camhy (ed.) *Philosophical Foundations of Innovative Learning*, (Saint Augustin, FL: Academia Verlag).

Sen, A.K. (1985) Well-being, agency and freedom: The Dewey Lectures 1984, *Journal of Philosophy*, 82(4): 169–221

Sen, A.K. (1987) *On Ethics and Economics*, (Oxford: Basil Blackwell).

Sen, A.K. (1992) *Inequality Re-Examined*, (Oxford: Clarendon Press).

Sen, A.K. (1997) Human capital and human capability, *World Development*, 25(12): 1959–1961.

Sen, A.K. (1999) *Development as Freedom*, (Oxford: Oxford University Press).

Sen, A. (2000) A decade of human development, *Journal of Human Development*, 1(1): 17–23.

Sen, A.K. (2007) Children and human rights, *Indian Journal of Human Development*, 1(2): 1–11.

Sen, A.K. (2009) *The Idea of Justice*, (London: Allen Lane).

Trani, J-F, Bakhshi, P., Bellanca N.,Biggeri M. & Marchetta F. (2011), Disabilities through the Capability Approach Lens: Implications for public policies, ALTER. *European Journal of Disability Research*, 5: 143–157.

UNDP (1990) *Human Development Report*, (New York: Oxford University Press).

UNESCO (2003) *Education for All: Is the World on Track?* EFA Global Monitoring Report, Paris: UNESCO.

UNICEF (2002) *State of the World Children 2003*, (New York: UNICEF).

Unterhalter, E. (2009) Education, in S. Deneulin, L. Shahani (eds) *An Introduction to the Human Development and Capability Approach: Freedom and Agency*, (London: Earthscan/IDRC).

Walker, M. (2010) Capabilities and socially just [lifelong] education for vulnerable youth, paper presented at the conference on Human Development, Education and Vulnerable Youth, Pavia, 28–29 May.

Walker, M. (2012) Egalitarian policy formulation in lifelong learning: two models of lifelong education for young people in Europe, in D. Aspin, J. Chapman, K. Evans, R. Bagnall (eds) *Second International Handbook of Lifelong Learning*, (Dordrecht: Springer).

Walker, M., Unterhalter, E. (2007) The capability approach and its potential for work in education, in M. Walker, E. Unterhalter (eds) *Amartya Sen's Capability Approach and Social Justice in Education*, (New York: Palgrave Macmillan).

White, S.C. (2002) Being, becoming and relationship: conceptual challenges of a child rights approach in development, *Journal of International Development*, 14(8): 1095–1104.

World Health Organization (1997) *Life Skills Education in Schools*, WHO/MNH/PSF/93.7A.Rev.2, Geneva: WHO.

3

The Capability Approach and Children's Rights

Daniel Stoecklin and Jean-Michel Bonvin

Introduction

This chapter explores issues central to the children's rights debate, in particular the right to be heard (Art. 12 CRC),[1] from the perspective of the capability approach. Participation rights contained in the *United Nations Convention on the Rights of the Child* (CRC) challenge traditional conceptions of childhood. Their translation into enhanced capabilities depends on methodologies that are sensitive to cultural and personal diversity. The outline of our research problem is presented with an emphasis on outcomes of an already tested methodology which highlights the children's own constructions of reality. It is based on a systemic theory of the social actor, linking together an individual's activities, relationships, values, images of self and motivations. This new model, called 'the actor's system' tries to overcome the agent/structure dichotomy. Empirical tests done so far with children in Switzerland, Finland, Slovakia, Moldova and France confirm the heuristic value of the method that is used to understand the individual and social factors that convert the formal liberties contained in the CRC into real freedom and enhanced capabilities for children. Child participation and human development are thus assessed in new ways.

The subject of rights and the social actor

The rights contained in the UNCRC challenge traditional conceptions of childhood. Beside protection and provision rights, the UNCRC also includes 'participation rights': the right to be heard (Art. 12), the right to freedom of expression (Art. 13), the right to freedom of thought, conscience and religion

(Art. 14), the right to freedom of association and peaceful assembly (Art. 15), the right to privacy (Art. 16), the right to have access to information (Art. 17), and the right to participate freely in cultural life and the arts (Art. 31). This chapter concentrates on Article 12 CRC that reads as follows:

1.   States Parties shall assure to the child who is capable of forming his or her own views the right to express those views freely in all matters affecting the child, the views of the child being given due weight in accordance with the age and maturity of the child.

2.   For this purpose the child shall in particular be provided the opportunity to be heard in any judicial and administrative proceedings affecting the child, either directly, or through a representative or an appropriate body, in a manner consistent with the procedural rules of national law.

This article can be qualified as 'revolutionary' (Zermatten, 2005) because its introduction in the CRC means that children are not just protected, they are not just guaranteed some provisions, but there is also an *obligation* made to States parties to guarantee that they are listened to.

The articles of the CRC are interdependent. For instance, the best interests of the child (Art. 3 CRC) must be defined by integrating the child's point of view (Art. 12 CRC). This integration should be sensitive to forms of communication, written (including drawings) and oral, through which children express their opinions. The 'due weight' given to the views of the child according to age and maturity is a limitation. But it should also be understood as the consideration that is due to the child so that he/she can be effectively heard through appropriate procedures and hearing techniques. Therefore, the limited but evolving capacities of the child become a '*de facto*' criterion (to be assessed on a case-by-case basis) linked to the '*de jure*' subjective right attached to the child of seeing his/her best interests considered (Art. 3 CRC) in any decision affecting him/her. As procedural rights, Article 3 and Article 12 call for participative procedures: the child should be heard (Art. 12) in the definition of actions aimed at serving his/her best interests (Art. 3 CRC). Article 12 is also linked to Article 5 (evolving capacities) whereby parents or guardians have to provide guidance to the child on the exercise of the CRC rights until the child is able to exercise these rights directly. The CRC therefore constitutes a holistic system where all articles are interdependent, and it is within this interplay of rights that an implicit theory of the social actor can be identified whereby the child is considered as a subject of rights with evolving capacities.

Although the CRC does not contain the concept 'social actor', it has become common sense in the field of children's rights, with the consequence that 'subject of rights' and 'social actor' are sometimes used as equivalents, as if one could stand for the other or explain it. Yet, and paradoxically, the underlying theories of action are not discussed, and there is an increasing number of articles and books using the concept 'social actor' as taken-for-granted. Consequently, children's agency remains a rather vague notion, sometimes even reduced to a slogan for militant movements. In reaction to overprotective or paternalistic conceptions of childhood, there is a tendency to consider children as competent agents regardless of their age. However, 'children' is probably one of the most confusing categories, as it applies to individuals whose experiences are so different. What does a one-week old baby have in common with a teenager? Mainly the fact that they are both considered as 'children', as defined by the CRC (0–18 years). The ways in which 'children' experience the world, and can act upon it, are certainly more diversified than the experiences of adults, even at ages as different as 20 and 80 years old. Hence, it is certainly relevant to consider that 'children act as agents in various ways at any one time in the course of their development; and certainly the range of sophistication of their agency changes over time' (Pufall and Unsworth, 2004: 9). Nevertheless, this range is not well documented, and still leaves too much room for speculation.

The capability approach offers an illuminating perspective to explore issues central to the children's rights debate, in particular the right to be heard (Art. 12 CRC). This chapter begins with considerations on the capability approach applied to children's rights, underlining the existing gap between a child's rights and his/her actual capabilities. The distinction between the subject of rights and the social actor points to the importance of what we call the 'participative capability'. It tackles the issue of agency and shows that children develop their own ways of making sense of reality. This is illustrated with a systemic theory of the social actor which has been empirically tested in a series of small-scale applications which will be described later in the chapter. This methodology brings in several considerations for further research on the 'participative capability' of children and young people. It has been used in the field of organized leisure activities in order to highlight the factors converting a child's formal right (to be heard) into real and increased freedom in the field of leisure. Some concrete examples will be given in the following sections. As a matter of fact, such participative capabilities developed in the field of leisure impact on, and are impacted by, educational activities in schools or other informal educational settings.

Translations of children's rights into real freedom

The capability approach (Nussbaum, 1997, 2004; Sen, 1999; Alkire, 2002; Vizard, 2006; Bonvin and Farvaque, 2006; Duray-Soundron, 2008; Comim *et al.*, 2008; Deneulin, 2009) is a rather new perspective in the field of children's rights. Applying the capability approach to children (Biggeri *et al.*, 2011) is a promising path, because children's rights can be seen as formal resources or entitlements that need to be transformed into real rights or capabilities. Consequently, the gap between formal liberties (rights) and real freedom (capability) can be more precisely highlighted and explained by emphasizing the individual and social conversion factors that allow for transforming rights into capabilities. A person's capability depends on the interplay between his/her personal skills and the available social opportunities in a given context. Therefore, the capability set is the outcome of a person's rights (entitlements) and resources (commodities), and of his/her ability to convert them into what Sen calls 'valuable functionings' (Sen, 1999). In this perspective, what should be promoted via public policies is not outcomes but an appropriate environment for the development of capabilities, or, in other words, for the real freedom to choose the life one has reason to value (Bonvin and Farvaque, 2006).

Transposed to our field of study, the capability approach emphasizes the relevance of the child's 'participative capability', which can be described as the capacity of the child to effectively participate in the definition and fulfilment of choices that affect his/her own life. Children's participative capabilities result from the combination of individual skills and available opportunities in the environment. The observation reveals that there is a gap between the child's legal status (subject of rights) and his/her social status (social actor) regarding participation in decision-making. The question is: how can these rights, considered as formal freedoms, be translated into real freedoms? What individual and social factors favour or impede the conversion of these rights into capabilities?

A one-size-fits-all top-down implementation process of the CRC is irrelevant (Archard, 1993; Lücker-Babel, 1995; Verhellen, 1996; Freeman, 1997; Van Bueren, 1998), as the translation of 'participation rights' into enhanced capabilities for children depends on methodologies that are sensitive to cultural and personal diversity. The way people define situations is especially central to understanding the choices they make, as well as their motives. This applies to children too. As the capability approach places great emphasis on freedom of choice, the methodologies that are needed to understand these choices must highlight the children's own constructions of reality.

The different definitions of situations do not only depend on individual points of view but also on collective constructions of reality. The word 'participation' itself does not mean the same in countries with western-liberalist value traditions as in countries with collectivist value systems: some see participation as an individual right, while others see it as a social obligation (Mason and Bolzan, 2010). These cultural differences are important to bear in mind when talking about children's agency defined as 'an individual's or a group's capacity to make decisions, act, and interact with other people in a socially competent way' (Nibell *et al.*, 2009: 264).

This leads us to critically consider the confusion between 'social actor' and 'subject of rights', which actually may be linked to the history of western liberal traditions. Individualism was a nineteenth century 'novel idea', as Tocqueville stressed in *Democracy in America* (1835). Later on, Simmel (1950) distinguished the individualism of uniqueness ('*Einzigkeit*') of the nineteenth century as opposed to the individualism of singleness ('*Einzelheit*') (Lukes, 2006: 31). This new conception, arising with the Romantic Movement, sees individual interests from a qualitative angle. It detaches itself from the previously quantitative conception of the abstract singleness of individuals, seen primarily as members of a totality, be it the species or the community. The idea of children having individual rights could hardly develop if there had not been this 'qualitative individualism' that has been conducive to individual rights, hence human rights instruments.

Consequently, when we refer to the child as being a 'subject of rights', the uniqueness of the person predominates over the singleness of the member of a community. Nevertheless, individuals act as social actors in all cases, also when they are not perceived as unique persons. Therefore 'subject of rights' and 'social actor' cannot be equated: whereas the subject is entitled to individual rights, the actor acts through families and broader social groups. In other words, the child, as a subject of rights, has a right to participation, and as a social actor, this same child has a capability through participation. This important distinction gives us an insight in the discrepancy, and sometimes tension, between the 'subject of rights' and the 'social actor'. The CRC may give a formal right to any individual child to fully participate in society; nevertheless real children will always have real limitations as social actors. Acting socially is a learned process whereby the sociocultural representations of normative frameworks (including children's rights) are progressively internalized by the actor who then actively transforms them and expresses them in renewed ways (Berger and Luckmann, 1966). One is not born with the articles of the CRC in mind, one learns how to behave according to the place given by society to these normative standards.

Therefore, confusing the subjects of rights and the social actor leads to conclusions that are epistemologically and ethically problematic. The equation does not work. Being formally a subject of rights does not mean that one is automatically a social actor with fully-fledged agency. Conversely, one cannot say that because the actor has agency (the capacity to influence things), therefore he/she has a right (upon things). This is a mistaken view, as agency, or the sole capacity to do something, cannot be the principle underlying any right. However, a limitation to act in a given respect (limited ability) may be a reason to restrict a given right. This is the case of Article 12 CRC, as the right to be heard is assured 'to the child who is capable of forming his or her own views'.

While the CRC sets no age limit on participation rights, real participation of children depends on their abilities, which are in turn constitutive of their agency. Therefore, we have to consider the individual and social factors promoting (or obstructing) the conversion of the right to be heard (Art. 12 CRC) into capabilities or vectors of possible functionings. In our case, the individual entitlement is the right of the child to be heard (Art. 12 CRC) in decisions over leisure activities. This framework allows an emphasis to be given to the factors converting the children's right into increased freedom. To identify what personal and social factors help (or not) in converting the right to be heard into vectors of possible functionings in the realm of leisure activities, we interviewed children and young people aged 12–18 about the influence they think they have over issues that are supposed to be in their reach.

Among the social factors, we considered public policies regarding children and youth, institutions and procedures through which children can participate and be heard, and especially their accessibility and adaptability to different groups of children (according to age, gender, ethnicity, geography) possessing different kinds of capital: economic, social and cultural (Bourdieu, 1994). The unequal distribution of these forms of capital is however not the sole explanation to the variability of children's participative capability. One should also look more closely at how the child as a 'social actor' perceives reality and gives meaning to his/her actions in relation to others. Actually, the personal characteristics are crucial to see how the child converts the right to be heard into a functioning.

The child's ability to make sense of the right to be heard and to use and shape the existing means to achieve this right is the focus of our study. How and why the actor makes choices has to do with both objective sociocultural influences and subjective perceptions. To have a capability approach to children's rights is therefore a very good way to critically look at the so-called cultural bias of the CRC, whereby the western conception of childhood would pervade the developing world. The question is: what levels of autonomy, capability or agency is the CRC conveying to children? There will always be some gap between the status ascribed to a child – a subject of rights as soon as born, and the effective competence to ask and obtain respect for personal rights. The extent to which subjects of rights can be agentive and influence their environment, depends on their ability to transform their ascribed roles into achieved roles. An ascribed role is conferred to an actor whereas an achieved role is conquered by the actor. This distinction corresponds to role-taking and role-making (Mead, 1934). The social actor is anyone able to transform the roles ascribed to him/her by others into new ways of performing or achieving things (achieved role). This leads us to see that agency might be captured through the observation of achieved functionings. These aspects have been incorporated in the systemic theory of action and corresponding methodology which we present in the next section.

A systemic theory of action and methodology

According to Sen (1985), focusing on people's agency implies observing how committed they are in actions that are beneficial not only to their own well-being but also to others. In other words, agency is about bringing change that affects oneself and others. This applies to children too and can be observed in the achievements of specific actors. The concept of agency then becomes clearer: a child's agency depends on how he/she makes use (choices) of institutional structures (family, education, law, etc.) and personal skills (cognitive and social competences).

Applied to our topic, we may observe a child's achievements regarding organized action. These achievements (choices) depend on the child's participative capability. In other words, the child's freedom to achieve organized actions can be specified through the observation of real achievements. This is how we can approach the child's real freedom to participate (participative capability). This is an operational way to observe how concrete functionings can be explained by specific participative capabilities, and eventually how conversion factors (social opportunities and individual capacities) are constitutive of people's capabilities (Nussbaum, 1997; Sen, 1999). We can evaluate agency through the child's achieved functionings, as the result of the child's choices constrained by his/her own evolving capacities and the social context. Attention must be paid to both social and individual conversion factors. How children 'make sense' of what is happening to them is a crucial component that is often overlooked.

In order to get closer to the actor's reflexivity, a new model called the 'actor's system' has been developed and consolidated (Stoecklin, 2009a, 2009b). It stems from former research with children in street situations in several countries, showing that they develop pragmatically their own ways according merely to subjective assessments (Stoecklin, 2000, 2007; Lucchini, 2007). Stoecklin has used Lucchini's framework 'Child-Street System' to analyse the accounts of children living in the streets of Shanghai during a 14-month fieldwork (1993–1996).[2] He then adapted it as a tool for intervention or consultation with various international non-governmental organizations (INGOs), local associations and networks from 1998 to 2005,[3] with the support of its conceptor. This tool has been used mainly for bottom-up identification of needs and capacities of children living in the streets and/or victims of trafficking. The samples varied from around 10 to 50 children per city, according to the contacts made by the social educators of the respective NGOs, and the age of respondents ranged from 8 to 20, with techniques going from semi-structured interviews to focus group discussions and individual drawings.

The new model called 'actor's system', elaborated later on by Stoecklin, is a simplified and more general version of the 'Child-Street System' that allows reconstructing how the actor makes sense of whatever situation (and not only the 'street situation') by using common notions, linked together in a systemic way, namely: activities, relations, values, images of self and motivations (see Figure 3.1).

The model is called the 'actor's system' because it is assumed that one's own system of action is the constantly evolving outcome of the links among these components of personal experience. The concepts used in this model are what Blumer calls 'sensitizing concepts', which act as propositions with a content that is not given beforehand. These are concepts open to the definition of their content by the respondents, concepts which therefore only suggest directions to look at (Blumer, 1969: 148). This approach also corresponds to the claim for interdisciplinary active listening using 'interpenetrating language', which 'comes down to employing terms that an intelligent inquirer can understand without knowing the shorthand that every academic discipline develops for itself' (Pufall and Unsworth, 2004: 7). The 'actor's system' is not a deterministic theory tightening together abstract concepts. On the contrary, it is a heuristic tool with daily-used concepts in order to let individuals reflect how they are (re)structuring their own experience.

Following Berger and Luckmann's (1966) conception of reality as both objective and subjective, the five dimensions of experience in our model are not

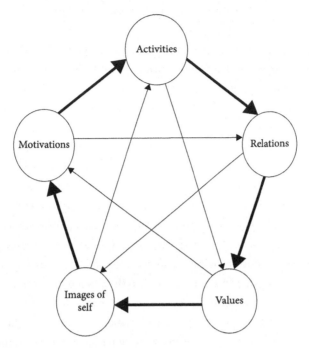

Figure 3.1 The 'actor's system'
Source: Stoecklin (2009a)

considered as things *per se*. This would be a reification of social forms as if they had an existence of their own. In a constructionist approach, these elements are rather seen as meanings attached to items of experience as they are conceptualized by the actor. The concepts are general sensitizing concepts through the lenses of which the actors may read and give meaning to reality. They can identify concrete elements in their own experience, see them through these lenses, and make comments about the links between them.

With its recursive chain of causality, this model corresponds to and reflects the cumulative nature of experience (Dewey, 1910; Mead, 1934), whereby the social actor can be defined as anyone able to transform assigned roles into new ways of performing or achieving things. It also integrates the double structuration theory (Giddens, 1984), as each dimension of experience (activities, relations, values, images of self and motivations) is at the same time structured and structuring. Through observations of subjective assessments of situations, one may reconstruct specific social configurations (Elias, 1991), and their influence on children's capabilities.

Assessing child participation

In all the applications of the 'actor's system', we have always respected the ethical requirements regarding consent and confidentiality when doing interviews with children and young people (Morrow, 2008). The tool was first used in an empirical testing in 2009 with 34 adolescents (17 boys and 17 girls), aged from 12 to 18, in the French-speaking part of Switzerland (Stoecklin, 2009b). The sample was randomly selected in four French-speaking counties, and included respondents from rural and urban settings and from different walks of life. As the rationale was to see how the tool would stimulate and give value to the child's reflexivity, the statistical representativeness of the sample was not requested. Nevertheless, the diversity of respondents gave an acceptable degree of validity to the results. The test first started with a very wide open question: 'What is important in life?' before moving on to semi-structured questions that invited respondents to locate their preferences within the concepts of activities, relations, values, images of self and motivations. It showed that respondents used different dimensions to describe similar experiences, which attracted our attention to the 'permeability' of these concepts. For instance, when speaking about their 'friends', some respondents would talk about activities, while others would insist on relations or values. The same was observed with 'travelling'. In other words, experience appears as highly permeable to conceptual choices made by respondents to reflect on it. Consequently, realities like 'child participation', 'children's rights' or 'the right to be heard' should also be kept open to children's definitions, stimulated by a tool that helps respondents to reflect more deeply about their own experiences. Following these observations, the tool was then used in focus-group discussions to assess child and youth participation in Finland (2010), Slovakia (2011) and Moldova (2011) for the Council of Europe project 'Building a Europe for and with Children' (Council of Europe, 2009, 2011). The sample in each country was selected by an in-country team responsible for conducting the focus-group discussions under the supervision of the international *ad hoc* group that was elected by the COE for an evaluation of the child participation policies of these three countries. Respondents were chosen among children and young people already active in children's parliaments or 'participatory projects'. In Finland, the discussions were held with a group of 9 girls and 9 boys from different parts of the country, aged between 10 and 21, including six children involved in children's parliaments or NGOs. In Slovakia, the group was composed of 8 girls and 7 boys, aged 9 to 18 but with the majority (8) aged 17 and above, and coming from different regions and backgrounds. In

Moldova, 14 girls and 8 boys between the age of 11 and 17 took part. As a first task, the participants were asked to write down activities they usually do. Then they were asked to specify the persons (relations) with whom they connected during these activities. Next, the participants were asked to underline those people whom they considered did not take into account their opinions when making decisions concerning them. Eventually, they were asked to think of the reasons why these people did not listen to them (values), what feelings they had about it (image of self) and what could be done (motivation) to change the situation. The tool helped keep open considerations for a large range of relationships, values, images of self and motivations, before (or instead of) reducing participation only to 'activities'.

For instance, a whole range of activities were raised by the children in Finland:

- School: attending school, homework, studying.
- Home: gardening and work in the yard, walking the dog, home, resting, lounging, watching television.
- Friends and relatives: meeting friends, spending time with family, spending time at granny's, visiting relatives.
- Eating, food.
- Hobbies: reading, visiting the library, drawing, cooking, cleaning.
- Sports: jogging, swimming, stables, driving, downhill skiing, scouts, gym, ballroom dancing.
- Music: composing music, song writing.
- Travel: travelling, tourist activities, visiting the summer cottage, going abroad, travelling by train.
- Being alone, spending time alone, wondering about the world.
- Playing on the computer, internet, hobbies.
- Participation activities: youth council, organizations, meetings, wielding influence, the youth work facility, student council, participation, sharing information, town hall, the youth services office, having a say in municipal affairs, having a say through the Finnish Children's Parliament.
- Going out: partying, music, shopping, visiting cafés, nightclubs (Council of Europe, 2011: 32–33).

The tool therefore helped children to reflect on a wide range of activities that allowed them to not only focus on activities that are seen as 'participative', which would have prevented inclusion of situations that set the wider picture whereby the question of status proximity was a central feature. In other words, the 'actor's system' framework has made it possible to include a key concern for children, that could otherwise have remained hidden, namely the distance they feel towards adults in charge of education and the corresponding necessity of linking teaching (and generally speaking, all professions linked to childhood) not solely to disciplinary expertise but also to skills in listening to all stakeholders, including children (Council of Europe, 2011: 38).

Using the tool in our research on the right to be heard in leisure activities suggests that child participation is mainly induced by professional adults working in youth associations and leisure centres, while knowledge of 'participation rights' is rather low. It confirmed the importance of relationships in the experience of young people. The tool made it possible for 14 respondents in Switzerland and 5 respondents in France to reflect on concrete aspects of their participation in a collective project (see Table 3.1).

The playful shape of the 'actor's system' helped to integrate questions on their knowledge about their right to be heard in a rather discrete way. The method fostered open discussions about the respondents' activities, relations, values,

Table 3.1 Young people interviewed according to the types of participatory projects

Participatory projects and locations	Number of young people interviewed	Ages of young people interviewed	Gender of young people interviewed
A website for young people of the city of Sion, Switzerland	1	14	M
A hip-hop scene in the city of Sion, Switzerland	1	17	F
The organization of a students' party, in the city of Sion, Switzerland	1	13	M
A music scene in the city of Romont, Switzerland	1	14	M
Animation of a cultural centre for young people in the village of Marly, Switzerland	1	18	F
A discotheque for young people aged 12–17 of the village of Marly, Switzerland	1	18	M
A children's parliament in the village of Romanel, Switzerland	4	15	M
A video centre in the village of Romanel, Switzerland	4	15	M
A journey in Senegal for students from Montreuil (Paris), France	5	13, 13, 12 15, 13	F M

images of self and motivations, allowing proxy questions that helped avoid the side-effect of social desirability, which is the tendency to answer in a way thought to be socially acceptable and desirable (McBurney, 1994). We observed that our respondents very seldom used the narrative of 'children's rights' to reflect upon their praxis. This typical line of conduct, or 'system of action', indicates that social relations play a greater role than children's rights in their subjective evaluation of participatory projects. Conversely, experience shapes children's knowledge of their rights which they roughly know, without needing to quote the articles contained in the UNCRC. In order to test their knowledge about children's rights, a question directly addressed their knowledge about their right to be heard (Art. 12 CRC). No respondent was able to tell exactly what this right was about, while in their descriptions of their participatory experiences they referred to values such as respect for people's (and their own) opinions. This shows that the actor does not need to be clearly informed about or aware of his/her rights before acting in a rightful way. This is due to the complex set of peer influences in the elaboration of one's preferences. Hence, the child's 'own views' are pragmatically formed when the child is able to actively participate in social life. Participation rights become real only through the exercise of participation, which may eventually contribute to gradual capacities gained by children as social actors having voice and agency.

These pilot attempts to explore the usefulness of the tool in practice have led to some early findings. These include the hypothesis that agency is bound to a recursive system of action, reflecting subjective assessments of situations that help reconstruct specific social configurations (Elias, 1991) that are more or less conducive to children's active participation. So far, the applications of the 'actor's system' have helped identify a cross-cultural trend regarding agency, namely that the child does not conceive participative rights in a rational-choice oriented way but rather through the double mediation of group sociability and their own reflexivity about concrete experiences. The metaphor of stage and backstage (Goffman, 1959) indicates that there may be large discrepancies between the presentation of self in everyday life (rational and socially desirable discourses) and subjective understandings or feelings about such a socially constructed notion as 'children's rights'. It is assumed that the tool gives a possibility to overcome the bias, so often encountered, of linking competence with rational discourse. It is however too early to speak of a real theory of the 'actor's system' and further research is needed to reconstruct how children, in different settings and with different capacities, develop their agency through participation.

These heuristic features and outcomes of the tool help in deconstructing taken-for-granted conceptions such as the equivalence between the child as a subject of rights and the child as a social actor. They help us to understand how specific actors make sense of their own social environment and how this environment is in-built in their identity. This confirms that the individual/society dichotomy is a social construct and not a reality (Elias, 1991). Seeing society as 'surrounding' and the individual as 'inside' is linked to the historical movement analysed by Elias whereby external constraints are progressively replaced by self-constraints. The 'actor's system' helps conceive this in a more concrete way: what social actors identify as their 'real experience' is made up of activities, relations, values, images of self and motivations, all elements that are at the same time 'inside' and 'outside' the individual. Another outcome is that the common-language notions used in the model help understand the systemic nature of action by observing how the actor shapes diverse settings according to their command over symbols. Our observations reveal the centrality of the respondents' relations, and the emotional appeal of these interactions challenges the artificial separation between objective acting and subjective reflexivity:

> Sociologists now generally recognize that emotional processes are crucial components of social experience. Although this turn toward including emotions within the domain of sociology has been a useful corrective to the dominance of rational-actor models of human nature, most of the work on emotions has been restricted to issues of conceptualization or debate over theoretical frameworks.
>
> Ellis and Flaherty, 1992: 2

Therefore, the actor's system helps to overcome the bias whereby one considers child participation only through the lenses of so-called mature decision-making processes. We still need to get closer to subjective understanding or feelings, and not just to observe discourses expressed 'on the stage' through presentation of self in everyday life (Goffman, 1959).

Our hypothesis is that child participation depends on their subjective assessments of situations and that these cannot entirely be grasped with the ladders of participation (Hart, 1992; Treseder, 1997). Children's agency starts with their own reflexivity about concrete experiences, and the decision not to participate in a given process is also an agency. Measuring 'child participation' therefore requires that processes and not just outcomes are considered. What is innovative in the model of the 'actor's system' is its potential to assess child participation not in terms of *visible* participation but in terms of *subjective* participation. Assessments of participation remain fragile and possibly ethnocentric as long as we do not have a clearer understanding of the participants' subjective sense of reality. Children develop their capacities to build and voice their own views through social networks. We could say that children actually participate *through* rather than *in* activities. But participation with the outside world, through the mediating effect of a group, first implies a subjective internalization of the outside world as it appears to oneself and also as others make it appear to be (Berger and Luckmann, 1966). Therefore, two central issues must be addressed: the mediating role of social groups through which one experiences the world, and the role of personal reflexivity through which one gives meaning to these social activities. In this way, this methodology allows one to come closer to the individual and social factors that help (or do not help) to convert the formal rights and liberties contained in the CRC into real freedom and enhanced capabilities for children.

Conclusion

The rights of the child need a good arsenal of procedures (Lücker-Babel, 1995), and improvements in hearing procedures (Art. 12 CRC) is definitely an area of concern. The procedures through which the right to be heard is to be implemented, in any setting (be it leisure or formal or informal educational settings), all too often neglect the question of their accessibility to the understanding and ways of expression of children at different ages. While the 'burden of proof' regarding the child's maturity is not with the child but with the decision-makers, the procedures and tools that are concretely used to 'prove' a child's maturity or immaturity remain too much bound to adult rationality.

Both a subjective right (right to be heard) and a procedural right, Article 12 CRC is open to interpretations and conflicting views, as is the case for other objects of discourse. Going back to Giddens' (1984) structuration theory, procedures to hear children can be seen as both structured and structuring. Hearing procedures are structured in a certain way because rights must be granted independently of the actual capacity of children to actively influence them. Such procedures are also structuring the way the child may express her/himself. The 'due weight clause' regarding 'age and maturity of the child' and the impossibility of objectively proving that one is 'mature enough' leave the door open to the arbitrariness of capacity evaluation. This is part of the collective power against which the international human rights treaties wanted to preserve the individual.

To be considered eligible (subject) to Article 12, the child must be recognized as competent ('the child who is capable of forming his or her own views'). What is generally overlooked is that 'to have one's own views' is also a socially defined (structured) and therefore recognized (structuring) concept. Therefore, power relationships are mostly overlooked by the 'competent child' discourse. Paradoxically, the 'competent child' discourse falls into the trap it wanted to escape, because 'being competent' equates to being competent in the ways that are recognized as competency, maturity and rational thinking. All these notions are social constructs, and the 'competent child' is another construction which is both stemming from and strengthening the false equivalency between 'subject of rights' and 'social actor'.

This confusion between subject and actor leads to distorted debates that are not conducive to child participation. The sociological perspectives in the field of children's rights may have played a significant role in this biased debate, probably because the notion itself, the 'social actor', has not been all too clear. As a consequence, there all too often arise some biased debates over competences where arguing that the child is an actor at birth (ignoring the progressive internalization and externalization of norms and values) turns out to be accepted just in order to grant him/her participatory rights. If rights are attached to competence, then the child, as a subject of rights, must be a 'generally competent child'. The other side-effect of this problematic stance is the opposite conclusion that participation rights cannot be granted before the child demonstrates a sufficient level of competence. How can we measure 'a sufficient level of competence' or 'maturity'?

As we have seen, the CRC does not make any explicit reference to the 'social actor'. But if participation rights are granted only to those who are able to actively make use of these rights (those with a sufficient level of reflexivity to express their 'own views'), then the CRC implicitly holds that some children are not yet social actors. It does not mean that these children are not holders of the right contained in Article 12; on the contrary, Article 12 may be seen as based on the expectation that *all* children will, at some stage in their development, be able to express their own view freely. This possibility is not only bound to individual competence but, again, to the combination of individual ability and social opportunity (capabilities).

Therefore the CRC does not imply that one can just wait until the child is able to form his/her own views, but must see to it that procedures and techniques are developed to include children's voices as much as possible. Declaring that the child is 'generally competent' or a 'social actor' at birth is not a way to make any progress in the design of these techniques and procedures. Rather, recognizing the differentiated stages of capacity development is conducive to elaborate, more accurate and appropriate tools to make Article 12 accessible to children placed in different situations.

Considering the child as a 'social actor' is a way to say that he/she is 'generally competent', but the problem is that it is impossible to be a 'generally competent' social actor at any age and in any setting. One should better acknowledge that giving 'due weight' to the child's opinion can also mean bringing the hearing techniques and procedures closer to the child and not just the child closer to the socially constructed sense of 'maturity' prevailing in a specific context and in a specific period.

Non-distinction between 'subject of rights' and 'social actor' ignores the problem of capability and the complex interaction between individual competences and social opportunities. Whereas the subject has *rights*, the actor is developing *capabilities*. These two aspects are interdependent: rights may enhance capabilities, and conversely capabilities are needed to actively make use of one's rights. Recognition of this specific interplay between rights and capabilities makes participative rights granted to children a quite relevant movement towards personal and social development. The child can therefore participate in the objective definition of reality, which is not reducible to a single point of view but rather the outcome of a social construction. The social actor is participating in the daily construction of social reality; therefore the subject is entitled to a right on the definition of social reality, including the definition of rights themselves. Here, the subject is recognized as having the capacity to act as a social actor, and therefore is entitled to develop this capacity to the fullest extent. But the power conferred is not upon things but upon processes.

Any social actor, whether or not he/she is declared a subject of rights, acts through relationships with others. What is different when one considers children as rights-holders is the importance attached to their own views. The attention for children in terms of their real freedom might change dominant conceptions of power: from oppressive power over things and people to an enhanced and shared capability to participate in the reshaping of social interactions. This indeed makes a big difference.

Notes

1 Full details on the UNCRC can be found at www.unicef.org/crc.
2 Daniel Stoecklin (2000), *Enfants des rues en Chine* (*Street Children in China*). Paris: Karthala.

3   Aparajeyo-Bangladesh (Bangladesh), Arsis (Greece), Associaçao Curumins (Brazil), Association Appert (Chad), Fastenopfer (Switzerland), ECPAT (Luxemburg), Institut international des Droits de l'Enfant (Switzerland), Médecins Sans Frontières (Switzerland), NPF (Albania), Pro Victimis (Moldova), Rede Amiga da Criança (Brazil), Rede Rio Criança (Brazil), Samu Social (Mali), Songes-Niger (Niger), Terre des hommes – aide à l'enfance (Switzerland).

References

Alkire, S. (2002), *Valuing Freedoms: Sen's Capability Approach and Poverty Reduction.* Oxford: Oxford University Press.

Archard, D. (1993), *Children, Rights and Childhood.* London: Routledge.

Berger, P.L. & Luckmann, T. (1966), *The Social Construction of Reality: A Treatise in the Sociology of Knowledge.* New York: Anchor Books.

Biggeri, M., Ballet, J. & Comim, F. (eds) (2011), *Children and the Capability Approach.* Basingstoke: Palgrave Macmillan.

Blumer, B. (1969), *Symbolic Interactionism: Perspective and Method.* Englewood Cliffs, NJ: Prentice Hall.

Bonvin, J.M. & Farvaque, N. (2006), Promoting capability for work: the role of local actors, in S. Deneulin *et al.* (eds), *Transforming Unjust Structures: The Capability Approach.* Dordrecht: Springer, pp. 121–143.

Bourdieu, P. (1994), *Raisons pratiques. Sur la théorie de l'action.* Paris: Le Seuil.

Comim, F., Qizilbash, M. & Alkire, S. (eds) (2008), *The Capability Approach. Concepts, Measures and Applications.* Cambridge: Cambridge University Press.

Council of Europe (2009), *Ad Hoc Advisory Group on Child and Youth Participation (MJ-S-CYP)*, www.coe.int/t/dg3/children/default_en.asp.

Council of Europe (2011), *Child and Youth Participation in Finland: A Council of Europe Policy Review*, www.coe.int/t/dg3/children/participation/PolicyReview_en.pdf.

Deneulin, S. (2009), *An Introduction to the Human Development and Capability Approach: Freedom and Agency.* London: Earthscan.

Dewey, J. (1910), *How We Think.* Lexington, MA: Heath & Co.

Duray-Soundron, C. (2008), *Repenser l'action collective: une approche par les capabilités.* Paris: L'Harmattan.

Elias, N. (1991), *La société des individus.* Paris: Fayard.

Ellis, C. & Flaherty, M. (1992), *Investigating Subjectivity. Research on Lived Experience.* London: Sage.

Freeman, M. (1997), *The Moral Status of Children: Essays on the Rights of the Child.* Dordrecht: Martinus Nijhoff.

Giddens, A. (1984), *The Constitution of Society: Outline of the Theory of Structuration.* Cambridge: Polity.

Goffman, E. (1959), *The Presentation of Self in Everyday Life*. Edinburgh: University of Edinburgh, Social Sciences Research Center, Anchor Books Edition.

Hart, R. (1992), *Children's Participation from Tokenism to Citizenship*. Florence: Innocenti Research Center.

Lucchini, R. (2007), 'Street children': deconstructing a category, in: I. Rizzini, U. Mandel Butler & D. Stoecklin (eds), *Life on the Streets: Children and Adolescents on the Streets: Inevitable Trajectories?* Sion: Institut International des Droits de l'enfant, pp. 49–75.

Lücker-Babel, M.-F. (1995), The right of the child to express views and to be heard: an attempt to interpret Article 12 of the UN Convention on the Rights of the Child, *The International Journal of Children's Rights*, 3: 391–404.

Lukes, S. (2006), *Individualism*. Essex: ECPR Press.

Mason, J. & Bolzan, N. (2010) Questioning understandings of children's participation: applying a cross-cultural lens, in B. Percy-Smith & N. Thomas (eds) *A Handbook of Children and Young People's Participation: Perspectives from Theory and Practice*. London: Routledge.

McBurney, D.H. (1994) *Research Methods*. Pacific Grove, CA: Brooks/Cole.

Mead, G.H. (1934), *Mind, Self, and Society* (ed. C.W. Morris). Chicago: University of Chicago Press.

Morrow, V. (2008), Ethical dilemmas in research with children and young people about their social environments, *Children's Geographies*, 6(1): 49–61.

Nibell L.N., Shook, J.J. & Finn, J.L. (2009), *Childhood, Youth, and Social Work in Transformation: Implications for Policy*. New York: Columbia University Press.

Nussbaum, M. (1997), Capabilities and human rights, *Fordham Law Review*, 66: 273–300.

Nussbaum, M. (2004), Beyond the social contract: capabilities and global justice, *Oxford Development Studies*, 32(1): 3–18.

Pufall, P. and Unsworth, R. (2004), *Rethinking Childhood*. London: Rutgers University Press.

Sen, A. (1985), Well-being, agency and freedom, *The Journal of Philosophy*, LXXXII(4): 169–221.

Sen, A. (1999), *Development as Freedom*. Oxford: Oxford University Press.

Simmel, G. (1950), Individual and society in 18th and 19th century views of life: an example of philosophical sociology (1917), in K.H. Wolff (ed.), *The Sociology of Georg Simmel*. Glencoe, IL: The Free Press, pp. 78–83.

Stoecklin, D. (2000), *Enfants des rues en Chine*. Paris: Editions Karthala.

Stoecklin, D. (2007), Children in street situations: a rights-based approach, in I. Rizzini, U. Mandel Butler & D. Stoecklin (eds), *Life on the Streets: Children and Adolescents on the Streets: Inevitable Trajectories?* Sion: Institut international des Droits de l'Enfant, pp. 77–97.

Stoecklin, D. (2009a), L'enfant acteur et l'approche participative, in J. Zermatten & D. Stoecklin (eds), *Le droit des enfants de participer. Norme juridique et réalité pratique: contribution à un nouveau contrat social*. Sion: IUKB/IDE, pp. 47–71.

Stoecklin, D. (2009b), Réflexivité, participation et capabilité, in J. Zermatten & D. Stoecklin (eds), *Le droit des enfants de participer. Norme juridique et réalité pratique: contribution à un nouveau contrat social*. Sion: IUKB/IDE, pp. 75–109.

Treseder, P. (1997), *Empowering Children and Young People*. London: Children's Rights Office/Save the Children.

Van Bueren, G. (1998), *The International Law on the Rights of the Child*. The Hague: Martinus Nijhoff Publishers.

Verhellen, E. (1996), *Monitoring Children's Rights*. The Hague: Martinus Nijhoff Publishers.

Vizard, P. (2006), *Poverty and Human Rights: Sen's Capability Perspective Explored*. Oxford: Oxford University Press.

Zermatten, J. (2005), *Les enfants ont des droits: une révolution?* Sion: Institut Universitaire Kurt Bösch/Institut international des Droits de l'Enfant.

4

Agency, Participation and Youth Inequalities

Zoë Clark

Introduction

The capabilities approach as developed by Amartya Sen (for example, 1987, 1999) and Martha Nussbaum (2006, 2007) delivers a metric of well-being defining people's standard of living. Individual choices are socially embedded and as individuals tend to adapt their preferences to their given life circumstances, the yardstick of well-being is not defined in terms of happiness, but in terms of what people are free to do and to be. Thus well-being is evaluated independently of the fact that people might also be happy under more restrictive or oppressive conditions, and 'objective' criteria are developed. The term 'objective' does not indicate that these criteria are fixed, i.e. not open for deliberative debates. It rather points out that the subjective well-being of the individual is not the metric for the standard of living. Rather the metric relates to positive freedoms to realize a life one has reason to value. The positive freedoms as criteria for a standard of living are called 'capabilities'. Realized freedoms into actual states of being or doing are described with the term 'functionings' (Sen, 1992).

The main contribution of this chapter is an adaption of the capabilities approach for young people in order to identify pathways of the reproduction of social inequality during this biographical period.[1] In order to discuss if and how we can apply and investigate capabilities for young people, the theoretical groundings of this approach have to be analysed with respect to this target group. While it is not obvious to include young people in Sen's (2010) version of the capabilities approach, it seems to be sensible to do so in Nussbaum's (2007) version. Beyond the general concerns about the question of 'justice for whom?' some clarification concerning the relationship of functionings and capabilities is required, too. In the early sections of this chapter, I will argue that the often-made suggestion of a functionings approach for young people, which implies that there can be a functioning without a previous capability, opens up the doors to all kinds of education, including authoritarian and oppressive modes of education. But insisting on a capabilities rather than a functioning approach for young people leads to a range of methodological challenges. Measuring capabilities as distinct from functionings as latent and counterfactual opportunities is difficult and rarely done. Due to such difficulties this chapter investigates the limitations of access to certain (age-specific) capabilities. A structural equation model (SEM), which is developed based on the theoretical discussion of the early sections, will be presented in the latter part of the chapter. The suggested SEM relates intergenerational inequalities to the capabilities and future aspirations of young people.

Equality of what and justice for whom?

The questions of 'justice for whom?' and 'equality of what?' (Sen, 1992) are closely connected to each other within liberal ideas and in particular within the capabilities approach. Amartya Sen (cited in Saito, 2003: 25ff.) and Martha Nussbaum (Nussbaum, 2006: 90, 2007: 172) suggest a focus on functionings instead of capabilities for young people. This suggests that young people are not autonomous and self-responsible human beings by birth, but that they are still vulnerable and dependent beings. In particular Nussbaum developed a version of an ethical (instead of a political) contractualism, which offers an approach to justice which includes each and every person, independent of their state of rationality and autonomy. While Sen presumes autonomous actors within his notion of agency freedom (for example, Sen, 2010: 286ff.), Nussbaum (for example, 2007: 96ff.) has an idea of ethical equality which includes all human beings regardless of their different kinds of abilities. In other words, as Des Gasper (2004: 182ff.) puts it, in particular Nussbaum takes into account that human beings are not 'pre-social' agents, who make choices right from the start, at birth, but that they are in an ongoing process of human development.

This philosophical approach of ethical contractualism results from Nussbaum's reflections on Rawls' (cf. 2001, 2005) political contractualism, which can be classified as a liberal way of thinking. Yet looking at Nussbaum's (2007: 99ff, 156ff.) critique of Rawls' contractualism, this surplus of a functioning approach for young people (compared to the capability approach for adults) does not seem to be necessary within her version of contractualism. Nussbaum claims that justice is not to be reduced to a political state of fairness in the form of a contract between only those who are free and equal in their abilities and in their willingness to participate and who are furthermore the ones who do fully participate. Instead she argues for an ethical contractualism, which defines the social as a relationship between moral equals, who are interdependent on each other. Instead of a political definition of an addressee and author of social justice she gives an essentialist answer to the question of justice for whom. Nussbaum suggests an ethical individualist perspective, which includes each and every human being on the basis of moral instead of political equality of human beings with dignity. Within her claim for a moral instead of a political equality she rejects the Kantian definition of a person through the person's rationality (Nussbaum, 2007: 155ff.). Instead of this political notion of a person, she regards interdependency and vulnerability as essential characteristics, which constitute human beings as social beings. Within this context it seems to be redundant to find a special answer to the 'equality of what' (Sen, 1987) question for young people.

Next to the question of whether a functioning approach is consistent with this form of ethical contractualism, there are some problems for the question of 'equality of what' from a perspective of educational science. If we define a functioning as anything else than the result of a real freedom, this category loses the critical and political progressive impact it could have, in particular with respect to education. An example of the German welfare state may clarify this issue: on the basis of the German welfare reform in 2005 the welfare state is no longer founded on a needs-based approach, but the fulfilment of basic needs is conditional in respect to people's achievements (including young people from the age of 16). The character of welfare institutions can no longer be described as redistributing resources (in order to reduce the harms of capitalism). Nowadays it also fulfils the task of evaluating people's achievements as a precondition for their social right to welfare. After this seemingly meritocratic welfare reform, young people in particular have to take part in different kinds of 'trainings', where they are supposed to learn how to write applications or to use certain computer software. This is not to be understood as a selectable opportunity for education, but as an obligation related to sanctions. Non-participation can lead to a temporary cut-off of their entire benefits. If we now have the possibility to define these competencies developed within a repressive welfare sanction as a functioning, this category is too fuzzy for analytical ends and not helpful from a political perspective. This potential fuzziness and tolerance for all kinds of political implication in respect of education is due to the definition of a functioning as a pure outcome. If young people can have functionings without capabilities, then these do not seem to be necessarily related to capabilities and particular ways of human development. Hence the kind of education becomes arbitrary, if the source of the doings and beings does not have to be defined in order to take it into account as a functioning. A comprehensive capabilities approach offers the opportunity to elaborate a concept of education in terms of cultural and social self-formation – a process of human development which should at best lead to autonomy and always have the source of a 'functioning' within a choice based on real freedoms. However, an isolated focus on functionings is not only confining the capabilities approach with respect to young people, but it is also changing the implications of the term 'functioning'. This does not mean that each ability has to be developed in the same way a functioning does, but paternalistic ways of competence development have to be justified in a different way. In other words, if the category of a functioning is open to any kind of authoritarian ideas of education, there is little justification in this newly-created category beyond the term of a competency.

Agency as an endless pathway of capabilities and functionings

The claim of inconsistency of a functionings approach demands for a systematization of the relationship between functionings and capabilities. I would like to suggest a rewriting of a systematization by Des Gasper and what he calls 'endless pathways of functionings and capabilities' (2002: 448) as shown in Figure 4.1. Gasper criticizes Sen for his overly economistic notion of human development. Analysing the conversion of a capability into a functioning as choice-making implies a construction of subjects as pre-social beings (Gasper 2002: 451ff.). Before looking at the background of Gasper's discussion of how to include an understanding of subjectivation (the socially embedded process of identity formation) into the capability approach as a theoretical frame for human development, a systematization of capabilities and functionings is made in Figure 4.1.

Following Des Gasper (2002, 2004), one of the main points of this model is that it is not a one-way track converting one capability into one functioning, but that realized functionings are again a precondition for capabilities as part of a circular progression of human development. From this perspective the development from a capability towards a functioning is not only regarded as an act of choice-making, but as an educational process in the sense of human development. Part of this circular way of analysing human development is to

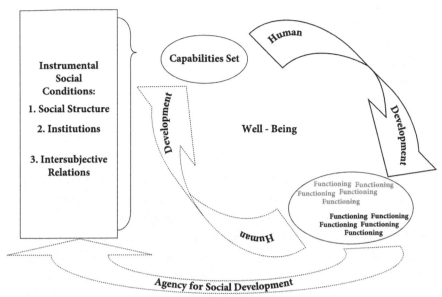

Figure 4.1 Modified 'endless pathways of functionings and capabilities'.
Adapted from Gasper 2002/4

conceptualize functionings not only in terms of the results of a capability, but at the same time as utilities for the enhancement of a capability set. Unlike Gasper's model, this modified model of 'endless pathways of functionings and capabilities' starts from a person's capabilities instead of their functionings. While Gasper (2002: 448) classifies any current state of being or doing as a functioning, the argument in this model is to classify only those doings and beings as functionings which result from capabilities in terms of real freedoms. From this perspective there can be a meaningful distinction of functionings from competences in that education is recognized as a process of cultural self-formation. Whether there can be a functioning without a preceding capability is an essential question in order to develop a capability oriented educational (*Bildung*) theory.

But an isolated focus on the level of well-being would be a social decontextualization in the sense that social conditions (class belonging, gender relations, family relations or schooling conditions) play a major role in access to central capabilities (as illustrated on the left-hand side of Figure 4.1). These conditions are instrumental, yet belonging to a certain class, to a certain gender or to a certain nation state is not necessarily intrinsically valuable to the individual, but is related to standard of living and hence influences and shapes the opportunities for individual well-being (which is illustrated in the oval on the right-hand side of Figure 4.1). If we assume that capabilities are intrinsically valuable, it is worthwhile knowing which opportunities people have under which instrumental conditions. Within such a model we can go beyond the question of whether people are under or above a universal threshold, to analyse under which conditions privileges and disadvantages, in terms of access to capabilities, are developed.

The crucial point is, now, how we describe and analyse the process of human development which is taking place between the transformations from counterfactual freedoms to an actual state of being or doing. Within this construction of well-being Gasper (2002) is criticising Sen for his description of the process between a capability and a function as a pure choice. According to Gasper (2004: 181ff.) this economic rhetoric of autonomous choice-making actors leads to a notion of subjects as pre-social beings, ignoring the social conditions under which people are not just choosing their capabilities, but where a social process of human development also takes place. The question he is addressing to the capabilities approach concerns the character of humanity within the notion of human development. It is a major task to analyse how individual actions are shaped through social structures and vice versa (structure-agency debate). It may be argued that the two are inseparable and yet humans must be analysed as social beings rather than as autonomous choosers.

Young people's choices are often limited, and yet their development and flourishing are key concerns for society. In order to decide how appropriate capabilities can be used as an evaluative scale for the well-being of young persons in contrast to a mandatory preparative achievement of competences, a debate about paternalism (in close relation to different concepts of education) comes into play. This cannot be fully elaborated upon here, but some hints will be made.

Andresen *et al.* (2008) claim in their article called '*Bildung* as human development', that there should be critical alliances between the capabilities approach and critical theories on education. Education is understood in a particular tradition of an educational concept, which is not necessarily related to schooling, but implies the meaning of social and cultural self-formation. One advantage of this concept of *Bildung*, which makes this alliance reasonable, is grounded in the educational goal of autonomy. In terms of the capabilities approach this could be translated into the ability to have reasons to value the things one values. This does not mean that autonomy as a major goal of education has to be fulfilled in order to speak about capabilities and functionings instead of competences. But it does mean that the paternalistic compulsion to develop particular skills or competences has to be justified through the educational outcome of self-determination.

Being consistent with Nussbaum's (2007: 212ff.) notion of interdependency as a constitutive part of the human social condition, a critical concept of *Bildung* cannot assume a fully autonomous subject, who can make reasonable choices in each and every situation. In order to avoid falling back again behind the idea of fully autonomous persons, paternalism might not be fully rejected for young people, but has to be justified in respect to particular abilities.

The whole picture is complete as capabilities and functionings are the basis for agency in terms of the influence on social conditions, which are outside personal life:

> When more capability includes more power in ways that can influence other people's lives a person may have good reason to use the enhanced capability – the larger agency freedom – to uplift the lives of others, especially if they are relatively worse off, rather than concentrating only on their own well-being.
>
> Sen, 2009: 289

Sen's perspective highlights the necessity of conceptualizing the term 'agency' when we discuss the capabilities of young people. The definition of agency formulated by Sen is one where people with fewer capabilities are dependent on the goodwill of those with more freedom. This suggests a one-way trap of dependency of young persons on adults. Within bottom-up deliberative practices, it is those people with fewer freedoms (already problematic if they are produced and reproduced through and within social conditions) who have the greatest need of being the ones with the agency to influence the structures and social conditions by which they are oppressed.

Methodology

Taking the capabilities approach seriously as a scale for the well-being of young people, the next challenge is the methodological link to social science. There are already some qualitative and quantitative examples of how research about the well-being of young people in terms of the capabilities approach can be done. The following is an example of a path model (using Mplus and SPSS) as an instrument in order to link structural conditions to the well-being of young people in terms of capabilities and linking the latter to their future aspirations as well as to their subjective well-being. The empirical basis of this study is a sample of 780 young people in the ninth grade (aged between 15 and 17). The demographic factors school type, gender and migration background are distributed as shown in Table 4.1.

Table 4.1 Distribution of relevant demographic factors

School type[2]	Gymnasium (academic track/A level)	45.38%
	Realschule (non-academic track)	26.41%
	Hauptschule (non-academic track)	17.31%
	Comprehensive school (academic and non-academic tracks)	9.49%
	Special school	1.41%
Gender	Female	49.1%
Migration background[3]		23.1%

The data was collected by the 'North Rhine-Westphalian Research School Education and Capabilities' as a panel study with 37 schools in the state of North Rhine-Westphalia, Germany. The following analysis is based on the first wave of this panel data, collected by the end of 2009.

Structural equation modelling

SEM (see for example, Kline, 2001; Di Tommaso *et al.*, 2004; Di Tommaso, 2007) is used in order to analyse the link between structural backgrounds and the circle of capabilities and functionings. The main advantage of this method is a relation between factor analysis and regression analysis. Within SEM the confirmatory factor analysis is the so-called measurement model, which is for estimating latent variables. This means that we have the hypothesis in our measurement models that a certain phenomenon exists, but we cannot observe it directly. For example, if we believe that people do have a certain degree of autonomy, we cannot simply ask them 'how autonomous are you?' Instead we have to operationalize the different aspects of autonomy, such as, 'I often have to do what other people want me to do' as indicators of being non-autonomous. The confirmatory factor analysis is the instrument to test, if and to what degree our items do explain the latent construct. With the help of regression coefficients, weighted impacts on the construct are measured; hence we can test which items explain most in relation to the ones which explain least.

In the second step within the structure model we can calculate the regressions between different latent variables. While the dependent variable of the factor analysis is the unobserved latent construct with items as independent predictors, latent constructs within the structural model can be predictors as well as independent variables. Unlike the usual multivariate regression, SEM offers the opportunity to have more than one outcome variable and mediating variables. If variable *a* is the predictor of variable *b* and variable *b* is at the same time the predictor of variable *c*, then *b* is the mediator between *a* and *c*.

Beyond the mediating effects, moderation effects can be estimated too. This means that we can calculate the effect of variables on parameters, instead of on other variables. This can be done amongst others with a multiple group analysis as we will now see.

Within the language of SEM there are certain standards regarding presentation of the data. If the measurement model is done simultaneously with the structural model, the latent constructs should be presented as ovals. In this case all latent constructs (migration background, language brokering, privacy, autonomy and subjective well-being) are calculated as separate factors. These factors are included in the structural model as manifest variables and are therefore illustrated as boxes (see Figure 4.2) as is required for path models (see Reinecke, 2005).

Results: The social conditions of youth

Consistent with 'the endless pathway of functionings and capabilities', the model presented in Figure 4.2 includes three layers: one layer with variables about instrumental structural dimensions of inequality (migration background, gender, parents' socioeconomic status and school type); followed by a layer of mediating variables, which are interpreted in the rationality of the capabilities approach (language brokering, privacy and autonomy) and which are again related to the final layer of the model, including variables about current well-being and future aspirations (subjective well-being, job aspirations, job versus family aspirations).

In the next section a description of the basic idea of the model (related to its layers, variables and constructs) is given. Subsequently the central results of the model will be summarized.

The stars within the model indicate three levels of significance: * indicates a 0.05%, ** indicates a 0.01%, and *** indicates a 0.001% level of significance. An additional part of the model results are the fit-indices: chi² p-value: 0.2735; CFI: 0,991; TLI: 0,986; RMSEA estimate: 0,014 / 90% C.I.: 0,000, 0,034; SRMR: 0,029. These results indicate that the model fits the data well. The amount of explained variance of each dependent variable is reported with the following R² values: school-type: 0,188***; job aspirations vs. family aspirations: 0,021*; job aspirations: 0,222***; language-brokering: 0,105***; autonomy: 0,098***; life-satisfaction: 0,224***.

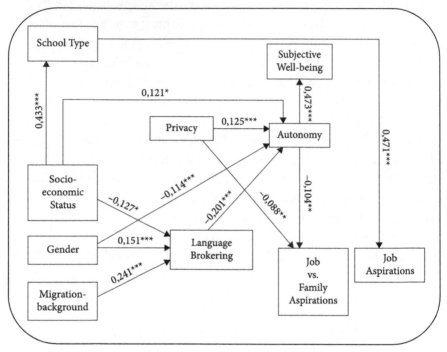

Figure 4.2 Structured youthfulness

Capabilities as mediators between (intersecting) structural categories and future aspirations

Structural backgrounds

The initial points on the left-hand side of the estimated SEM shown in Figure 4.2 are the socioeconomic status (SES), gender and migration background. In capitalist, patriarchal and nation-state based societies, these seem to be the three main categories which are structuring people's lives. Gender is based on common binary codes of male and female and hence is a simple manifest variable with no latent construct behind it. The socioeconomic status of young people is also a manifest variable as it consists of the occupations of the participants' parents, which are matched into the International Socio-Economic Index of Occupational Status (ISEI) provided by Ganzeboom and Treiman (1996) (ISEI08 – see Ganzeboom, 2010).[4] Migration background is a latent construct, operationalized by the parents' place of birth and the interviewees', as well as the language(s) spoken at home. The latter include the questions, if they never, sometimes or always speak another language than German at home.

Following a methodological paradigm of intersectionality, a multiple group analysis was conducted in order to find out if the parameters of the model differed significantly between groups with intersecting characteristics regarding gender, class (SES) and migration background. This comes close to McCall's methodological systematization of an intercategorical approach (whereby she distinguishes between an anti- and an intracategorical approach): 'The categorical approach focuses on the complexity of relationships among multiple social groups within and across analytical categories ... The subject is multigroup, and the method is systematically comparative' (McCall, 2005: 1781). Instead of analysing only the separated impacts of class, gender and migration background, the multiple group analysis can show if there are moderation effects within these three variables and furthermore if they explain parameters between different aspects of well-being.

Capabilities for youth

The second layer of the model, the mediating variables, refers to the well-being of young people in terms of capabilities. Within the second layer of the model there are different dimensions, which are age-specific operationalizations in respect to Martha Nussbaum's (2007: 76, 77) list of Central Human Capabilities, measured as latent variables. Measuring capabilities in the sense of positive freedoms is difficult and has rarely been done until now (Comim, 2010). These are not directly observable and hence have to be modelled as latent constructs, but as they are also counterfactual, they are even harder to identify (see Comim, 2010: 173ff.). On the one hand, this implies identifying doings and beings persons *could* have realized, even though they have not done so yet, and indeed may never realize. On the other hand, the meaning of the term 'capability', based on choice-making, includes the opportunities people have had to *refuse* the achievement of certain doings and beings they *have* realized.

There are few works by researchers to measure capabilities and relate them to functionings (Van Ootegem and Verhofstadt, 2010) and to well-being (Anand and Van Hees, 2005; Anand *et al.*, 2009; Van Ootegem and Verhofstadt, 2010). Due to these difficulties the latent constructs of the second layer of the model (language brokering, autonomy and privacy), are proxies for the capability for youth and are in fact asking for issues that are assumed to be obstacles to young people realizing a period of youth in a sociological sense.

The concept of language brokering (see Buriel *et al.*, 2006; Burton, 2007; Faulstich Orellana, 2009; Antonio, 2010; Bauer and Coram, 2010; Guske, 2010) is used as an indicator of the responsibilities young people have for their families. Language brokers mediate communication with others. The work of language translation and mediation for others in private, but also in institutional contexts, is defined as language brokering. For example, one item in the questionnaire was about whether they had to support their parents in their direct interaction with institutions, whether they helped them with reading and understanding their correspondence or with making telephone calls (Jurkovic *et al.*, 2000). This latent variable is reinterpreted on the basis of the concept of youth as a moratorium in terms of structured irresponsibility in the historical context of expansion of education. Opposed to a transitive youth concept, which focuses on the instrumental value of youth, the concept of a moratorium insists on the intrinsic value of youth as an autonomous life-period of self-development. The concept of youth as a moratorium is often only attached to temporary non-participation in the labour market. Distinctively, to this strong focus on labour-market inclusion, this period can also be defined by the absence of the responsibility for one's own reproduction, and the reproduction of other persons, and at the same time by the possibility of relying on non-reciprocal, but asymmetric relations of responsibility (not necessarily within traditional family patterns). These kinds of responsibilities may include, for example, the responsibility for emotional and psychological stability of other family members, the responsibility for administrative tasks, like mediating interaction with institutions for family members, or reproductional tasks, like raising siblings. Formulated differently, the access to a moratorium should not be reduced to the status of young people within the labour market, but also to their option of relying on adult care instead of being a responsible care worker themselves. Being not responsible to act as a care worker can be understood as a negative freedom as a precondition for the capability for youth, while the privilege to be dependent on adult care is a positive freedom and a basis to realize the capability for youth as a state of being.

With respect to the capabilities approach I am arguing that youth in itself is a state of being, a real freedom of human development and that it can hence be as an age-specific capability in itself. Language brokering is a construct, which is set in contrast to the concept of an intrinsically valuable period of youth which implies on the one hand negative freedom of the absence of responsibility for (labour) work and on the other hand the positive freedom to rely on asymmetrical relations of responsibility. Hence the absence of language brokering is theoretically embedded as an obstacle to the free choice of a youth moratorium; or in other words, the negative freedom of being responsible as a language broker is regarded as one aspect of the positive freedom of youth as a capability. This is particularly relevant for those young people whose parents have a migration background and do not fluently speak the prevalent language of the country they live in.

While language brokering refers to youth as a capability, the other two latent constructs in the layer of meditating variables are about control over their own environment. Privacy is used as an indicator of the control over one's own material environment. This includes questions regarding, for example, whether other people knock on the door before entering their room or if they are allowed to lock their room. The autonomy scale[5] indicates how far young people can govern their own life as it is formulated in Nussbaum's capability number 10a: 'being able to participate effectively in political choices that govern one's life; having the right of political participation, protection of free speech and association' (Nussbaum, 2007: 77). Even though this autonomy scale does not directly concern political decisions, it measures to which degree the interviewees felt governed or under social pressure within their social relations.

Subjective well-being and job aspirations

Future aspirations as well as current life satisfaction (see Dalbert, 2010) are outcome variables illustrated on the right-hand side of the model (Figure 4.2) and are at the same time the third layer of the model. In order to know if these current capabilities have any impact on future living conditions, I included two open questions about employment aspirations in the model, which are matched into the metric ISEI scale (see Ganzeboom, 2010). Furthermore the participants were asked if they put greater emphasis on having a future family or a future job. Beside these variables about aspirations, the other outcome of this model was about current subjective well-being.

Responsibility and agency of young people within the public and the private sphere

After the description of each of the three layers of the model, the structural conditions, the obstacles for certain capabilities, and their future aspirations, I now summarize the whole picture and elaborate on the hypotheses and the results of the different links between those layers.

As Biggeri *et al.* (2006) pointed out, the capabilities set of young people is not independent of that of their parents. In other words, young people depend on the freedoms of their parents, which are based on the class-belongings that produce intergenerational inequality. The gender relations and the migration background are also taken into account in respect of their potential effects on the capabilities sets of the participants. I assumed that language brokering is a gender-, class- and migration-related phenomenon, which indicates an absence of a youth moratorium. It can be argued that such a youth moratorium is intrinsically valuable as a matter of human development, but at the same time it has instrumental effects on the reproduction of social inequality. If the access to a youth moratorium is regarded as a capability, it is an object of distribution too. Furthermore it affects future aspirations (see Zinnecker, 2003) or, in other words, the state of being during a period of youth is adapting the preferences of young people.

The results of the model show that language brokering is predicted by the whole triad of class (which only has a weak effect), gender and migration background, while the latter has the strongest effect. The estimations indicate that being a boy and being from lower classes and having a migration background make involvement in language brokering responsibilities more likely. While the class and migration specificity is not surprising, the direction of the gender parameter demands explanation. That boys are the ones who tend to be more involved in language brokering makes sense if this kind of reproduction work is embedded in a broader context of filial responsibility. The participants were also asked about chores they do at home. A regression analysis showed that it is more likely for boys to be involved in language brokering, but less males are likely than girls to be involved in housework ($-.114^{***}/R^2$ 0.05). As the language brokering items mostly refer to tasks where persons appear in public, while the chores are not, it seems to be plausible that there is a traditional gender gap, maybe not in terms of the the amount, but in the *kind* of responsibilities along a boundary between public and private tasks.[6]

This assumption of gendered kinds of reproductive work is further verified by the fact that reading letters to the parents is gender neutral, while making phone-calls for them or helping them in their interactions with institutions is not. Hence it does not seem to be related to language itself, but to the question of whether the brokering takes place in public or private spheres. In the next step I analysed language brokering as a mediating variable. I assumed that language brokering would increase the amount of autonomy as it includes being involved in 'adult issues' and that it would lower job aspirations, as early involvement in high amounts of responsibility might adapt aspirations towards early adulthood and hence early labour market involvement. But the results show that language brokering *decreases* the amount of autonomy young people feel they have, rather than increasing it.

Being involved in language brokering is assessed with lower evaluations of one's own autonomy. This can be explained through an adaption of preferences. Qualitative research (see Guske, 2010: 337) indicates that language brokering stands in a conflicting relationship to the parents' authority. Guske (2010) shows in her research that those young people who are involved in 'adult issues' resist more strongly accepting their parents' authority. The data from this study indicate that language brokers assess their own autonomy less highly than other young people do. It is plausible that they develop a greater desire for autonomy due to adult responsibility or that they feel constrained in developing autonomy.

Analysing the whole sample in one model, the job aspirations are not predicted by language brokering involvement. But if the data is analysed from an intersectional perspective, it indicates that this is not true for boys from the lower classes. Within this group the data shows that those who are doing language brokering tend to have higher job aspirations ($-0.231^{**}/R^2$ 0.05).[7]

Concerning privacy, covered by the questions about whether young people were allowed to lock their doors or if other people would knock before entering, as a matter of being able to control one's own environment – my hypothesis was that privacy is predicted by structural background and that in turn it affects job aspirations, assuming that a lack of privacy will cause a desire for early independence of the household of origin. The data showed that there is no correlation with any kind of structural group-belonging and also no correlation with job aspirations. This might be due to the variables in this construct, which only asked about matters of power relations. There were only a few young people in this sample who did not have their own rooms; hence the material basis of privacy could not be included in the analysis. But privacy is still a precondition for feeling autonomous, and the data shows that a sense of feeling autonomy is more likely if the family members allow the young person to control access of others to their own room.

Concluding remarks

This chapter is not to be misunderstood as a judgement of the better way of spending one's youth and finding ways of adapting each and every person to models of youth which were developed in privileged contexts. One central result of the data analysis is the structured inequality in the amount and, in particular, the kinds of responsibility young people have to take. The same holds true for future aspirations: it is not my task to judge the aspirations, but to unmask unequal freedoms and conditions of job aspiration formation.

Looking at the data analysis through the glasses of Nussbaum's capabilities approach, two major issues are worth problematizing. First, the unequal distribution of responsibility for reproductive work concerning language brokering as well as housework is an obstacle on the way towards a youth moratorium. If a youth moratorium is regarded as an age-specific capability then this inequality of responsibility can be criticized as capability deprivation of young people. Secondly, the division in the kind of tasks between public and private spheres is an inequality of control over young people's environments. This is also articulated in the higher amount of desire for autonomy of language brokers and in the significantly positive correlation between language brokering and job aspirations among boys from the lower classes.

Notes

1   The participants of this empirical investigation are mainly aged 15.
2   The German school system is a tracking system, which selects pupils after Grade 4, at the age of 10, into an academic track or into a non-academic track. Additionally Germany has comprehensive schools where young people can either qualify for university or for vocational training. Furthermore there are special schools for children who are diagnosed with special needs.
3   For this frequency distribution an item is used asking if they never, sometimes or only speak another language then German at home. In the following model further information is included.
4   Only 52 per cent of the parents gave information about their occupation and therefore this model is based on a multiple imputation in order to get plausible values for the relations between different factors. These 14 items are derived from the questionnaires filled in by the young people and include cultural goods at their respective homes (like how many books they have at home), joint activities (like going to the opera with their parents), and a self-description in respect to their consumerism.
5   For the autonomy scale a selection of items of the Basic Psychological Needs Scale (http://www.psych.rochester.edu/SDT/measures/bpns_scale.php) was used.
6   Research conducted in the USA (Buriel *et al.*, 2006) showed different results. They found that girls have an overall higher amount of responsibility within families and that they are also more involved in language brokering tasks. It seems to be necessary to differentiate this further, e.g. with respect to the question of whether they broker for their mother or father.
7   The R^2 of the job aspirations is not significant for the multiple group analysis. This might be due to less power because of the smaller sample size of 227 participants within this group.

References

Addabbo, T., Di Tommaso, M. L., & Facchinetti, G. (2004) To What extent fuzzy set theory and structural equation modelling can, measure functionings? An application to child well being, *Materiali di Discussione del Dipartimento di Economia Politica*, 468, www.dep.unimore.it/materiali_discussione/0468.pdf, accessed 9 May 2012.

Anand, P. & Van Hees, M. (2005) Capabilities and achievements: an empirical study, *Journal of Socio-Economics*, 35: 268–284.

Anand, P., Hunter, G., Carter, I., Dowding, K., Guala, F. & Van Hees, M. (2009) The development of capability indicators, *Journal of Human Development and Capabilities*, 10: 125–284.

Andresen, S., Otto, H.-U. & Ziegler, H. (2008) *Bildung* as human development: an educational view on the capabilities approach, in Otto, Hans-Uwe & Ziegler, Holger (eds) Capabilities –Handlungsbefähigung und Verwirklichungschancen in der Erziehungswissenschaft, Wiesbaden, VS Verlag für Sozialwissenschaften.

Antonio, R. (2010) The study of child language brokering: past, current, and emerging research, *mediAzioni*, 10, http://mediazioni.sitlec.unibo.it, accessed 25 January 2010.

Bauer, E. & Coram, T. (2010) Language brokering: practicing active citizenship, *mediAzioni*, 10, http://mediazioni.sitlec.unibo.it, accessed 30 February 2011.

Biggeri, M., Libanora, R., Mariani, S. & Menchini, L. (2006) Children conceptualizing their capabilities: results of a survey conducted during the first Children's World Congress on Child Labour, *Journal of Human Development*, 7(1): 59–83.

Buriel, R., Love, T. & De Ment, T. (2006) The relation of language brokering to depression and parent-child bonding among Latino adolescents, in Bornstein, M. & Cote, L. (eds) *Acculturation and Parent-Child Relationships – Measurement and Development*, London, Psychology Press.

Burton, L. (2007) Childhood Adultification in economically disadvantaged families: a conceptual model, *Family Relations*, 56: 329–345.

Comim, F. (2010) Measuring capabilities, in Comim, Flavio, Qizilbash, Mozaffar & Alkire, S. (eds) *The Capabilities Approach – Concepts, Measures, and Applications*, Cambridge, Cambridge University Press.

Dalbert, C. (2010) General wellbeing, http://www.erzwiss.uni-halle.de/gliederung/paed/ppsych/TWBI.pdf, accessed 2 May 2011.

Di Tommaso, M. L. (2007) Children's capabilities: a structural equation model for India, *Journal of Socio-Econiomics*, 36(3): 436–450.

Faulstich Orellana, M. (2009) *Translating Childhoods: Immigrant Youth, Language, and Culture*, New Jersey, Rutgers University Press.

Ganzeboom, H. (2010) *International Standard Classification of Occupations ISCO-08, with ISEI-08*, http://home.fsw.vu.nl/hbg.ganzeboom/isco08, accessed 21 December 2010.

Gasper, D. (2002) Is Sen's capabilities approach an adequate basis for considering human development? *Review of Political Economy*, 14(4): 435–461.

Gasper, D. (2004) *The Ethics of Development*, Edinburgh, Edinburgh University Press.

Guske, I. (2010) Familial and institutional dependence on bilingual and bicultural go-betweens – effects on minority children, *mediAzioni*, 10, http://mediazioni.sitlec. unibo.it, acessed 20 February 2011.

Jurkovic, G. J. *et al.* (2000) Adolescent Filial Responsibility Questionnaire – revised, Available from Gregory J. Jurkovic at Department of Psychology, Georgia State University, MSC 2A1155, 33 Gilmer Street, SE, Unit 2, Atlanta, GA 30303-3080 or TUgjurkovic@gsu.edu.UT.

Kline, R. (2011) *Principles and Practice of Structural Equation Modeling*, New York, Guildford Press.

McCall, L. (2005) The complexity of intersectionality, *Signs: Journal of Women in Culture and Society*, 30(3): 1771–1800.

Nussbaum, M. (2006) *Women and Human Development – The Capabilities Approach*, Cambridge, Cambridge University Press.

Nussbaum, M. (2007) *The Frontiers of Justice – Disability Nationality Species Membership*, Cambridge, MA, Harvard University Press.

Rawls, J. (2001) *Justice as Fairness – A Restatement*, Cambridge, MA, Harvard University Press.

Rawls, J. (2005) *Political Liberalism*, New York, Columbia University Press.

Reinecke, J. (2005) *Strukturgleichungsmodelle in den Sozialwissenschaften*, Oldenburg, Oldenbourg Verlag.

Saito, M. (2003) Amartya Sen's capability approach to education: a critical exploration, *Journal of Philosophy of Education*, 37(1): 17–33.

Sen, A. (1987) *The Standard of Living*, Cambridge, Cambridge University Press.

Sen, A. (1992) *Inequality Reexamined*, Cambridge MA, Harvard University Press.

Sen, A. (1999) *Development as Freedom*, Oxford, Oxford University Press.

Sen, A. (2010) *The Idea of Justice*, Cambridge, MA, Harvard University Press.

Van Ootegem, L. & Verhofstadt, E. (2010) Using capabilities as an alternative indicator for well-being, working paper, Genf University, http://www.feb.ugent.be/nl/Ondz/ wp/Papers/wp_10_677.pdf, accessed 13 March 2011.

Zinnecker, J. (2003) Essay zur Geschichte und Bedeutung eines Forschungskonzepts, in Reinders, H. & Wild, E. (eds) *Jugendzeit – Time Out? – Zur Ausgestaltung des Jugendalters als Moratorium*, Opladen.

5

Child Poverty from a Capability Perspective

Ortrud Leßmann

Introduction

This chapter discusses the application of the capability approach (CA) to child poverty. First, the usual approach to measuring child poverty is explained. Most efforts to measure child poverty rely on data on household incomes. Children living in income-poor households are counted as poor. While the focus on income in poverty measures is disputed in general, it is particularly inadequate for children. Typically, income poverty measures account for the special needs of families by using equivalence scales. However, these mostly assign high economies of scale to large households and thus calculate high equivalence incomes for families, resulting in an underestimation of child poverty rates. Further, this so-called indirect approach to measurement by looking at income is praised for respecting freedom of choice and not prescribing a way of life to poor households. This seems cynical even in the case of adults, but for children who do not have an income at their command the argument is questionable.

Secondly, the chapter introduces the CA as a basis for the 'direct approach to measuring poverty' by looking at the various conditions of life and determining poverty lines for each dimension, while at the same time respecting freedom of choice by referring to the capabilities of people. However, measuring poverty directly on the basis of the CA demands first of all the selection of relevant dimensions. This is always a difficult task, but in the case of child poverty the question arises whether the dimensions are the same for children and adults. Further, there is no easy way to measure the capabilities of people, what they can be and do.

Thirdly, the chapter discusses the cogency of the concept of capability in the case of children. Sen and Nussbaum suggest concentrating on achieved functionings (beings and doings) rather than on capabilities in the case of children. But then, how will they grow up to be responsible agents? At the end of the chapter a research agenda is sketched in order to answer this question.

Income poverty of children

Although most children do not earn an income of their own, their standard of living is mostly assessed by looking at income figures, namely household income (Roelen and Gassmann, 2008). The standard procedure of income poverty measurement identifies the poor by setting a poverty line and then aggregates individual poverty to indicate the extent of poverty at the social level (Sen, 1979), for example, by calculating the head-count ratio. Before this can be done, individual incomes have to be calculated with the help of equivalence scales.

Equivalence scales

In general, income data is available at the household level, not at the individual level. The poverty line is applied to the distribution of individual incomes, however. This amounts to either assigning the actually achieved income to individuals, which would leave children without any income at all, or taking the household income and assigning a portion of it to the household members. Which part of the household income should be assigned to its members? Equivalence scales try to answer this question while taking the needs of children into account. As Muellbauer puts it, equivalence scales deflate budgets in order to 'calculate the relative amounts of money two different types of household require in order to reach the same standard of living' (see Pollak and Wales, 1979: 217).

In doing so, equivalence scales such as the Organization for Economic Cooperation and Development (OECD)-modified scale try to capture two effects: (a) differences in needs and (b) economies of scale. The more members a household has, the more needs are to be fulfilled. Some equivalence scales further differentiate between the needs of household members according to their age, assuming that children's needs are smaller than adults',[1] that is, that their needs can be fulfilled with less income. For example the, OECD-modified scale assigns a value 1 to the first household member and 0.3 to a child (up to 14 years) as opposed to 0.5 to an adult (14 years and older). Economies of scale refer to the fact that a household double the size of the reference household needs more but not twice as much income to achieve the same standard of living as the reference household. For example, larger households can use facilities such as the washing machine, the TV set, bathroom and kitchen jointly. Thus, there is widespread agreement that doubling the size of the household necessitates an income higher than that of the reference household and lower than twice that income, but there is no agreement about the exact size of needs differences and of economies of scale (see Buhmann *et al.*, 1988 for a comparison of various scales).

Implicitly, calculating equivalent incomes relies on two assumptions: first, the household members pool their income. Secondly, all household members achieve the same standard of living. This is often not true (for example, Haddad and Kanbur, 1990; Agarwal, 1994), but it is hard to get data on intra-household distribution.

The overall outcome of this method is to assign larger households higher equivalent incomes, emphasizing economies of scale. This emphasis is especially questionable in the case of poor households. Koulovationos *et al.* (2005) show that equivalence scales depend on income levels. A poorer household needs relatively more additional income than a rich household to maintain the same standard of living when it grows. They explain this phenomenon by (1) an increasing share of goods that have a public goods character within the household in richer households, i.e. goods that can be used together like a TV, a washing machine etc., and (2) the deliberative restriction of children's expenses by the adults. Hence, there is a tendency to overestimate the income of large poor households and in consequence to underestimate the extent of child income poverty.

Poverty lines

By creating data on individual (equivalence) incomes, it is possible to identify the poor by introducing a poverty line. In the European Union (EU) it has been agreed to use 60 per cent of the median income[2] as the poverty line. This is called a 'relative poverty line' because it is defined relative to the income distribution of a society. While there are good reasons for defining poverty relative to the society, it can be disputed whether the relative poverty line has any meaning beyond grasping income inequality. The value of 60 per cent is completely arbitrarily chosen. Sometimes it is referred to as the 'at-risk-of-poverty line' while the 50 per cent median income is called the poverty line, for example, by the OECD (2008) and UNICEF (2012).

Poverty lines refer to the needs of a single adult and are implicitly adjusted for children by equivalence scales. For comparing numbers of different studies on child poverty it is important to notice which concept of a poverty line was chosen and which equivalence scales. De Vos and Zaidi (1997) show how the choice of equivalence scales affects the poverty measure. Using lines that emphasize economies of scale results in measuring more poor households and less poor people, because large households are thought to benefit from the economies of scale. Thus, it also tends to de-emphasize the problem of child poverty.

Databases and conclusions on income poverty of children

In addition to conceptual choices, empirical researchers who measure poverty have to pick a database (household survey). Information on income is notoriously hard to get from those placed at the upper and lower ends of the income distribution. Thus, some databases are more representative than others with respect to the incomes of poor and rich people. Further, databases differ with regard to the information on age of household members. Finally, the frequency of household types in the database should match that in the overall population in order to ensure representativeness.

To conclude, the data on child poverty based on income is flawed in several ways. Children usually do not have an income of their own and do not have a say in how household income is spent. Yet, by applying equivalence scales an income is assigned to children and adults alike. This presupposes that the household pools its income and aims at an equal standard of living of all its members.

For these reasons, the first postulation is to make the assumptions behind equivalence scales explicit. Secondly, equivalence scales tend to underestimate child poverty in monetary terms when they assume large economies of scale. The definition of the poverty line and the choice of the database further contribute to obscuring the meaning of data on child poverty. Thirdly, the whole approach does not pose the question of whether infantile needs can be represented in monetary terms at all. Fourthly, it is necessary to determine infantile needs in order to overcome these problems.

Direct measurement of poverty based on the CA

Looking directly at a person's conditions of life is called the 'direct approach to poverty measurement' whereas the income approach is termed indirect since income is taken as a proxy for the opportunity to lead a decent life. The following subsection addresses the pros and cons of both approaches. If the direct approach is favoured, the relevant conditions of life must be chosen. Further, there is the general question of whether these should be the same for adults and children. This question is tackled in the second subsection. Thirdly, the CA is presented as an approach that lends itself for direct measurement while emphasizing the value of freedom of choice.

Direct versus indirect measurement of poverty: The argument of paternalism

Though poverty is mostly measured as income poverty, what matters are the conditions of life. Income is a means to achieve a good life by buying food, education, health services and so on. This idea lies at the heart of poverty measurement as can be seen when poverty lines are justified by referring to a minimum living standard. Referring to income instead of directly looking at whether people have all necessities comprised by the minimum standard at their command, avoids prescribing them a way of life. What people regard as 'necessary' may differ from person to person and by setting a poverty line in the income space the decision of what to buy to make ends meet is left to them. If the poverty line is determined relative to consumption patterns or income distribution, there is even less need to name the elements of a decent life. It is not the valuation of the researcher or of some experts but rather a standard set by the behaviour of normal people. A further argument for using the income approach is the availability of data for almost all countries. Income may not always reflect the standard of living properly, but it can serve as a first proxy for estimating the size of the problem and to monitor changes over time.

A drawback of the income approach is that income data is not always accurate. Home production, in-kind benefits and public services are contributing to the standard of living without being accounted for in income data. Furthermore, the income method relies on a functioning market where all the relevant goods can be purchased and have a market price that can be observed. In many countries this is not the case (Sen, 1979).

As we have seen, income data is individualized by equivalence scales. This is a way to take the needs of household members into account along with economies of scale. But often the needs are not specified further. The underlying aim seems to treat everyone the same. Yet, this is hardly satisfying and leaves the impression that equivalence scales are a means to downplay the problem of poverty in large households and thereby child poverty.

In contrast, the direct approach to measurement looks at the lives people lead, whether they actually have the goods deemed necessary at their command, and searches for direct signs of deprivation. It seems much easier to check if, for example, a child is adequately nourished by measuring their height and weight (Sen, 1985) than to calculate household equivalence income, the monetary value of home production, to determine a diet and compute the monetary price for it. But what else is necessary in a human being's life?

This approach urges us to state explicitly what we deem necessary and where deprivation sets in. Thus, spelling out the underlying normative concept is unavoidable. Several approaches in philosophy come to mind, focusing on resources (Dworkin, 1981a, 1981b), primary goods (Rawls, 1971), functionings (Sen, 1985) or capabilities (Nussbaum, 2000). Apart from choosing one of these evaluative spaces it is necessary to determine minimum standards for all dimensions. The philosophical approaches argue for one or the other evaluative space, but usually fall short from stating minimum standards explicitly. Nussbaum (2000: 73) develops her conception of a threshold without giving guidelines or illustrations concerning the operationalization. Rawls (1971: 83) refers to 'the worst off' but does not go into the technicalities of measuring primary goods and comparing various levels of those goods (Gibbard, 1979). Sen (1985) at least illustrates his approach, but deliberately leaves open many questions as well, for example, which functionings are basic[3] and how to determine the minimum standard.

What should be noted is that the direct approach to measuring poverty will always define poverty multidimensionally. This gives rise to a lot of further difficulties into which I will not go here (for an overview on multidimensional inequality measurement see, for example, Savaglio, 2002).

The special case of children

Whatever approach is chosen, with respect to children the question arises whether their conditions of life should be evaluated by the same standard as that of adults. 'The same standard' refers to (1) the same dimensions (which might be a subset of the evaluative space deemed essential for having a decent life) and (2) the same minimum standard.

Having the picture in mind that children are 'small adults' and 'persons to be', the intuitive answer may be to treat them like adults, but to assign them smaller amounts than adults, thus arriving at the same procedure as equivalence scales. However, if we take the example of rights, children are treated differently from adults (Lansdown, 2005). They are shielded from harm more carefully than adults, for example, by the prohibition of child labour, but at the same time they do not have the same rights as well, for example, to participate in elections and to set up a company.

Hence, it will be necessary to consider this question thoroughly in relation to the chosen evaluative space. There are at least three different questions: (1) Which is the right evaluative basis for measuring child poverty? (2) Which dimensions are relevant in this context – are they the same for adults and children, are the children's dimensions a subset, a superset or simply a different set of the adults'? (3) Is the minimum standard the same for children and adults? If not, do children need more or less of the particular dimension in question?

The existing studies (see Roelen and Gassman, 2008 for an overview; UNICEF, 2012) take a more pragmatic approach. Mostly they disregard the first question and answer the second, depending on data availability. However, they maintain that children should be treated differently to adults.

The CA as a basis for direct measurement

As Sen (1993: 50) puts it, the CA argues for the cogency of the evaluative space of functionings and capabilities. Functionings are the various doings and beings a person can achieve such as being nourished, being healthy, riding a bike, walking, reading and appearing in public without shame. Thus, they range from rather elementary ones like being adequately nourished to complex ones like appearing in public without shame. The CA views functionings as constitutive of well-being.

Which functionings are feasible for a person depends on the interaction of two sets of conditions. The first is the budget set that determines which resources are at the person's disposal. The second is the set of conversion factors that determines whether and how a person can utilize the resources in order to achieve a doing or a being. For example, for being adequately nourished it is crucial that the person has access to nourishment (resources), but it is also important that she has got the means, time and knowledge to prepare a meal, that this meal matches her digestive needs (for example, she is not allergic to the available food) and that it is deemed seemly for her to prepare the meal. Thus, there are various kinds of conversion factors. Robeyns (2005) distinguishes personal, social and environmental conversion factors. The first allude to a person's skills, talents and handicaps, the second to social norms and values as well as institutions and infrastructure, and the third to geographical and climatic conditions and the like.

A functioning will never come alone or independent from other functionings. Rather it is always bundles or combinations of doings and beings that are feasible due to the interaction of resources and conversion factors. Each combination of functionings describes a way of life. The capability set consists of all combinations of functionings feasible for a person from which she can choose 'a life [she] has reason to value' (Sen, 1999: 74). The CA thus promises to serve as a basis for direct poverty measurement that meets the objection of paternalism by emphasizing freedom of choice. Yet it provides objective indicators of poverty and models freedom of choice by introducing the capability set.

In terms of evaluation, functionings are situated between resources on the one hand and utility (happiness or desire satisfaction) on the other hand: functionings depend on resources, but it is not sufficient to look only at resources or even at primary goods. Resources enable a person to lead her life, but it is not resources alone that have to be taken into account. Rather it is the interaction between resources and conversion factors that is crucial. Thus, it is also insufficient to look at the enabling social and environmental conditions, as reference to 'social capital' sometimes suggests. (Monetary) resources are important. At the same time functionings are intrinsically valuable, that is, their value does not derive from the utility or happiness they generate, but well-being consists of achieving functionings.

In order to use the CA as a basis for direct poverty measurement one has to select relevant functionings. Sen does not provide a list of functionings necessary for leading a decent life. As mentioned earlier he gives some examples and

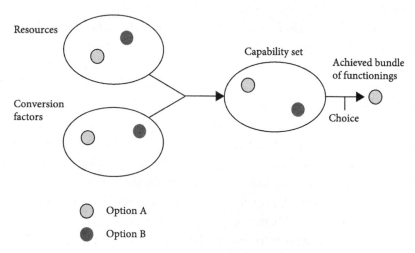

Figure 5.1 Resources, conversion factors and the capability set

illustrations. He envisages public participation as a means to arrive at a list of valuable functionings (Sen, 2005: 158). In the case of poverty measurement he maintains that it is often sufficient to look at some basic functionings – for example, the set of relevant functionings may be smaller in the case of poverty measurement than for measuring the standard of living (Sen, 1999: 103).

Nussbaum (for example, 2000: 78), in contrast, set up a list of 10 'Central Human Functional Capabilities' and holds that they are all relevant. She argues for a threshold that determines what is necessary for leading a life worthy of a human being. But she does not indicate how to operationalize her list, albeit pointing out that the capabilities have to be specified for the context at hand (Nussbaum, 2000: 105). In addition, Nussbaum falls short of elaborating thresholds or procedures for determining thresholds.

Many empirical studies based on the CA have been carried out despite the difficulties involved in operationalizing the approach (see Leßmann, 2013 for an overview).[4] Alkire (2007) summarizes the methods which have been used for selecting relevant functionings and Robeyns (2003) proposes procedural criteria for selecting functionings. There is also a growing number of studies related to children and child poverty based on the CA (for example, Biggeri *et al.*, 2011; Leßmann *et al.*, 2011; Chapter 1 of this book), but they are not systematically answering the three questions posed above. Hence, the next section looks at the theoretical and empirical treatment of children and childhood in the CA.

The CA and children

In general the CA is an approach to the evaluation of human well-being. Insofar as children are human beings the CA includes children in its considerations, but neither Sen nor Nussbaum, the two leading authors of the CA, specifically relate to children at any length. Rather, they sometimes use examples. Thus, the first part of this section presents the collected passages on children and childhood in their writings. The second part sketches how others have applied the CA to children and childhood. There is still a huge gap in the literature and the last part outlines a research agenda for filling that gap.

Sen and Nussbaum on children and childhood

In an exchange about the conception of freedom Cohen (1993) mentions the example of a baby who achieves the functionings of being well-nourished and warm without doing these things itself. It is the baby's parents who care for it, clothe and feed it. Sen (1993: 43) takes up this example to argue that it is nevertheless freedom that the baby enjoys. Here Sen maintains that children enjoy freedom, implicitly stating clearly that their well-being matters and that it should be evaluated in terms of freedom, just as adults' well-being. Liberal approaches (Rawls, 1971; Nozick, 1974) do not usually grant children the same evaluative status as adults, since they relate only to mature and rational persons. They rather hold that children have some rights as 'persons to be' (see Macleod, 2010). Children's rights are derived from the fact that they become rational agents later on.

Sen, however, also looks at children as 'adults to be' as this quote in an interview with Saito (2003: 25) shows:

> If the child does not want to be inoculated, and you nevertheless think it is a good idea for him/her to be inoculated, then the argument may be connected with the freedom that this person will have in the future by having the measles shot now. The child when it grows up must have more freedom. So when you are considering a child, you have to consider not only the child's freedom now, but also the child's freedom in the future.

In a similar vein he argues in *Children and Human Rights* (Sen, 2006: 10) that the idea of freedom is not 'entirely parasitic on the person taking control of the actual exercise of his or her freedom'. Sen refers to control and procedural rights as the process aspect of freedom and distinguishes the opportunity aspect from it which refers to having a choice among several options. He claims that this difference is important with regard to children and argues:

> Insofar as the process aspect of freedom demands that a person should be making his or her own choice, that aspect of freedom is not particularly relevant to the human rights of children, except in some rather minimal ways (such as a child's freedom – and perhaps right – to get attention when it decides to scream the house down). But the opportunity aspect of freedom is immensely important for children. What opportunities children have today and will have tomorrow, in line with what they can be reasonably expected to want, is a matter of public policy and social programmes, involving a great many agencies.
>
> Sen, 2006: 10

Thus, it seems that though Sen does not deny children freedom completely, he maintains that in the case of children the question is not whether children can take decisions (Sen, 2006: 9). Instead he emphasizes the opportunities they will have as adults over their right to choose themselves and hence over their opportunities in childhood. Thus, he does not finally answer the question of whether we owe freedom to children or not. This position raises the question of how children who are not allowed to choose themselves grow into adults able to make choices and take decisions (Leßmann, 2009).

More than Sen, Nussbaum (2000: 89–90) points out the importance of preparing children for their later role and of urging or even forcing them to exercise certain functionings in childhood: 'if we aim to produce adults who have all the capabilities on the list, this will frequently mean requiring certain types of functioning in children since exercising a function in childhood is frequently necessary to produce a mature adult capability'. This argument leaves open whether children should be granted freedom at all, but at the same time it hints at the necessity of educating children in order to enable them to be mature adults later on. When Nussbaum elaborates her view on education for democratic citizenship, she embraces the relevance of freedom for children: 'education must begin with the mind of the child, and it must have the goal of increasing that mind's freedom in its social environment rather than killing it off' (Nussbaum, 2006: 393). But it is unclear how this relates to freedom in the sense of capabilities.

In this essay she argues for the importance of three capacities that have to be built into people for democratic citizenship: (1) critical self-examination, (2) the ability to see themselves as citizens of the world, and (3) narrative imagination. She describes these capacities in more length:[5]

> ... living what, following Socrates, we may call 'the examined life' ... means a life that accepts no belief as authoritative simply because it has been handed down by tradition or become familiar through habit, a life that questions all beliefs, statements and arguments, and accepts only those that survive reason's demand for consistency and for justification.

> Citizens who cultivate their capacity for effective democratic citizenship need, further, an ability to see themselves as not simply citizens of some local region or group, but also, and above all, as human beings bound to all other human beings by ties of recognition and concern.

> [Narrative imagination] means the ability to think what it might be like to be in the shoes of a person different from oneself, to be an intelligent reader of that person's story, and to understand the emotions and wishes and desires that someone so placed might have.

> Nussbaum, 2006: 388, 389, 390–91

Though Nussbaum refers in this context to freeing the child's mind and mentions 'capabilities' in the title she does not relate the capacities for democratic citizenship to the concept of freedom embraced by the CA. In my view, these capacities mainly describe desirable propositions of mature adults, a goal to be aimed at, but do not constitute the basis for the right to exercise one's freedom.

To conclude, in both Sen's and Nussbaum's work the special case of children is lacking. They do not deny the right to well-being to children, but concerning the right to freedom otherwise closely intertwined with human well-being in the CA they are less assuring and tend to reserve the benefits of freedom to children's later lives as adults. It seems that Sen and Nussbaum imagine small children, too small to decide for themselves or to exercise their freedom, when writing on childhood (Graf, 2012). Apart from that they give some hints about the goal of a mature adult life without, however, sketching the transition from childhood to adulthood.

Other authors on capabilities of children

Despite these omissions in Sen and Nussbaum, children have been asked about their goals and values in empirical studies (Biggeri *et al.*, 2006; Young, 2006; Babic *et al.*, 2011). The authors do not simply assume children to have some powers to deliberate about their goals and values, but justify their approach by hinting at the basic ideas of the CA as well as at the literature in educational science on participation of children (Babic *et al.*, 2011).

Whenever the CA is applied to children, and there is a growing number of empirical studies on child well-being based on the CA, its application has to be justified and its suitability for the case of children carefully assessed. For example, Volkert and Wüst (2011) muse about the meaning of 'agency' in the case of small children; Di Tommaso (2007) argues that the set of dimensions relevant for children differs from that for adults and emphasizes the importance of play in their case (taken from Nussbaum's list of Central Human Functional Capabilities, see as well Addabbo and Di Tommaso, 2011). Studies that refer to the CA mainly as a basis for multidimensional direct measurement of child well-being (for example, Phipps, 2002; Apablaza and Yelonetzky, 2011; Alkire and Roche, 2012) focus on the question of which dimensions to select, too. They derive the demand for data on deprivations and combinations of deprivations at the individual level as an important characteristic of the CA and point out that data availability often constrains the selection of dimensions. They also hint at the impact of deprivation in childhood on a person's well-being in the long run as one argument why it is important to investigate child poverty.

More theoretical research points to the shortcomings of the CA with regard to children and childhood (Walker and Unterhalter, 2007; Brighouse and Unterhalter, 2010; Macleod, 2010; Graf, 2012). Despite the growing literature on education as well as children and the CA, the statement of Unterhalter (2001) that the CA is undertheorized when it comes to these issues is still valid.

A research agenda

From this short summary of the writings on the CA and children, a research agenda emerges that contains several elements or steps towards a comprehensive view of the subject. First, the question of the *concept of personhood* in the CA has to be answered. This question has been raised by Nussbaum (1988) and triggered the dispute on listing functionings (or capabilities) between her and Sen. But the discussion was going astray in focusing on the question of a list instead of that of personhood. Nussbaum (2006) herself has set out her idea of citizenship without really linking the term 'democratic citizenship' to the CA. Several papers (Giri, 2000; Giavonola, 2005; Qizilbash, 2006; Davis, 2007; Teschl and Derobert, 2008; Leßmann, 2011) tried to refocus the debate towards what it essentially means to be a person or human being according to the CA, but the dispute is not settled yet. Without having a clear idea of the essence of maturity it is, however, difficult to develop a proper idea of how to educate children towards this goal.

The question of when childhood ends and adulthood starts seems to be innocuous or even trivial, but it is crucial to define, secondly, the *limits of childhood and adulthood* for getting a clear grip on the issue (Lansdown, 2005). The usual approach is to use the age as a proxy. For example, the *United Nations Convention of the Rights of the Child* (UNCRC) defines children to be below the age of 18 years. One may also refer to conditions of maturity such as economic independence. If more than one condition has to be met, a person can be described as a child in some respects and as mature in others. For the CA the ability to take decisions and to choose a life one values (and has reason to value) seems crucial for drawing a line between childhood and adulthood, but we may well find that people are able to deliberate and choose with respect to some aspects but not to all at a time.

This brings us to the third item on the agenda: *selecting functionings for child well-being*. First, the question of whether the list of functionings relevant to children is the same as that for adults in principle has to be answered. Nussbaum

(2000: 82–83), for example, generally argues that all items on her list of capabilities are relevant for being human and leading a life in dignity, but she allows for specifying the dimensions differently in different contexts. In contrast, Sen (2005: 157–160) does not embrace the idea of a complete list of dimensions and urges us to select functionings in relation to the task at hand. Hence, secondly, dimensions of child well-being have to be specified or selected (see Robeyns, 2003 and Alkire, 2007 on possible criteria for selection). In the case of children, educational and psychological theory should have some important insights to contribute and provide further criteria.

The fourth item on the list is *freedom in childhood*. Though Sen and Nussbaum seem to reserve fully-fledged freedom to mature adults, they both speak of freedom in relation to children. Thus, the question is what role freedom plays in childhood. Nussbaum (2000) seems inclined to demand a minimum of functioning achievements for children without specifying the idea further. Brighouse (2003) argues that in the case of agency the responsibility always lies with the adults whereas children have full well-being rights (cf. Lansdown, 2005).

Hence, the question of freedom in childhood entails two further questions: first, the *relation between parental and child freedom* and, secondly, the *development of freedom in the course of time*. The former is important for determining the extent of a child's freedom since it is restricted but also enhanced by parental (and governmental) freedom. This is why Apablaza and Yalonetzky (2011) include household-specific characteristics in addition to individual characteristics in their study of child poverty. Volkert and Wüst (2011) model how children's capabilities depend on the resources and conversion factors of their parents. Miller (2009) hints at the dependence of children with respect to socialization in a broader sense. The interdependence of capability sets is obvious in the case of children and parents. In fact, the issue of conflicting capability sets has not received much attention so far (only the related discussion of collective capabilities, see Stewart and Deneulin, 2002 and the response of Sen, 2002). In the case of children there are often three parties involved: the child, the parents and the state.

Finally, the issue how the capability set develops in the course of time is undertheorized in the CA despite some efforts to change this (Grasso, 2002; Comim, 2004, 2008; Teschl and Comin, 2005; Leßmann, 2009; Clark and Hulme, 2005; Bartelheimer *et al.*, 2011). This issue has general relevance with regard to the question of what the agent herself can do to enhance her capability and how this relates to the opportunities provided by her social environment. In the case of children, the specific relevance of how capabilities 'evolve' has been acknowledged by Biggeri *et al.* (2011), but has not been tackled in detail.

Concluding remarks

Measuring child poverty by the number of children living in income-poor households seems inadequate for several reasons. All in all, income data does not tell us much about the well-being of children. This could be done by using a direct approach of poverty measurement which amounts to defining a 'good life' for children and controlling whether the children actually enjoy the features of this concept. The CA lends itself as a conceptual basis for the direct approach. However, the operationalization of the CA as a direct approach to poverty measurement is challenging in any case and particularly challenging in the case of children, since the CA is almost silent on the special situation of children. Hence, the long research agenda in the last subsection highlights the main conclusion. There is a lot of work ahead of us.

Acknowledgements

Many thanks to Daniel Neff, Tanja Munk, Bernhard Babic, Gunter Graf, Anca Gheus, an anonymous referee and the audiences at the Philosophical Seminar of the RWTH Aachen, ifz in Salzburg and the Discussion Group on the CA in Hamburg for their comments and encouragement. I wrote this paper during a stay in Salzburg and would like to thank the ifz as well as the American-Austrian Foundation in Salzburg for their hospitality.

Notes

1 Or even worse, they view children as consumption goods of their parents (Bojer and Nelson, 1999).

2 The median income is the income of the person in the middle if the persons are ordered by increasing income. The median is not apt to adjustments due to changes in the income of rich people. Thus, it is more stable than the average income. The EU developed a set of indicators at a meeting in Laeken, see Atkinson (2003) on these Laeken-indicators.

3 Sen does not use his terminology consistently and refers to those functionings which are essential in life and should be feasible for all people as 'basic capabilities' (1980, 1999). In order to avoid confusion, I prefer to stick to 'functionings' also in this context.

4   See also Hart, Chapter 1 in this volume.
5   In her book *Cultivating Humanity* Nussbaum (1997) has outlined these cornerstones of 'liberal education' for the case of higher education in the US.

References

Addabbo, T. & di Tommaso, M.L. (2011) 'Children's Capabilities and Family Characteristics in Italy: Measuring Imagination and Play', in Biggeri, M., Ballet, J. & Comim, F. (eds.) *Children and the Capability Approach*. Palgrave MacMillan, Basingstoke, 222–243.

Agarwal, B. (1994) *A Field of One's Own: Gender and Land Rights in South Asia*, Press Syndicate of the University of Cambridge, Cambridge.

Alkire, S. (2007) 'Choosing Dimensions: The Capability Approach and Multidimensional Poverty', in Grusky, D. & Kanbur, R. (eds) *Poverty and Inequality*, Stanford University Press, Stanford, CA.

Alkire, S. & Roche, J.M. (2012) 'Beyond Headcount. The Alkire-Foster Approach to Multidimensional Child Poverty Measurement', in Ortiz, I., Moreira Daniels, L. & Engilbertsdóttir, S. (eds) *Child Poverty and Inequality: New Perspectives*, UNICEF Division of Policy and Practice, New York, 18–22.

Apablaza, M. & Yalonetzky, G. (2011) 'Measuring the Dynamics of Multiple Deprivations Among Children: The Cases of Andhra Pradesh, Ethiopia, Peru and Vietnam', OPHI – research in progress rp 26a.

Atkinson, A.B. (2003) 'Developing Comparable Indicators for Monitoring Social Inclusion in the European Union', in: Hauser, R. & Becker, I. (eds) *Reporting on Income Distribution and Poverty*, 175–191, Springer, Berlin.

Babic, B., Germes Castro, O. & Graf, G. (2011) 'Approaching Capabilities with Children in Care – An International Project to Identify Values of Children and Young People in Care', in Leßmann, O., Otto, H.-U. & Ziegler, H. (eds) *Closing the Capabilities Gap – Renegotiating Social Justice for the Young*, Barbara Budrich, Leverkusen, 267–276.

Bartelheimer, P., Büttner, R. & Schmidt, T. (2011) 'Dynamic Capabilities – A Capability Approach to Life Courses and the Case of Young Adults', in Leßmann, O., Otto, H.-U. & Ziegler, H. (eds) *Closing the Capabilities Gap – Renegotiating Social Justice for the Young*, Barbara Budrich, Leverkusen, 147–164.

Biggeri, M. Libanora, R., Mariani, S. & Menchini, L. (2006) 'Children Conceptualizing Capabilities: Results of a Survey Conducted During the First Children's World Congress on Child Labour', *Journal of Human Development*, 7(1), 59–84.

Biggeri, M., Ballet, J. & Comim, F. (eds) (2011) *Children and the Capability Approach*, Palgrave Macmillan, Basingstoke.

Bojer, H. & Nelson, J. (1999) 'Equivalence Scales and the Welfare of Children: A Comment on "Is there a Bias in the Economic Literature on Equivalence Scales?"', *Review of Income and Wealth*, 45(4), 531–534.

Brighouse, H. (2003) 'How Should Children be Heard?', *Arizona Law Review*, 45(3), 691–711.

Brighouse, H. & Unterhalter, E. (2010) 'Education for Primary Goods or for Capabilities?', in Brighouse, H. & Robeyns, I. (eds) *Measuring Justice*, Cambridge University Press, Cambridge, 193–214.

Buhmann, B., Rainwater, L., Schmaus, G. & Smeeding, T. (1988) 'Equivalence Scales, Well-Being, Inequality and Poverty: Sensitivity Estimates Across Ten Countries Using the Luxembourg Income Study (LIS) Database', *Review of Income and Wealth*, 34, 115–142.

Clark, D. and Hulme, D. (2005) 'Towards a Unified Framework for Understanding the Depth, Breadth and Duration of Poverty', Global Poverty Research Group, GPRG-WPS-020.

Cohen, G.A. (1993) 'Equality of What? On Welfare, Goods and Capabilities', in Nussbaum, M. & Sen, A.K. (eds) *The Quality of Life*, Clarendon Press, Cambridge, 9–29.

Comim, F. (2004) 'Time and Adaptation in the Capability Approach', proceedings of the Capability Conference, Pavia 2003.

Comim, F. (2008) 'Measuring Capabilities', in: Comim, F., Qizilbash, M. & Alkire, S. (eds) *The Capability Approach: Concepts, Measures and Application*, Cambridge University Press, Cambridge, 157–200.

Davis, J.B. (2007) 'Identity and Commitment', in: Peter, F. & Schmid, H.B. (eds) *Rationality and Commitment*, Oxford University Press, Oxford, 313–336.

De Vos, K. & Zaidi, M.A. (1997) 'Equivalence scale sensitivity of poverty statistics for the member states of the European Community', *Review of Income and Wealth*, 43(3), 319–33.

Di Tommaso, M.L. (2007) 'Children's Capabilities: A Structural Equation Model for India', *Journal of Socio Economics*, 36, 436–450.

Dworkin, R. (1981a) 'What is Equality? Part 1: Equality of Welfare', *Philosophy and Public Affairs*, 10, 185–245.

Dworkin, R. (1981b) 'What is Equality? Part 2: Equality of Resources', *Philosophy and Public Affairs*, 10, 283–345.

Giavonola, B. (2005) 'Personhood and Human Richness: Good and Well-Being in the Capability Approach and Beyond', *Review of Social Economy*, 63(2), 249–267.

Gibbard, A. (1979) 'Disparate Goods and Rawls' Difference Principle: A Social Choice Theoretic Approach', *Theory and Decision*, 11, 267–288.

Giri, A.K. (2000) 'Rethinking Human Development: A Dialogue with Amartya Sen', *Journal of International Development*, 12, 1003–1018.

Graf, G. (2012) 'Realizing the Life chances of Children – An Application of the Capability Appoach', in: Hawa, B. & Weidtmann, N. (eds) *The Capability Approach on Social Order*, LIT-Verlag, Münster.

Grasso, M. (2002) 'A Dynamic Operationalization of Sen's Capability Approach', working paper 59, Dipartimento di Sociologia e Ricerca Sociale, Università degli Studi di Milano Bicocca.

Haddad, L.J. & Kanbur, R. (1990) 'Is there an intra-household Kuznets curve? Some evidence from the Philippines', *Public Finance*, 47(suppl.), 77–93.

Hart, C.S. (2014) 'The Capability Approach and Educational Research'; in: Hart, C.S., Biggeri, M. and Babic, B. (eds.): *Agency and Participation in Childhood and Youth*, Chapter 1.

Koulovatianos, C., Schmidt, U. & Schröder, C. (2005) 'On the Income Dependence of Equivalence Scales', *Journal of Public Economics*, 89, 967–996.

Lansdown, G. (2005) *The Evolving Capacities of the Child*, Innocenti Insight, UNICEF Innocent Research Centre, Florence.

Leßmann, O. (2009) 'Capability and Learning to Choose', *Studies in Philosophy and Education*, 28, 449–460.

Leßmann, O. (2011) 'Adaptive Preferences, Identity and Reflection', paper presented at the annual conference of the Human Development and Capability Association in The Hague.

Leßmann, O. (2013) 'Empirische Studien zum Capability-Ansatz auf der Grundlage von Befragungen – ein Überblick', in Graf, G., Kapferer, E. and Sedmak, C. (eds) *Der Fähigkeitenansatz und seine praktische Anwendbarkeit in der Arbeit mit Kindern und Jugendlichen*, VS-Verlag, Wiesbaden.

Leßmann, O., Otto, H.-U. & Ziegler, H. (eds) (2011) *Closing the Capabilities Gap – Renegotiating Social Justice for the Young*, Barbara Budrich, Leverkusen.

Macleod, C. M. (2010) 'Primary Goods, Capabilities, and Children', in: Brighouse, H. & Robeyns, I. (eds) *Measuring Justice*, Cambridge University Press; Cambridge, 174–192.

Miller, D. (2009) 'Equality of Opportunity and the Family', in Satz, D. & Reich, R. (eds) *Towards a Humanist Justice: The Political Philosophy of Susan Moller Okin*, Oxford University Press, New York, 93–112.

Nozick, R. (1974) *Anarchy, State and Utopia*, Basic Books, New York.

Nussbaum, M.C. (1988) 'Nature, Function, and Capability: Aristotle on Political Distribution', *Oxford Studies in Ancient Philosophy* (supplementary volume), 145–184.

Nussbaum, M.C. (1997) *Cultivating Humanity: A Classic Defense of Reform in Liberal Education*, Harvard University Press, Cambridge, MA.

Nussbaum, M.C. (2000) *Woman and Human Development: The Capabilities Approach*, Cambridge University Press, Cambridge.

Nussbaum, M.C. (2006) 'Education and Democratic Citizenship: Capabilities and Quality Education', *Journal of Human Development*, 7(3), 385–396.

OECD (2008) *Growing Unequal? Income Distribution and Poverty in OECD Countries*, OECD, Paris.

Phipps, S. (2002) 'The Well-being of Young Canadian Children in International Perspective: A Functionings Approach', *Review of Income and Wealth*, 48(4), 493–515.

Pollak, R.A. & Wales, T.J. (1979) 'Welfare Comparisons and Equivalence Scales', *American Economic Review*, 69(2), 216–221.

Qizilbash, M. (2006) 'Well-Being, Adaptation and Human Limitations', *Philosophy*, 59 (supplement), 83–109.

Rawls, J. (1971) *A Theory of Justice*, Harvard University Press, Cambridge, MA.

Robeyns, I. (2003) 'Sen's Capability Approach and Gender Inequality: Selecting Relevant Capabilities', *Feminist Economics*, 9(2–3), 61–92.

Robeyns, I. (2005) 'The Capability Approach: A Theoretical Survey', *Journal of Human Development*, 6(1), 93–114.

Roelen, K. & Gassman, F. (2008) 'Measuring Child Poverty and Well-being: a Literature Review', Maastricht Graduate School of Governance, working paper MGSoG/2008/WP001.

Saito, M. (2003) 'Amartya Sen's Capability Approach to Education: A Critical Exploration', *Journal of Philosophy of Education*, 1, 17–33.

Savaglio, E. (2002) *Multidimensional Inequality: A Survey*, Quaderni del Dipartimento di Economica Politica, 362, Università degli Studi di Siena, Siena.

Sen, A.K. (1979) 'Issues in the Measurement of Poverty', *Scandinavian Journal of Economics*, 81, 285–307.

Sen, A.K. (1980) 'Equality of What?', in Sen, A.K. (ed.) (1982) *Choice, Welfare and Measurement*, Blackwell, Oxford, 353–369.

Sen, A.K. (1985) *Commodities and Capabilities*, North-Holland, Amsterdam

Sen, A.K. (1993) 'Capability and Well-being', in Sen, A.K. & Nussbaum, M. (eds) *The Quality of Life*, Clarendon Press, Oxford, 30–53.

Sen, A.K. (1999) *Development as Freedom*, Alfred A. Knopf Inc., New York.

Sen, A.K. (2002) 'Response to Commentaries', *Studies in Comparative International Development*, 37(2), 78–86.

Sen, A.K. (2005) 'Human Rights and Capabilities', *Journal of Human Development*, 6(2), 151–166.

Sen, A.K. (2006) *Children and Human Rights*, Institute for Human Development, New Delhi.

Stewart, F. & Deneulin, S. (2002) 'Amartya Sen's Contribution to Development Thinking', *Studies in Comparative International Development*, 37(2), 61–70.

Teschl, M. & Comim, F. (2005) 'Adaptive preferences and capabilities: some preliminary conceptual explorations', *Review of Social Economy*, 62(2), 230–47.

Teschl, M. & Derobert, L. (2008) 'Does Identity Matter? On the Relevance of Identity and Interaction for Capabilities', in Comim, F., Qizilbash, M. & Alkire, S. (eds) *The Capability Approach: Concepts, Measures and Application*, Cambridge University Press, Cambridge, 125–156.

UNICEF (2012) *Measuring Child Poverty*, UNICEF Innocent Research Center report card no. 10, Florence.

Unterhalter, E. (2001) 'The Capability Approach and Gendered Education: An Examination of South African Contradictions', Paper presented at the Conference on Justice and Poverty (2nd Capability Conference), Cambridge.

Unterhalter, E. & Walker, M. (eds) (2007) *Amartya Sen's Capability Approach and Social Justice in Education*, Palgrave Macmillan, New York.

Volkert, J. & Wüst, K. (2011) 'Early Childhood, Agency and Capability Deprivation: A Quantitative Analysis using German Socio-economic Panel Data', in: Leßmann, O., Otto, H.-U. & Ziegler, H. (eds) *Closing the Capabilities Gap – Renegotiating Social Justice for the Young*, Barbara Budrich, Leverkusen, 179–198.

De Vos, K. & Zaidi, M. A. (1997) 'Equivalence Scale Sensitivity of Poverty Statistics for the Member States of the European Community'; *Review of Income and Wealth* 43 (3), 319–333.

Walker, M. & Unterhalter, E. (2007) 'The Capability approach: Its Potential for Work in Education'; in: Walker, M. and Unterhalter, E. (eds.): *Amartya Sen's Capability approach and Social Justice in Education*; Palgrave Macmillan; NewYork, 1–18.

Young, M. (2006) 'Defining Valued Learning and Capability', download HDCA-website.

Part 2

Developing Agency and Capabilities in Schools and Beyond

Pedagogies to Develop Children's Agency in Schools

Marina Santi and Diego Di Masi

Introduction: The agency-based paradigm

The 1970s saw a rise in the importance of 'agency', one of the key theoretical contributions to childhood studies (James, 2009). The notion of 'agency' emphasizes a child's role as a social agent and introduces a radical change of perspective whereby children are seen as people who, through their actions, both individual and collective, influence their relationships and decision-making processes (Mayall, 2002; Biggeri *et al.*, 2006).

The agency-based paradigm spread primarily due to scientific research and studies on intelligence and learning that built the conditions for a new approach to childhood. The work of Vygotsky (1962) and his colleagues at the Russian sociocultural school of psychology (Kozulin, 1998), as well as the activity theory paradigm (Engeström *et al.*, 1999) and situated cognition theory (Resnick *et al.*, 1991), paved the way for researchers to understand the role a child plays in human development. Indeed, both approaches highlight the human ability (or capability) to construct knowledge and how such ability (or capability) is strictly connected with the real social context where the human being lives, in such a way as intelligence and learning are not a product but a process where the human being, and even the child, becomes a social actor, or rather an *agent*, of their own development. The difference between an 'actor' and an 'agent', and the ensuing theoretical shift, is important because the actor (see Mayall's definition) is an individual who does something, while the agent is an individual who does something with other people; this *doing* makes things happen, thus contributing to wider social and cultural reproduction and transformation processes (James *et al.*, 1998; Mayall, 2002; James, 2009, 2010).

These processes are neither linear nor an exact copy of the internalized model. In each one, a child is faced with a multitude of misunderstandings, ambiguities and difficulties that must be solved and interpreted, and it is within this process that children carry out their own agency (James, 2009), transforming reality creatively. Children should be seen as active constructors of their own reality, one that contributes to the processes of social and cultural reproduction. Here, 'reproduction' does not mean a passive process of internalizing social and cultural habits, but a dual process in which a child actively promotes cultural production and change (Corsaro, 2005) and acquires the knowledge and skills conveyed by his or her own culture.

Childhood sociological perspectives on children's actions played a fundamental role in shaping this concept of agency applied in the study presented here. It focuses on how children's actions can change the structures that continuously shape our everyday experiences (e.g. school, work and institutions). Childhood sociology sees children as a social category rather than as an individual one, and highlights how every concept of childhood is socioculturally dependent and politically determined (Qvortrup, 2005). However, the new perspectives of political philosophy and economics on human development within the capability approach (CA) are also fundamental in defining the meaning of individual child agency in this study (Ballet *et al.*, 2011), and these perspectives are emphasized by Amartya Sen's interpretation of agency based on reason and finalized to action; 'I am using the term *agent* . . . in its older sense as someone who acts and brings about change, and whose achievements can be judged in terms of her own values and objectives, whether or not we assess them in terms of some external criteria as well' (Sen, 1999a: 18–19).

In our pedagogical framework, the capability approach (CA) emphasizes agency's transformative role in a bid to enhance the potential of children, young people and adults to promote change and to rethink the power relations in which we are involved as individuals. In emancipation discourse terms, giving a person the chance to change the world, both as an individual and as a member of a community, is a significant break from the idea that only those with institutional, leadership or even authoritarian power have the prerogative to decide.

The concept of agency in deliberative democracy: The capability approach perspective

According to Crocker (2008) a person is an 'agent' only when he/she carries out an action by i) deciding to act autonomously, ii) basing his/her decisions on rational grounds, iii) playing an active role in them and producing a change and making a difference in the world. We are agents when we are not forced to carry out an action by forces outside our own will and act without any external restriction; when we decide to act on aims and interests, being motivated by reasons for acting; when we actively participate, directly or indirectly, in individual or collective actions; and when we achieve our objectives intentionally and our actions produce an effect or a change. Extending agency to children is not an automatism, nor is it problem-free. In fact, children's ability to judge autonomously and rationally, take decisions and act without external restrictions is made possible only under specific constraints and a revised notion of development. Nevertheless, the idea of children as active agents is well established in literature, and defining their scope for autonomous choice and deliberation still remains a crucial point, one also discussed within the CA (Ballet *et al.*, 2011). However, a degree of child agency is a fundamental premise for defending a child's right to make a difference and to free self-determination. We should also evaluate whether attributing agency to children is consistent with the idea of agency when it is viewed as an ability 'expressed through political participation in democratic decision-making' (Deneulin and Shahani, 2009: 186) by an individual as a member of a community and as a participant in economic, social and political action (Sen, 1999a). This direction is taken by the studies and experiences in a range of countries where the CA is applied to child development policies (Biggeri *et al.*, 2011). Its strength is its adoption of bottom-up methodologies that identify a tentative list of relevant capabilities for children in order to legitimize the view that children are not simply recipients of freedom, but also participants in delineating the capabilities which give meaning to their daily agency; thus they self-contribute to their own development and to child development policies (Biggeri, 2007).

When the CA is taken in these terms, political participation in democratic settings and procedures becomes a key domain of human development in that it is a tangible example of the mechanisms through which people exercise their own agency in the public sphere. Drèze and Sen (2002) put forward a form of democratic governance based not only on the smooth working order of representative democracy, but also on the participation mechanisms that enable citizens to make themselves heard even outside the electoral process; these mechanisms also include people who live on the margins of society and have no contact with those who are supposed to represent them. This concept of democracy sees children transformed into 'marginal individuals' in the deliberative process as they are excluded from participating in their society. Thus, it is crucial to promote children's active participation in society (Comim *et al.*, 2011) and to redefine both democracy and citizenship, making them 'child size'[1] so that children may be considered capable agents.

According to Sen, participation in public discussion and in the institutions that make this participation possible is not an optional aspect of democracy, but a requisite. He affirms that 'democracy is a demanding system, and not just a mechanical condition (like majority rule) taken in isolation' (Sen, 1999c: 9–10), in which people can learn from each other and define their own social and political agenda. Following Sen's normative idea of democracy, Crocker (2008) suggests a scalar account of democracy by analysing four domains: breadth, depth, variety and control. 'Breadth' refers to the degree that all citizens, as well as those belonging to the most disadvantaged and marginalized groups, are included. 'Depth' is the capacity to create participatory paths that enable citizens to express themselves and to contribute their reasons to decision-making processes. 'Variety' refers to issues on which citizens may decide and what democratic institutions are involved. Finally 'control' is the degree of influence that citizens have over decisions. According to Drèze and Sen, the main domain of democratic participation in public life is the one that deals most directly with inclusion as a condition of political agency; all four domains, however, contain an inclusive component when dealing with democratic deliberative procedures (Young, 2000). The ways and extent to which children would be included in the different domains of public life as active agents are governed by their being recognized as active thinkers and being able to judge and choose values for themselves within a dialogue-based participative process (Biggeri and Libanora, 2011).

In line with the perspective outlined by Sen, Crocker (2008: 310) defines the two main aims of deliberative democracy. The first is 'to identify and solve concrete problems or to devise general policies for solving specific problems. Second, deliberation's goal is to provide a fair way in which free and equal members of a group can overcome their differences and reach agreement about action and policy'. We will draw upon Crocker's definition of these aims to look more carefully at four words whose meanings are highly relevant in education terms: problem, fair, group and action.

At the centre of deliberation lies the 'problem': the practical problem. In a deliberative democracy, citizens start a discussion about practical problems in order to find solutions. This type of discussion emphasizes the public use of reason and offers the members of a community the opportunity to share their opinions. According to Crocker, deliberative democracy offers a method for finding solutions to practical issues and also enables fair decisions to be taken.

Here 'fair' means an opinion of value not regarding the content of the decisions, but rather the procedure that envisages the involvement of all the decision-makers; this involvement enables all of the people who are entitled to express their opinion to be heard, as they are directly involved in the decision-making process. Again, the inclusive dimension of fair deliberation emerges as a fundamental component of the democratic process, and it is manifested in terms of opportunity for all people to be involved, both as entitled persons and as accountable points of view.

As deliberative democracy focuses on a 'group', namely the community, it offers an alternative model to the logic of aggregation of demand that is the hallmark of representative democracies, in which it is interest groups, rather than autonomy, freedom and individual well-being, that dictate the public agenda. Furthermore, the involvement of the community in decision-making processes enables it to exercise control in order to prevent the authoritarian and high-handed policies that may even tempt democratic regimes, especially in times of crisis.

Finally we come to 'action'. The objective of deliberation is to produce change, to transform and resolve what is felt and judged to be problematic. The result is not therefore a simple agreement based on a summary of different ideas or preferences, but a rationally built consensus that motivates people to act. Nevertheless, we believe people's actions should not be considered the result of a 'consensus-oriented' democracy, but that they should be governed both by the assumption that one could be constructed and by the inquiry procedure adopted to explore whether the two could be shared by the community and internalized by each member during the argumentative activity. Thus, deliberative democracy provides the context and the opportunity to develop and exercise individual agency by accepting the challenges that another person and the context offer in terms of limits and potential.

Despite criticism (Cooke and Kothari, 2001) and the limits of the participatory approach, deliberative democracy remains, for now, the only model that ensures citizens can make a social choice through public deliberation (Crocker, 2008). This opportunity is provided by the participation method created during discussion, information-gathering, implementation and evaluation by a group directly involved in an activity; it is a method through which the participants directly involved in the action are called upon to make a decision, to make a choice (Alkire, 2002). The intrinsic value of participation is that it offers a range of opportunities: it develops individual and collective agency; it develops friendship, sociability and community spirit (Alkire, 2002a); it promotes the introduction of values and responsibilities in that, through discussion, it makes participants aware of the decision's effects and consequences, not only for them but also for others (Drydyk, 2004). Participation is also a value because it develops what the CA calls 'the well-being of people'.

Philosophy for children as an opportunity for practical reasoning

Teaching democracy means educating citizens because citizens are its agents. Democracy is not simply an ideal, but a praxis, a way of acting, and a way of thinking; its main aim is not only to offer solutions to problems, but to promote a participation process which, starting with a problem, is able to produce and evaluate alternatives by using a form of public deliberation based on democratic values such as justice, respect, equality and freedom. Kelsen (2000) believed that modern democracies, i.e. those in the liberal tradition, are characterized by their critical and relativist concept of the world; accepting this stance entails teaching citizens about democracy to develop their critical and reflective thought.

According to Nussbaum (2002, 2010), philosophy is the best way to cultivate the skills required for democratic thinking. Nussbaum's words belong to a long tradition, dating back to Ancient Greece, which dealt with the educational benefits of philosophy; pragmatism and Deweyan thought were landmark moments in this tradition as they were an attempt to overcome the concept of the metaphysical which, according to its detractors, had become 'an attempt to impose a parochial scheme of values upon the cosmos in order to justify or undermine a set of existing social institutions by a pretended deduction from the nature of Reality' (Hook, 1939).

According to Dewey, the hallmark of the empirical method is experience, which has a dual nature, both active and passive; when we create an experience 'we do something to the thing and then it does something to us in return' (Dewey, 1916: 107). Not all of our actions, however, are experiences; an experience becomes such when it produces a reflective process that sees thought involved in understanding the connections between an activity and its consequences. Thus the use of the empirical method links philosophy with daily life and enables us to enhance the role of philosophy by turning it into a tool for social emancipation.

Despite the best intentions, developing critical and reflective thought, warns Nussbaum (2002), does not happen by magic, but through our education institutions and their curricula. One proposal that heads in this direction was made by Matthew Lipman and is known as 'Philosophy for Children' (P4C).[2] According to Lipman (2003), the most disappointing aspect of our schools is their failure to form reasoning people and thus, given the Deweyan framework behind his work, people capable of democratic thought. Lipman's criticism may be read on two distinct, yet complementary levels: the first looks at education institutions, focusing on their key role in democratic society, and the education system in general; the second focuses on the individual and on the curricula that can be used in class in order to foster reasoning skills. This perspective affords us a clearer insight into the innovative workings of P4C as an education movement and curriculum.

The capability to think for themselves between dialogue and community

P4C complies with the aforementioned view of agency for two main reasons: the first is P4C's emphasis on philosophical dialogue as a method for reflective agency; the second is its 'community of inquiry' as a setting for the agency of thinking. These two key aspects of P4C should be considered together to highlight the power of philosophical-inquiry dialogue to construct 'communities of agents'.

Philosophy's strong relationship with dialogue is rooted in its history and based on the argumentative nature of reflective thinking, as it emerged in the ancient Socratic tradition. The rational nature of philosophical speculation requires that positions, claims and perspectives, developed to respond to logical, ontological, aesthetical, ethical and epistemological issues about the world, knowledge and humanity, are sustained by a sufficient amount of 'good reasons', in terms of acceptable grounds, warrants and backings (Toulmin, 1958). These grounds are offered and submitted to the judgement of a 'generalized other' (Mead, 1966) who is supposed to be reasonable, trustworthy and involved in a hypothetical dialogue with a 'universal auditory' (Perelman and Olbrecht-Tyteca, 1958). In this sense, we can conceive the process of philosophical reflection as a sort of internalized dialogue that is experienced previously within a 'community of inquiry' (Lipman, 2003), in which all the interlocutors think aloud to the others, and then listen and take into account the other interlocutors' ideas. It is assumed that they are always able to question claims, to agree or disagree with a position and also to propose different problem constraints or views. The dialogue behind philosophical reflection distinguishes philosophical argumentation, for instance, from religious or scientific argumentation, as philosophy's intrinsic nature ensures that directions of inquiry and possible solutions are always open-ended. Indeed, philosophical dialogue means that any new questions arising are also open-ended, that there are multiple possible compatible frameworks, and that the criteria adopted to evaluate the answers are un-dogmatic and un-empirical.

Philosophical questioning works in two directions: it externalizes the states and feelings within the person, transforming them into shared concepts; and it internalizes meanings developed outside in social practice, integrating them into our own conceptual universe.[3] Philosophical questioning is always both self- and socially directed. From a methodological perspective, questioning is the linguistic expression of a cognitive doubt, which opens dialogue between a plurality of positions, assuming 'possibility' as a fundamental condition of the inquiry process.

According to Lipman (1988, 2003) the pragmatic experience of authentic dialogue could be learned and achieved only within a 'community of inquiry' and should be nurtured by philosophical wondering at the world and questioning of it. The decision to use philosophy is based on all the aforementioned features and constraints, but it depends mainly on Lipman's faith in the educational component of philosophy, which he derived from the pragmatism of Dewey and others. Lipman summarizes the strong link between philosophy and education in one claim, 'no true philosophy could be not educative, and no true education could be not philosophical' (Lipman, 1988). This equation is guaranteed in his programme by the 'effective members' status offered to all children from the beginning of the philosophical activity in the community of inquiry. This status legitimizes open access to discussion and gives children a range of different opportunities to become authentic 'participants', ones that are highly aware of the value of the inquiry process in which they are involved.

The inclusive dimension of philosophical inquiry

Stating that philosophical dialogue is not a spontaneous activity does not mean that it is not based on spontaneous thinking and being. The basic human functions of wondering at the world, looking for meaning, and aspiring to happiness and well-being are the implicit constraints which initially link community members to philosophical inquiry as a spontaneous intellectual experience based on questioning the world and its cultural meanings. Philosophical problems and issues have a controversial and interpretive nature and are based on a radical doubt of certainty as a thinking procedure; consequently they increase the opportunities to produce, take into account, and 'include' different positions, approaches and perspectives during dialogue, as well as focus on atypical stances that are usually 'excluded' by common sense and traditional habits. Moreover, the heterogeneity of the classroom population involved in the argumentation process benefits the development of both philosophical activity and participant capabilities. Firstly, the amount of possible rebuttals and counterarguments increases in such a context and consequently so does the depth of the argumentation, which could result in the tacit 'backing' of any idea or position being discussed. Secondly, interaction among the participants during philosophical problem-creating and solving is an opportunity for a 'cognitive apprenticeship' (Rogoff, 1990) in reflective thinking and inquiring, in which the learning potential of each community member is stimulated during novice-expert exchanges. Apprenticeship is an educational relationship based on reciprocal scaffolding between people with different levels of expertise who alternate between the roles of teacher, tutor or learner during a shared and mediated activity. The intellectual apprenticeship fostered in the community of philosophical inquiry optimizes the sociocognitive potential of interaction to create the 'zones of proximal development' (Vygotsky, 1962) for the higher-order thinking skills required to philosophize. These skills include formal and informal reasoning, which may be considered the cognitive condition, in terms of capabilities and functionings, for achieving authentic social participation. Involvement in classroom activities and scaffolding by teachers, peers and facilitators foster the internalization of the attitudes, values and competences which are fundamental for successfully implementing the inclusive dimension of philosophical dialogue. Its focus on questioning, openness to alternatives, non-predetermination of correct answers, and appeal to the power of good reason against the reason of dominant power are continuously fostered and maintained in the community of philosophical inquiry; furthermore they are the 'inclusive' constraints of this educational context and the guarantees of better conditions for intrapersonal and interpersonal agency in the community. The main activity of the 'community of inquiry' is philosophical discussion, i.e. a pragmatic experience of dialogue in which subjective and intersubjective identities are 'co-constructed', thus establishing the rational and communicative basis for non-violent coexistence and for liberation from the oppression of the dominant thought.

In the P4C curriculum, the epistemological aim and the moral aspiration of philosophical activity are closely related, and this is what links this proposal with the CA's analysis of democracy. Lipman's emphasis on the ethical-political dimension of education, which he took directly from Dewey, is explicit throughout his work, and it leads him to highlight the importance of children's participation in communities of philosophical inquiry, as they are an opportunity to experience the democracy of thinking. The trust in democracy behind the P4C curriculum is directly linked with the theme of inclusion that Lipman also uses in his philosophical novels and as the guiding idea in his manuals. The attention and attraction towards the value and richness of diversity is also clear in Lipman's choice of his novels' characters, who are often 'strange', disabled, children or elderly, and cause the 'normal' people to think differently. Moreover, the topics and activities proposed within the discussion plans and exercises are 'inclusive' as they encompass the triple perspective of complex thinking, i.e. encouraging 'caring', sensitivity and empathy towards differences; supporting creative imagination and plasticity within a provocative situation; and promoting critical analysis of dogmatism and prejudices towards people and cultures.

Considered from this procedural aspect, philosophical dialogue is thus a possible answer to the recommendations of many documents within international communities that underline the importance of promoting 'inclusive practices' to sustain human development and the agency of people and communities. UNESCO's 2007 document *Philosophy: School of Freedom* heads in this direction and highlights these features of philosophical reflection by including experiences and theoretical foundations for inclusive practices from around the world. The document depicts philosophy as a tangible, cultural way to engage people in open thinking, fostering conceptual innovation and moral sensitivity. In these terms, philosophical practice could contribute to clarifying the meaning of 'inclusion' and to better defining the tangible, effective action which should be promoted through participation. The risk, however, is viewing the inclusion process as mere acceptance of the minority by the majority, or as the assimilation of single parts into a homogeneous whole, in which differences are lost or simplified. But an inclusive process complexifies the inner relationships between interacting systems based on the 'principle of hospitality' and on co-evolution, in which each party is reciprocally changed by the encounter. According to this view, an inclusive practice is a peaceful process, not because differences and disagreements are avoided or forced to be univocally resolved, but because co-existence among differences is achieved by sharing consensual procedures to regulate disagreement on a rational basis.

If so, the role of dialogue is fundamental in 'inclusive practice', as pointed out by a recent UN (2007) document entitled *Participatory Dialogue: Towards a*

Stable, Safe and Just Society for All (PD-SSJS). This procedure is recognized as crucial in a country's commitment to promoting social integration by fostering stable, safe, just and tolerant societies that respect diversity. An inclusive society, a society for all, is one in which every individual, each with rights and responsibilities, has an active role to play (p. 1). Participatory dialogue is not a 'panacea' but a meaningful process that bridges the democracy gap still affecting many individuals. It also addresses,

> some important elements, such as overcoming exclusion, promoting inclusive institutions and promoting participation ... The challenge is to ensure that the concept of social integration is central to all policies and to find practical means of achieving a society for all. Participatory dialogue is an important policy tool that offers a range of practical means ... Such dialogue is based on and advances inclusion, participation, and justice, and enables the active engagement of all citizens in shaping their common future.
>
> p. xiii[4]

The PD-SSJS document also states that, 'a dialogic approach values the art of communication and planning as constituting a process of "thinking together" among a diverse group of people' (p. 4) with the aim not only of including 'someone', but to create a context in which 'everyone includes every last one' (p. 12). The PD-SSJS document explains this process in terms 'of coming together to build mutual understanding and trust across differences and to create positive outcomes through conversation' (p. 3). It also states that:

> whereas in many settings the term 'dialogue' implies various forms of conversations, the etymology of 'dialogue' – from *dia* meaning 'through', and *logos* translating as 'meaning' – suggests a synergistic fit with the concept of social integration. Within the context of social integration, dialogue refers to interactions for the purpose of uncovering shared meaning and mutual accommodation and understanding.
>
> PD-SSJS p. 3, 2007

The value of P4C for the CA

Recognizing children's rights to be included in participatory dialogue within their communities is perhaps the common denominator between P4C and the child-size CA (Biggeri *et al.*, 2011), although this view of inclusion as participatory dialogue is hardly problem- or paradox-free. Indeed, those excluded from a community are assumed to have previous knowledge of the value behind being included and to share the skills and procedures needed to participate in open dialogue. These common interests, competences and dispositions are exactly what the dynamics of exclusion lack, but they are the main achievements of the inclusion process. This risk of exclusion is avoided, however, by P4C's focus on reciprocal and unlimited questioning in a common space for inquiring, where questioning is a free, spontaneous need that is socially regulated and scaffolded in a dialogical activity.

From a CA perspective, the P4C curriculum is a pragmatic opportunity to go beyond the 'paradox of participation' (Calder, 2011), avoiding what Sen defines as 'unfavorable inclusion' (Sen, 2000) in which the functioning and capabilities of an individual and his/her community are not equally recognized, supported and distributed. Philosophizing within a 'community of inquiry' offers multiple opportunities, good circumstances, and the means to enhance the 'functioning' of participation as it fosters the social, procedural and cognitive capabilities involved in that process and nurtures the awareness which guarantees the freedom to participate. In other words, the 'community of philosophical inquiry' promotes both the final aim of participatory dialogue and the conditions for it to happen. According to Lipman, the 'community of inquiry' is the context in which children and adults can work together on their ability, and capability, to dialogue, an interactive, decision-making tool which is crucial for improving humanism within a democratic society. However, as participatory dialogue implies abilities and competences that are neither natural nor spontaneous, it must be taught and encompassed within lifelong learning.

The frameworks of P4C and CA share the same political and moral assumptions and direction. The philosophical discussion promoted by P4C in the community of inquiry strengthens complex thinking skills, such as reasoning, reflection and judgement, assuming that they are what a better society needs to empower its people and guarantee justice-based human development. Thus, the community of philosophical inquiry may be an educational answer to the inclusive recommendations of international communities. The inclusive dimensions of philosophical dialogue correspond to the refusal of all *a-priori* exclusion of alternatives, interlocutors, changes and possibilities. The egalitarian and democratic core of a community of inquiry is not based on the mere logic of presence, i.e. on the simple right to be in a place with others; nor is it based on the logic of majority, in which a minority is defended by rules and laws. Democratic justice based on respect of the proportional weights of the different parts contradicts the real meaning of egalitarianism, in which an equal weight for each party/member is fostered and guaranteed, and in which everyone, including children, has the right to judge and decide what to be and to do within the community (Biggeri *et al.*, 2011).

The link between P4C and Sen's perspective on human development seems justifiable and a source of interesting educational ideas. In her recent book, *Not for Profit*, Martha Nussbaum (2010) recommends P4C as an example of 'Socratic pedagogy' which, she argues, is a vital component of education in democratic societies. Although Lipman's 'community of inquiry' methodology is influenced by the Socratic dialogical approach to philosophical activity and by the ethical/ political dimension of Socrates' philosophizing, it is not merely reduced to a Socratic lesson. Lipman believes that it is the pragmatic nature of philosophical reflection, rather than the search for truth, that nurtures inquiry. Nevertheless, both Nussbaum and Lipman call for focus on the 'world-wide crisis in education' caused by its focus on national economic growth. This crisis involves the de-emphasis on and even elimination of teaching humanities and the arts. Nussbaum's own philosophy gives education three aims: prepare people for democratic citizenship, for employment and, most importantly, for meaningful lives. As her title indicates, the book focuses on the first of these aims, and its argument may be summed up in two statements: democracy requires three broad kinds of abilities: 'the ability to think critically; the ability to transcend local loyalties and to approach world problems as a "citizen of the world"; and … the ability to imagine sympathetically the predicaments of another person' (p. 7). With this in mind, P4C may be an answer which emphasizes the importance and need to cultivate the critical, creative, caring components of 'complex thinking' (Lipman, 2003). Socratic pedagogy combines a focus on 'the child's ability to understand the logical structure of an argument, to detect bad reasoning, [and] to challenge ambiguity' with a focus on the Socratic values of being 'active, critical, curious, [and] capable of resisting authority and peer pressure' (Nussbaum, 2010: 74), and consequently it is a hallmark that both P4C and CA share. But even Dewey, whom Nussbaum calls 'the most influential and theoretically distinguished American practitioner of Socratic education' (p. 64), 'never addressed systematically the question of how Socratic critical reasoning might be taught to children of various ages' (Nussbaum, 2010: 73). She points directly to P4C as a possible solution for creating capabilities for human development (Nussbaum, 2011).

P4C method that operationalizes children's
thinking capabilities

P4C is a breeding ground for the 'complex capabilities' involved in democratic citizenship, i.e. the *critical capability* to argue and judge, the *caring capability* to feel and respect, and the *creative capability* to invent and change. The results of many empirical studies (Santi, 2007, 2012; Di Masi, 2010a, 2010b, 2012; Di Masi and Santi, 2010, 2011, 2012; Santi and Di Masi, 2010, 2011; Santi and Oliverio, 2012) on the application of Lipman's curriculum at primary and secondary school[5] confirm the effectiveness of promoting democratic thinking and participatory dialogue in and out of school.

This suggests that the relationship between democracy, inquiry and dialogue is strong and inescapable. What the aforementioned studies demonstrate is that philosophizing is a powerful contextual and epistemological facilitator for promoting a range of democratic thinking skills in children, such as rational skills, cognitive dispositions and communicative styles of discourse.[6] In particular, when we reconsider the results of the empirical research in capability terms, the procedural, epistemological and substantial features of philosophical thinking and the corresponding abilities promoted in the P4C programme are interpreted as *components of functioning* and specific *sets of capabilities* offered to children as an inclusive experience of participatory dialogue. This perspective is possible because Lipman's curriculum considers philosophy to be, i) a reflective activity based on argumentative reasoning, such as forms of democratic *functioning*; ii) an example of procedural thinking that will help children decide by themselves what values to *be* and *do*; iii) a form of intellectual inquiry based on human wonder at the world as a condition of cultural, social and personal development. The dimensions shown in Table 6.1 are the procedures of a philosophical inquiry (Santi, 2009; Santi and Di Masi, 2010) and are also considered to be the functioning dimensions of human development.

These dimensions of philosophical thinking could be transformed and expressed in participatory dialogic functionings. These dialogic functionings, which range from communicative to argumentative, operationalize the different sets of capabilities, and constitute the cognitive backbone of human and community development.

The 'communities of inquiry' created in the classroom during the implementation of the P4C curriculum are, from the practical point of view of living together, an intersubjective entity and shaped like every democratic society. These communities are places where freedom and needs meet; they

Table 6.1 Procedural dimensions of a philosophical inquiry

Dimension	Description
1.	*Dialectical/dialogical*, which focuses on opposing dynamics as a social opportunity for people to recognize themselves in alterity/difference
2.	*Metacognitive*, which cultivates awareness of the thinking process and of oneself as a thinker, as a condition for new knowledge construction
3.	*Heuristic*, which considers doubts, questions and uncertainty as a guide when looking for meaning and solutions
4.	*Epistemic*, which aims to produce a conceptual generation and change
5.	*Self-corrective*, which adds value to the role of mistakes in knowledge falsification and production
6.	*Context-sensitive*, which contrasts the empty formalization of the reasoning logic with situated thinking
7.	*Values-oriented*, which emphasizes the basic moral nature and destination of all speculative thinking
8.	*Judgement-oriented*, which attributes a deliberative function to reflection, inquiry and imagination to assure cognitive conditions for human freedom

Source: Based on Santi (2009); Santi and Di Masi (2010)

encourage democracy through social negotiation and generate norms, agreed behaviour, and shared tasks and objectives (Salomon and Nevo, 2002). They are environments where students learn how to decide rules and to observe them. Being in a community-based classroom means joint understanding and learning through the use of instructional approaches, such as *reciprocal teaching* (Palincsar and Brown, 1984), *scaffolding* (Wood *et al.*, 1976) and *coaching* (Lipman, 2003). It also implies valuing plurality and diversity, and all members are expected to respect one another and to accept different perspectives and different points of view. Some research (Santi, 2007) has described and evaluated these connections in order to find out how the dialogic characteristics of philosophical discourse, argumentation theory and a socio-constructivist approach could be used to internalize discursive rules and develop collaborative and democratic attitudes in the members of a 'community of discourse' through a more meaningful and mediated use of explorative language. The central pedagogical tool is the community of inquiry where students work together through the use of dialogic, collaborative and explorative language. This form of dialogue, referred to here as 'inquiry talk', is designed to help community members to take responsibility for their comments, to motivate their ideas and positions with good reasons, to negotiate solutions and to take collective decisions. Furthermore, dialogue skills are believed to strengthen the development of specific functionings, such as thinking skills, and procedural and content knowledge, which are considered to be important for the progress and evolution of democratic living. Thus, education for democracy is promoted in a safe environment in which members can express their point of view, have the opportunity to generate more than one perspective on a problem, express the necessity to deliberate by considering different alternatives, learn to value ideas, and respect one another. These expressions of informal reasoning are usually displayed in the mediated form of verbal and symbolic discourse, which may include different communicative pragmatics, acquire dialogical or disputative conversational forms, have heuristic or expressive purposes, and adopt specific alternative styles. The discourse style that governs the specific interaction in the 'community of inquiry' is the above-mentioned 'inquiry talk' (Santi, 2007), a collaborative, heuristic discourse which is internalized by the participants during the philosophizing activity.[7] Inquiry talk is oriented towards shared inquiry, where the interlocutors exchange ideas and then offer constructive criticism. This process leads to statements and suggestions that reveal common ground on which problems can be both solved and created. Argumentative justifications and alternative hypotheses could be used to transform personal opinions into new ideas and theories worthy of further discussion (Wegerif *et al.*, 1999). The key to these rules is the participants' ability to use a range of argumentative skills and abilities during collaborative, heuristic and inclusive dialogue. These skills and abilities, however, do not only cover a person's capacity to evaluate propositional logic in order to understand objective reality (Habermas, 1981), as they are principally dialogical attitudes associated with the argumentative practices that focus on social and subjective knowledge. The internalization of rules, skills, capacities and attitudes constitutes the 'set of capabilities' implied in what Habermas calls 'communicative rationality', a process that is performed only through collaborative conduct and decentralized mechanisms. These mechanisms are favoured by argumentative practice, especially when activated as a rational socializing, individualizing and objectivizing tool, as proposed in P4C, which leads to an emancipative society based on free moral discourse between individuals and deliberative discourse among equal citizens (Habermas, 1981, 1999). In particular, the argumentative procedures established by Kline (1998) and implemented in the community of philosophical inquiry appear to be a better way to meet the need for inclusion in human development. These procedures encompass the capacity to create consensus, advocate proposals, facilitate commitment and integrate other identities, capacities that could be easily transformed into capabilities within children who choose *to be* citizens and *to do* so democratically.

Concluding remarks

In this chapter we argue that the practice of philosophical dialogue within a community of inquiry nurtures the capabilities and functionings which lead children and youths to flourish and to participate in decision-making processes, and thus to be agents and social actors. The inclusion of proposals such as P4C in the school curriculum goes in the direction of change. Here, an instructional design is needed, in order to offer an effective scaffolding of the children's evolving capabilities process and to establish and focus on the democratic and citizenship functionings they need to develop, in order to be recognized as agents and authentic participants in the society (Biggeri and Santi, 2012).

The value and role of philosophizing in communities of inquiry as an educational means to sustain the rights and the efforts of children to pursue flourishing lives, in and out of school, was discussed in this chapter. In particular, the critical, creative and caring dimensions of 'complex thinking' involved in the experience and practice of community philosophical dialogue were interpreted as possible conversion factors, which would help to achieve one of the main purposes of a democratic society, and to promote children's participation in social life in terms of *doings* and *beings*.

Furthermore, the P4C methodology and its application in educational contexts has been considered as a concrete example of how to promote values and good societies that are able to listen to children as full citizens and thus to actively engage with them to explore solutions for a better future (Biggeri and Santi, 2012; Di Masi, 2012). According to Freeman (1998), children's social participation needs to be visible in public contexts, in order to clearly manifest their citizenship and their inclusion in a society that includes a full range of rights and opportunities in the direction of the self-determination human rights approach. From this perspective, the P4C proposal and its applications can be considered as spaces in which such needs of visible participation find a response, creating 'communities of inquiry' in which children and youths might think about (and decide) what they want to be and become.

Further research perspectives may frutifully explore the social and cognitive potential of educational proposals in which the capability approach is operationalized in terms of the complex thinking dimensions and procedural rules, but we can say that philosophical practice geared towards developing the complex thinking functionings and capabilities in children is a core aim of education. It is also a tangible opportunity to operationalize the CA by focusing on contexts, the *community of inquiry*, and procedures, the *inquiry talk*, which develop both capabilities that children choose for themselves (Biggeri and Libanora, 2011; Biggeri *et al.*, 2011) and which each and every citizen needs for democracy.

Notes

1   This point may be considered an extension of the 'school of activity' movement, which is rooted in Europe's pedagogical tradition of the late 1800s and early 1900s. It encompasses educators such as Claparede, Montessori, Don Milani and Lodi, and is also emphasized in Dewey's experience-based pedagogy (Biggeri and Santi, 2012). All of these scholars point to the need to adapt an environment and ensure that it is 'child-size'; they also stress the importance of considering education as an opportunity for children to make a difference to the world in order to avoid exclusion and slavery in society.
2   See also Chapter 1 by Hart and Chapter 2 by Biggeri in this volume.
3   From this point of view, Socrates is a good example of why philosophical dialogue is two-way, as it moves an inquiry toward private knowledge of the self and toward the public good of the *polis*. In his experience, the personal and social dimensions of philosophical inquiry are continually interrelated, as private and public dialogue aimed at co-constructing a shared world-view, both at individual and community level.
4   The problem of a participation and justice 'gap' affecting young people is well addressed from a CA perspective by Leßmann *et al.* (2011).
5   The children involved were aged between 9 and 13.
6   A vast amount of literature is now available on the evaluation of the P4C curriculum, both from quantitative and qualitative perspectives. Many studies and much empirical research has been carried out to assess the effects of the curriculum's implementation in a range of school grades and within 'informal' contexts. For a complete database and review of studies on the topic, see the website of the Institute for the Advancement of Philosophy for Children (IAPC) at Montclair State University (NJ): www.montclair.edu/cehs/academics/institutes-and-centers/iapc/research.
7   The basic macro-pragmatic rules of inquiry talk (Santi, 2007) are: 1. Encouraging participants to put forward their own views in a group; 2. Reflecting before speaking; 3. Sharing and discussing relevant information; 4. Motivating their own reasoning;

5. Giving importance to the thinking structure; 6. Accepting challenges; 7. Building on others' ideas; 8. Discussing alternatives; 9. Proceeding in a self-correcting way; 10. Negotiating mediation; 11. Responsibly participating in decision-making. For further analysis of the role, impact, and internalization of inquiry talk, see Santi, 2007; Di Masi, 2010a, 2010b, 2011; Santi and Di Masi, 2010, 2011; Di Masi and Santi, 2011a, 2011b, 2010).

References

Alkire, S. (2002a) 'Dimensions of human development', *World Development*, 30(2), 181–205.

Alkire, S. (2002b) *Valuing Freedoms: Sen's Capabilities Approach and Poverty Reduction*, Oxford University Press, Oxford.

Ballet, J., Biggeri, M. & Comim, F. (2011) Children's agency and the capability approach: a conceptual framework', in M. Biggeri, J. Ballet & F. Comim (eds) *Children and the Capability Approach*, Palgrave Macmillan, Basingstoke, 22–45.

Biggeri, M. (2007) Children's valued capabilities, in M. Walker and E. Unterhalter (eds) *Amartya Sen's Capability Approach and Social Justice in Education,*, Palgrave, New York, 197–214.

Biggeri, M. & Libanora R. (2011) From Valuing to evaluating: tools and procedures to operationalize the capability approach, in M. Biggeri, J. Ballet & F. Comim (eds) *Children and the Capability Approach*, Palgrave Macmillan, Basingstoke, 79–106.

Biggeri, M. & Santi, M. (2012) The missing dimensions of children's well-being and well-becoming in education systems: capabilities and philosophy for children, *Journal of Human Development and Capabilities*, 13(3), 373–395.

Biggeri, M., Ballet, J. & Comim, F. (eds) (2006) *Children and the Capability Approach*, Palgrave Macmillan, Basingstoke.

Biggeri, M., Ballet, J. & Comim, F. (2011) Final remarks and conclusions: the promotion of children's active participation, in M. Biggeri, J. Ballet & F. Comim (eds) *Children and the Capability Approach*, Palgrave Macmillan, Basingstoke, 340–345.

Comim, F., Biggeri, M., Ballet, J. & Iervese V. (2011) Introduction: theoretical foundations and the book's roadmap, in M. Biggeri, J. Ballet & F. Comim (eds) *Children and the Capability Approach*, Palgrave Macmillan, Basingstoke, 3–21.

Calder, G. (2011) Inclusion and participation: working with the tension, *Studies in Social Justice*, 5(2), 183–196.

Cooke, B. & Kothari, U. (2001) *Participation: The New Tyranny*, ZED, London.

Corsaro, W.A. (2005) Collective action and agency in young children's peer cultures, in J. Qvortrup (ed.) *Studies in Modern Childhood: Society, Agency, Culture*, Palgrave Macmillan, New York, 231–247.

Crocker, D.A. (2008) *Ethics of Global Development*, Cambridge University Press, Cambridge.

Deneulin, S. & Shahani, L. (2009) *An Introduction to the Human Development and Capability Approach: Freedom and Agency*, Earthscan, London.

Dewey, J. (1916). *Democracy and Education*, Macmillan, New York.

Di Masi, D. (2010a) Polişofia a dialogic approach in community of philosophical inquiry for citizenship education, paper presented at Conference *Profundizando la Democrazia*, 13–16 May 2010, Rosario (Argentina).

Di Masi, D. (2010b) Friendship: a reflection about children participation in public space, *Childhood and Philosophy*, (6), 335–347.

Di Masi, D. (2010c) Converting Municipal Council of Children in community of philosophical inquiry to improve the competences for an authentic participation, paper presented at UNICEF Conference, Friendly Cities, 27–29 October, Firenze, Italy.

Di Masi, D. (2012) Dialogical and reflective activities in the classrooms to improve moral thinking, in D. Alt, R. Reingold (eds) *Changes in Teachers' Moral Role: From Passive Observers to Moral and Democratic Leaders*, Sense Publishers, Rotterdam, 133–146.

Di Masi, D. & Santi, M. (2011) Learning democratic thinking: philosophy for children as citizen, paper presented at EARLI conference Education for a Global Networked Society, 30 August–3 September, Exeter, UK.

Di Masi, D. & Santi, M. (2012) Polişofia: a P4C curriculum for citizenship education, in M. Santi, S. Oliverio (eds) *Educating for Complex Thinking Through Philosophical Inquiry: Models, Advances, and Proposals for the New Millennium*, Liguori, Naples, 151–167.

Drèze, J. & Sen, A. (eds) (2002) *India: Development and Participation*, Oxford University Press, Oxford.

Drydyk, J. (2004) The democratic capability, paper presented at the 4th International Conference on the Capability Approach: Enhancing Human Security, 5–7 September, Pavia, http://cfs.unipv.it/ca2004/papers/drydyk.pdf.

Engeström, Y., Miettinen, R. & Punamaki, R. (eds) (1999) *Perspectives on Activity Theory*, Cambridge University Press, Cambridge.

Freeman, M. (1998) The sociology of childhood and children's rights, *International Journal of Children's Rights*, 6(4), 433–444.

Habermas, J. (1981) *Theorie des kommunikativen Handelns* (vol. 1: *Handlungsrationalität und gesellschaftliche Rationalisierung*, vol. 2: *Zur Kritik der funktionalistischen Vernunft*), Frankfurt a.M.

Habermas, J. (1999) *Between Facts and Norms: Contributions to a Discourse Theory of Law and Democracy*, MIT Press, Cambridge, MA.

Hook, S. (1939) *John Dewey*, John Day, New York.

James, A. (2009) Agency, in J. Qvortrup, G. Valentine, W. Corsaro, M. Honig (eds) *Handbook of Childhood Studies*, Sage, London.

James, A. (2010) Dare voci alle voci dei bambini. Pratiche e dilemmi, trappole e potenzialità nella ricerca sociale con i bambini, *Cittadini in crescita*, nuova serie 2, 10–25.

James, A., Jenks, C. & Prout, A. (1998) *Theorizing Childhood*, Polity Press, Cambridge.

Kelsen, H. (2000) On the essence and value of democracy' in A.J. Jacobson & B. Schlink (eds) *Weimar: A Jurisprudence of Crisis*, University of California Press, Berkley, CA, Los Angeles, 84–110.

Kline, S.L. (1998) Influence opportunities and the development of argumentation competencies in childhood, *Argumentation*, 12(3), 367–385.

Kozulin, A. (1998) *Psychological Tools: A Sociocultural Approach to Education*, Harvard University Press, Cambridge, MA.

Leßmann, O., Otto, H.-U. & Ziegler, H. (eds) (2011) *Closing the Capability Gap – Renegotiating Social Justice for the Young*. Barbara Budrich, Leverkusen.

Lipman, M. (1988) *Philosophy Goes to School*, Temple University Press, Philadelphia, PA.

Lipman, M. (2003) *Thinking in Education*, second edition, Cambridge University Press, Cambridge.

Mayall B. (2002) *Towards a Sociology of Childhood*, Open University Press, Buckingham.

Mead, G.H. (1966) *Mind, Self, and Society*, Chicago University Press, Chicago.

Nussbaum, M. (2002) Education for citizenship in an era of global connection, *Studies in Philosophy and Education*, 21, 289–303.

Nussbaum, M. (2010) *Not for Profit: Why Democracy Needs the Humanities*, Princeton University Press, Princeton, NJ.

Nussbaum, M. (2011) *Creating Capabilities: The Human Development Approach*, Harvard University Press, Harvard, MA.

Palincsar, A.S. & Brown, A.L. (1984) 'Reciprocal teaching and comprehension-fostering and comprehension-monitoring activities, *Cognition and Instruction*, 1(2), 117–173.

Perelman, C. & Olbrechts-Tyteca, L. (1958) *Traité de l'argumentation: La novelle rhétorique*, P.U.F., Paris.

Qvortrup J. (ed.) (2005) *Studies in Modern Childhood: Society, Agency, Culture*, Palgrave Macmillan, New York.

Resnick, L.B., Levine, J. & Teasley, S.D. (eds) (1991). *Perspectives on Socially Shared Cognition*, American Psychological Association, Washington.

Rogoff, B. (1990) *Apprenticeship in Thinking: Cognitive Development in Social Context*, Oxford University Press, New York.

Salomon, G. & Nevo, B. (2002) *Peace Education: The Concept, Principles, and Practices Around the World*, LEA, Mahwah, NJ.

Santi, M. (2007) Democracy and inquiry: the internalization of collaborative rules in a community of philosophical discourse, in D. Camhy (ed.) *Philosophical Foundations of Innovative Learning*, Academia Verlag, Saint Augustin, 110–123.

Santi, M. (2009) Philosophers go to school: some constrains and shared remarks, in E. Marsal, T. Dobashi & B. Weber (eds) *Children Philosophize Worldwide: Theoretical and Practical Concepts*, Peter Lang, New York, 527–542.

Santi, M. & Di Masi, D. (2010) 'Inclusive citizenship? A philosophy for children project to promote student's activity and participation to political life', paper presented at pre-conference human development and capability approach, Children's Capability, 20 September, Amman, Jordan.

Santi, M. & Di Masi, D. (2011) Citizenship capability: a Philosophy for Children project to promote flourishing participation to political life, paper presented at HDCA SIG conference Children's Capabilities and Human Development: Researching Inside and Outside of Schools, 11–12 April, Faculty of Education, University of Cambridge, Cambridge, UK.

Santi, M. & Oliverio, S. (eds) (2012) *Educating for Complex Thinking Through Philosophical Inquiry: Models, Advances, and Proposals for the New Millennium*, Liguori, Naples.

Sen, A. (1999a) *Development as Freedom*, Knopf, New York.

Sen, A. (1999b) The possibility of social choice, *The American Economic Review*, 89(3), 349–378.

Sen, A. (1999c) Democracy as a universal value, *Journal of Democracy*, 10(3), 3–17.

Sen, A., (2000) Social exclusion: concept, application, and scrutiny, working paper, Social Development, Paper No 1, June, Asian Development Bank, Bangkok.

Toulmin, S.E. (1958). *The Uses of Argument*, Cambridge University Press, Cambridge.

UN (United Nations) (2007) *Participatory Dialogue: Towards a Stable, Safe and Just Society for All* (PD-SSJS), UN, New York.

UNESCO (2007) *Philosophy: A School of Freedom: Teaching Philosophy and Learning to Philosophize, Status and Prospects*, http://portal.unesco.org/shs/en/ev.php-URL_ID=11575&URL_DO=DO_TOPIC&URL_SECTION=201.html June 11/2008.

Vygotsky, L.S. (1962) *Thought and Language*, MIT Press, Cambridge, MA.

Wegerif, R., Mercer N. & Dawes L. (1999) From social interaction to individual reasoning: an empirical investigation of a possible socio-cultural model of cognitive development, *Learning and Instruction*, (9), 493–516.

Wood, D., Bruner, J. & Ross, G. (1976) The role of tutoring in problem solving, *Journal of Child psychology and psychiatry*, (17), 89–100.

Young, I.M. (2000) *Inclusion and Democracy*, Oxford University Press, Oxford.

7

Education and the Capabilities of Children with Special Needs

Cristina Devecchi, Richard Rose and Michael Shevlin

Introduction

This chapter focuses on the notion of voice in relation to expanding the capability of children with special needs and/or disabilities. While our focus is on the importance of voice, as a necessary prerequisite for the social, psychological and intellectual development of children, we are also interested in evaluating the role that education and schooling play in enabling children to develop their voice and in allowing them to use this effectively to speak out and participate fully in decisions which impact on their intellectual and social development and well-being. We consider respect for the individual voice as a means by which children are given the opportunity to enter a dialogue with those adults who have the responsibility to care for or educate them and to develop as citizens in their own right.

Rawl's (1971) concept of the 'citizen as a free and dignified human being' underpins many of the ideas developed by Nussbaum (2001) in her discussion of the capability approach. Nussbaum elucidates the notion of a rational and moral personhood as a state which embraces all of humanity with an emphasis upon the need to respect individuality and difference together with an obligation upon society to acknowledge the capability of the individual. This applies even when, as it is the case of children with special needs and disabilities, this might be conceived as differing from the norm. This chapter discusses these ideas in the context of empirical research conducted in partnership with students with a range of special educational needs (SEN). Data was collected by the authors in projects with children and young people from primary school age through to school leaving age. The research studies from which data were derived were conducted in both England and Ireland.

Education as a basic children's capability

If, as Nussbaum claims, when adults are concerned, 'capability, not functioning, is the appropriate political goal' (Nussbaum, 2001: 87), where children are involved adults tend to stress equipping them with functionings rather than capabilities. This is the case across many of their life domains, including education. Children's education is, in the broadest sense of being, a process of socialization (Durkheim, 1956), and in the narrower sense of schooling, is conceived as the preparation for the time when, as adults, they will be entitled to the freedom to choose amongst valuable functionings. Indeed, Sen (1992) recognizes education as one of the basic beings and doings which include ensuring the capability to be well-nourished and sheltered, to escape avoidable morbidity and premature mortality, and to participate in society without shame. Further Drèze and Sen (2002) argue that education is a basic capability with both instrumental and intrinsic value. As Terzi (2005: 6) argues, 'in this sense education, and specifically schooling, promotes the achievement of important levels of knowledge and skills acquisition, which play a vital role in agency and well-being'.

However, Unterhalter (2003) warns us that education itself can be a barrier to the expansion of capabilities unless its intent and application are clearly defined, and the necessity to focus upon the autonomy of the learner is taken into account. Likewise, Devecchi (2010) contends that such barriers are of different kinds and work at different levels. There can be physical and social barriers which prevent children's rights *to* education. In this sense children's access to education may be barred or limited. But there can also be social and pedagogical barriers which, while allowing access, do not fulfil the children's right *in* education, that is the right to participate fully in all aspects of their education. Finally, all such barriers concur to delimit children's rights *through* education, that is achieving outcomes of learning that expand children's capabilities. Walker (2010) identifies seven fundamental elements of just education, amongst which are the fact that education expands capabilities, functioning and valuable choices, but also that education fosters agency and well-being. In this chapter we argue that, in the case of children with special needs and/or disabilities, there is a need to ensure that their education does not limit present and future functioning and capability. We contend that, to do this in the light of the three rights outlined above, requires acknowledgement of one fundamental capability, that is the capability to voice what one has reason to value. The chapter therefore draws upon our research in partnership with young people with disabilities and SEN who have informed us of their personal experiences of education.

While all children are dependent on adults for safety, advice and guidance, those with special needs and disabilities are prone to being conceived as requiring total care and attention (Florian *et al.*, 2008). Partly, this is because their disability or special need construes their identity as vulnerable. Such vulnerability further reifies such children as needing care, but also as unable to gain independent living. As independence is not only about living without constant care, but also about being enabled and allowed to make informed decisions about one's life, the condition of vulnerability in which these children are placed prevents them being heard (Vorhaus, 2007). Their voices, here conceived as the expression of their agency, are silenced.

For many young people, described as having a disability or special need, their lives are lived apart from the majority of society. Whilst they may be physically present they are excluded by dint of their perceived difference from the majority and by suggestions that this makes them less likely to be able to contribute to or shape the society in which they live (Vorhaus, 2005). The voices of such individuals are often suppressed either in the belief that they are incapable of expressing an opinion which may be of value or through an inability of the majority to engage them in meaningful dialogue (Barton, 2005). Listening to these individuals, far from being a fruitless exercise, may often in fact provide useful insights not only into their world, but also into the kind of society which has been created and which denies these children of their basic rights of citizenship. By citizenship we mean the opportunity afforded to all children to learn, develop and exercise the three capabilities of practical reasoning, affiliation and control over one's environment, both political and material (Nussbaum, 2001). By presenting the opinions of young people about their life experiences and listening to the messages which they give, we have an opportunity to create citizens who are freed from oppression and dignified through the contributions which they make to their own quality of life and to our understanding of how we can bring it about.

Developing children's capabilities has to work simultaneously on the two meanings of capability. Firstly it must challenge the notion that children do not have the capability, that is the ability, to reason and make informed choices on what they have reason to value. Secondly it necessitates the consideration of the child's voice as one valuable capability, that is the freedom to express one's views and have them acknowledged as a means of informing educational provision, which is meaningful and effective at an individual and systemic level.

Capability, ability and voice

The definition and determination of children's capability, as 'the ability to', has inevitably been subject to the control of those individuals and organizations responsible for the development, interpretation and deployment of policy at local and national levels. There are varied conceptions of children's abilities to voice their views, concerns, dreams, aspirations, fears and hopes.[1] Many are linked to the notion that children, as individuals at an early stage of development, are less capable than adults, and thus not entitled to have a voice (Brighouse, 2003; Lansdown, 2005). The phrasing of Article 12 of The UN *Convention on the Rights of the Child* (UNCRC) (United Nations General Assembly, 1989) clearly demonstrates this dilemma. The article reads:

> Parties shall assure to the child who is capable of forming his or her own views the right to express those freely in all matters affecting the child, the views of the child being given due weight in accordance with the age and maturity of the child.

The *Convention* clearly establishes a set of principles with the intention of affording individual child rights and protection against exploitation and harm. However, the equivocal nature of the language used here allows for interpretation which, contrary to the intentions of the *Convention*, enables those with responsibility for the development and implementation of policy to justify the exemption of individuals and whole cohorts of children from the very protection which the documents intended to provide. The introduction of a caveat which in effect enables children to be identified as incapable of forming their own views is problematic in a number of respects. In particular it demands that judgements are made with regards to the ability of the individual child to make decisions based upon factors such as age, intellectual capacity or linguistic ability. Furthermore, it delegates the responsibility for decision-making to those organizations and individuals who oversee the lives of children without providing adequate guidelines or safeguards to ensure that their rights are protected and assured.

We do not suggest that children, regardless of need or ability, are necessarily fully competent to make decisions about all matters affecting their lives. Indeed, we would suggest that all individuals may benefit from the guidance and support of 'expert' individuals to enable informed choices and decisions in respect of personal welfare and needs. Experienced and educated adults often seek the advice of other more expert individuals when making decisions where individual expertise is seen as limited. Examples might include consultation with a doctor regarding our health, a mechanic with regards to a problem with a car or a computer specialist when a laptop fails. However, in reaching conclusions about a problem or need in any of these areas, we expect to be consulted and our opinions respected and considered in a rational manner. We are in effect acknowledging our personal limitations but expressing our rights to be fully consulted. The greater our experience, the more likely we are to be able to make an informed contribution to any discussion about our own needs. Inevitably, the child who has limited experiences is less likely to be able to demonstrate the confidence or competence which may be required to make informed choices or express considered opinions on a range of topics. It would be folly to suggest that children can be encouraged to make decisions about critical factors in their lives in isolation and without the guidance of experienced adults. It is also inconceivable that children will develop the capacity to gain greater autonomy in their lives unless they are encouraged to develop those skills necessary for decision-making from an early age.

Ignatieff (2001) asserts that one interpretation of the main purpose of human rights is to afford protection to individuals and recognizes that 'human beings have an innate or natural dignity, that they have a natural and intrinsic self-worth, that they are sacred' (p. 54). In scrutinizing this proposal, Ignafieff recognizes a number of challenges which may result in this interpretation being problematic when it is required to move beyond the theoretical presentation of an idea into the development of policy and practice. In particular he perceives difficulties with the language of human rights and the problematic interpretation of concepts such as natural dignity and self-worth, which are value laden, and subject to the exegesis of a third party. This challenge is of particular concern when we consider the needs of those members of our society, such as children or those with disabilities, who may be perceived as vulnerable and more easily subject to misrepresentation or marginalization within their communities.

Rawls (1971), building upon theories which expounded the 'lottery of birth', expressed the view that it was morally unacceptable to inhibit the opportunities of an individual simply because of any disadvantage acquired at birth. He discusses the importance of those charged with taking responsibility for others in society to recognize a need to ensure that the opportunities afforded to these individuals are enhanced rather than inhibited by any decisions taken. Likewise, Sen (2004) stresses our obligations towards enhancing the entitlement others have in pursuing their capabilities. While clearly espousing a strong ethical individualistic position, Sen recognizes the role society plays in fostering capabilities and carving spaces for a democratic dialogue and appraisal of what each and every one of us has reason to value.

The need to obtain the perspective of the individual and to ensure that they are fully engaged in the decision-making process is imperative. Whilst this may prove to be onerous in some instances it should not detract from the necessity to take those actions, which support the development of the individual as a self-determining being.

What children with SEN and disabilities say

Children described as having SEN are amongst those most likely to be denied opportunities to become effective independent decision-makers. The allocation of a negative label which identifies a child as having a learning difficulty or disability can in many instances have the effect of lowering expectations and leading to denial of personal capability. Yet in England, children with SEN and disabilities are entitled to be 'consulted' on matters that regard them. This is stated in the *Special Educational Needs Code of Practice* (DfES, 2001) which, under Part IV of the Education Act 1996, sets out guidance on policies and procedures aimed at enabling pupils with SEN to reach their potential, to be included fully in their school communities and make a successful transition to adulthood. Likewise in Ireland the EPSEN (Education for Persons with Special Educational Needs) Act (Oireachtas, 2004) stresses the need to provide for the inclusion of all children in mainstream school. Usually, this moment of consultation is carried out during an annual review of the child's progress against set targets during which parents, school staff and other professionals meet to review the provision which is made available to support children with a special need or disability. For the other children who do not have a formalized diagnosis, but who nonetheless exhibit difficulties with learning, legislation still valid today within England (DCFS, 2004) acknowledges the right of the child to be consulted, but without a statutory obligation to do so in a formal manner. This situation leaves many children in limbo with regard to expressing their views on matters that concern them, specifically the education they receive.

A number of innovations designed to ensure that children's voices are heard have made a major contribution in highlighting the need to listen to and have respect for their views. It is not the aim of this chapter to review the vast and complex literature on pupil voice, but suffice to say that including the views of children with regard to their education is now common practice in many schools in England. Supporters of the practice suggest that consulting children on teaching and learning can lead to school improvement and better learning opportunities and results (Munby, 1995; Wehmeyer *et al.*, 1998; Lawson, 2010). Others, such as Fielding (2001) and Deuchar (2009), have warned against tokenistic approaches in which the child's voice is heard but not listened to, or where children are consulted on minor issues while adults still maintain power and authority over major decisions. For others, such as Arnot and Reay (2007), it is important to understand which child's voice we are listening to as children address adults knowing, as Bernstein (1990) argued, the deep pedagogical discourse adults use and value.

Children have been for many years the subjects of educational, social and psychological research. Such research has been conducted on them, but rarely for them, and with them. Students as researchers (SARs) has shifted the focus of some research by empowering children to be as fully as possible involved in all aspects of research agenda. While this is a positive albeit fraught development (Fielding, 2007), little has changed for children with special needs and disabilities (Dowse, 2009). Even when included in research, these children are still mainly listened to simply as sources of data. Yet, if we were to listen more carefully, their voices could tell us much about their condition of disenfranchisement and silence.

Recent research into pupil participation for pupils with SEN in schools has demonstrated a willingness on the part of some teachers and other professionals to explore the means by which greater participation can be achieved (Shevlin and Rose, 2003; Rose and Shevlin, 2004; MacConville, 2007; Paige-Smith and Rix, 2011). In many instances the researchers involved in these studies have collated the experiences of young people, which often demonstrate how they have been marginalized or excluded from the everyday experiences which are afforded to other individuals. Over a number of years Rose and Shevlin have worked with young people described as having SEN who have shared their recollections of an educational experience that, far from including them as learners, has limited their opportunities.

The Encouraging Voices project (Shevlin and Rose, 2003) gathered research from a variety of sources that focused on the perspective of children and young people with SEN. Data were collected through the use of semi-structured interviews in order to construct narratives of the experiences of young people using only their own words. These narratives were verified by the young people in order to ensure the trustworthiness of the data and the authenticity of the expressions reported. Voluntary participation by young people ensured that the sample from whom the data was obtained was one that represented young people who had confidence in expressing their experiences and were prepared to provide reflective insights into these. All data were categorically analysed in order to develop themes under which experiences could be discussed. One powerful contribution from a group of young people with disabilities in Northern Ireland (Horgan, 2003) demonstrated very clearly how young people with disabilities feel excluded from consultation.

The children's accounts give a comprehensive view of how adults' perspectives on disability restrict their achieved and potential beings and doings. For example, this is the case when perceptions about disability conflate with those of ability to determine future career and life pathways, resulting in a lowering of expectations and a patronising interpretation of their individuality. As one young man interviewed for the Encouraging Voices project stated:

> No one expects us to do well in exams and go on to have a career or even a decent job. Changing this means challenging a mindset that sees the disability not the person, and that fails to recognize that while it might take a young person with a disability longer to achieve, we can still do it.

A further respondent who was a co-researcher in the Educable project (which explored experiences of young people in special schools) reflects on his own experiences and comments that:

> I find it very patronizing to be told 'you shouldn't do that because it's not for you and wouldn't suit you'. And 'we're really thinking about you, you know'. And actually it's not us that has to change. It's the environment that has to change; it's the exam system that has to change; it's the schools and the teachers that will have to reorganize themselves to allow young people with disabilities get a decent education.

Another young person in the Educable project makes a comparison between his sister and himself and is able to identify how educational systems replicate injustices in relation to potential life outcomes:

> My sister is at grammar school now and I can see the choice she gets and I realize what a bad deal I got. We're forced to go on to further education really because the education we got at school wouldn't get us a job.

Such differential outcomes are often highlighted, as in the examples below.

> It's not that I couldn't do them [exams], they just never gave me a chance to do them and I had seen other people doing exams and I thought, why can't I do them? Every time I asked them, it was like 'because' all the time.

From a beginning in education where the expectations of what I could achieve were very limited, I feel that I have now progressed to a position where I can influence others to have much higher expectations of all children.

Young adult with cerebral palsy

Lowered expectations were sometimes associated with particular 'conditions', such as dyslexia, as reported by the following young person who participated in the Encouraging Voices project: 'if you're dyslexic you won't be going anywhere so let's not bother ... So there was an attitude that if you have something wrong with you, you don't have to reach the same standards that others do ...'.

The setting of artificial limits and limiting possibilities and potential is clearly demonstrated by the following extract from Kathleen O'Leary (2003: 278), a person who has a physical disability and uses a wheelchair:

I was advised [by a university careers officer] to be proud of my achievement, frame my certificate but not to expect a place in the world of work. It was evident that there were two tracks – two sets of expectations for people with and without disabilities. This dual reality exists in the twenty-first century.

Kathleen qualified as a teacher and eventually secured a job as the head of department in a secondary school.

The consequences of a failure to consult and involve these young people in critical decisions has left them frustrated and with a feeling of exclusion from the very educational process that should be focused upon enhancing their independence. It is evident from interviewing these and other young people that they are capable of expressing their views but are subjected to the narrow interpretation of gatekeepers who are denying them an opportunity for full participation and, Booth (2002: 2) claims, 'active engagement with what is learnt and taught, and having a say in how education is experienced'.

Those responsible for the education of these young people are unlikely to have excluded them from decision-making through any malign intent. It is more likely that a focus upon disability has resulted in a lowering of expectation and a false interpretation of what their pupils can achieve. In Sen's terms, the focus upon pupil capacity has been made without consideration of the ways in which activity might enhance personal autonomy and increase opportunities for self-fulfillment.

Voice as a means to expand children's capabilities

The examples above bring to light the complex connection between the two meanings of capability, also outlined above. This lack of capability is both academic and agentic. Firstly it reiterates a factual or perceived inability of the child to formulate reasonable views, as the subject is deemed less intellectually able to make informed decisions. Their very identity as children restricts the potential achievement of functioning, being able to speak out, and the fulfilment of the opportunity to participate. Secondly the refusal to acknowledge their intellectual capacity determines the range of self-determination. The experiences of these children show how their identity as human beings is determined by a myopic mindset which reinforces the view that children are 'immature' and 'irrational' (Edwards, 1996: 47). The two reinforce each other into an infinite loop within which the child's identity as disabled or with special needs is framed and reframed in a condition of vulnerability, ignorance and hopelessness.

As a consequence, denying children a voice, here understood as acknowledging the connection between voice and agency, is denying them the fulfilment of valuable adult functionings and future capabilities. This is particularly the case at the stage of transition from education into employment. Here the mindset of adults is such that, 'no one expects us to do well in exams and go on to have a career or even a decent job'. The young person in question is here denied not only the opportunity to fulfil what he/she has reason to value, but also to dream and aspire to what he/she might achieve. Without the possibility of having a job, the young person's future functionings and quality of life are further limited by the restriction of those essential resources that he/she can convert into valuable functionings and capabilities. The inability by adults to acknowledge children's views destines them to a life of dependency in which, as Riddell *et al.* (1997) contend, disabled people become eternal children.

What the young person perceives as a 'patronizing' attitude is thus the consequence of social and cultural perceptions and practices that continuously support the view of disabled children as in need of care which becomes oppressive, smothering and totalizing. Far from Biggeri *et al.*'s (2010) notion of care as relational, that is as the acknowledgement that we are all vulnerable and needy of each other's support, in the case of children with SEN and disabilities, care becomes the only available option. In a situation in which adults decide what choices are reasonable and valuable, children are left with a shrivelling set of possible capabilities and functionings, and a limited ability to convert the resources made available through complex and no doubt well-meaning educational provision. While not without the possibility of making choices, but without real choices to choose from, their frustrated voices fall silent.

Sen (2009) recognizes that capability establishes the relationship between an initial capacity and the provision of activity which enhances the opportunities and autonomy of the individual. His development of the capability approach, along with the ideas expressed by Nussbaum (2006, 2009) in relation to disability and the right of all disabled people to education, urges the development of 'effective social institutions' that achieve social justice on the basis of recognizing and enhancing the dignity of each individual regardless of need or ability. By positioning difference not as a mark of ostracism, but as the very nature of human beings, Sen acknowledges that disabled people and disabled children have a rightful place to take in the debate about how social institutions are effective in broadening their capabilities. Essential in this process is, as he argues, the notion of freedom, since 'freedom is concerned with processes of decision making as well as opportunities to achieve valued outcomes' (1999: 291).

Enhancing a space for voice: Teachers' practices in supporting self-advocacy

So far we have contended that education for all children is a basic capability which has intrinsic value, but also extrinsic value in as much as it is instrumental in achieving future valuable functionings and capabilities later into adult life. We have also contended, through the use of empirical evidence, that while one of the aims of education is to foster the ability to make future decisions about what constitutes a valuable life, children with SEN and disabilities are frequently denied a voice, and thus agency and self-determination in planning a life-course. A lack of consideration for the process of enabling voice and acknowledging the content of what is said, is, in the words of Kittay (2005: 103), a denial of human dignity as she says, 'it appears that we deny people dignity to the extent that we place them in circumstances in which they are denied the possibility of making choices that they may have made in situations more under their control'.

This section of the chapter, therefore, will focus on the features of those circumstances which put children under more of their control. This will mean going beyond the evaluation of educational provision by measuring the quantity of human, material and financial resources available, and asking more pertinent, and no doubt more challenging, questions on how such provision can convert resources into valuable and valued capabilities. Terzi (2005: 3) argues that 'seeking equality in the space of fundamental educational capabilities helps substantially in considering the demands of educational equality for disabled children and children with special educational needs'. If this is the case, then we need to ask what part voice plays in meeting the demands of equality. Unlike Terzi (2005: 11) we partly disagree that, 'there are levels of choice that, given their status, are unavailable to children'.

Rather we contend that, while adults have the responsibility to 'protect their [the children's] interests and meet their needs' by ensuring a meaningful and appropriate education, this does not necessarily lead to acceptance that being a child 'does not allow for agency freedom or the exercise of autonomous choices' (Terzi, 2005: 11). Denying children the opportunity to exercise their freedom to choose would be tantamount to denying them their dignity as humans, let alone a safe environment in which they can learn how to make informed choices. However, we agree that adults play an important and vital part in creating those empowering circumstances.

It is at this point appropriate to give space to the voice of teachers as well. The Encouraging Voices project consulted teachers across phases of education in relation to the advantages, which they perceived to accrue from listening to the voices of their students. When interviewed, many recognized the particular challenges faced in enabling young people with SEN and disabilities to participate fully in this process. However, in several instances they demonstrated a determination to safeguard the rights of children to be fully engaged, as the following three teachers show:

Teacher 1

I think that teaching and learning of self-advocacy is one of the most difficult and complex areas for both staff and students, whether in mainstream or special education. However, I would argue that it is one of the most important issues in education as it enables students to feel empowered and to have to take on board the idea of ownership. Education is not just something that is done to them as a passive audience and self-advocacy requires students to take responsibility for themselves.

Teacher 2

...the benefits of self-advocacy are immense. For example Thomas' mum told me recently how weekly target-setting this term has had a very positive impact on him and how proud he was when he achieved a target.

Teacher 3

We cannot just expect any pupils to suddenly become target-setters within the context of an individual educational plan. Thus we give them choices in as many areas as possible and more importantly we try to let them see the consequences of their choice; we help them to develop a range of skills and develop their self-confidence and self-esteem. In this way it is hoped that they will be ready in the senior years to become more independent learners, whatever their levels of ability.

The issues these teachers raise are multiple. While all being positive about the merits of self-advocacy, they acknowledge the difficulties of teaching children how to be advocates for themselves. Indeed, as one teacher said, 'We cannot just expect any pupils to suddenly become target-setters'. Indeed, 'any' pupil requires to be educated and her voice to be trained. When this happens, 'the benefits of self-advocacy are immense'. Exercising one's voice leads to immediate functionings such as the ability to set targets and review them. But it also broadens future capabilities, such as becoming more independent learners. It further supports the broadening of immediate capabilities such as that of practical reason and social participation (Nussbaum, 2000), by developing their self-confidence and self-esteem. Because of such benefits of self-advocacy, agency and voice are to be construed as basic and foundational capabilities as they are the founding stones for the human development of children.

Listening to voices of children also has the consequence of broadening the teachers' professional functioning and capabilities. We contend that without a recognition of the importance of children's voice, the pedagogical and practical dilemmas teachers raised would have not been evident. Thus, enabling children to formulate their choices, to think about the consequences of such choices, and, ultimately, take responsibility for them, are all valuable lessons for both children and teachers alike. In this light, the very fact that teachers have to confront themselves with the voice of the child can be a reason for changing the mindset in which children with SEN and/or disabilities should have reduced opportunities to lead the life they value.

While inspirational, the teachers who took part in the research do not necessarily reflect the educational experience of many of our children. Rather, they show what can be achieved if the circumstances in which both adults and children operate appreciate and acknowledge the importance of children's voice. It is such circumstances that the final section of this chapter will explore.

Broadening children's capabilities: Enhancing voice for all

So far we have focused on how the capability approach can offer a different perspective with which we can evaluate the importance of listening to children. The quotes from the young people in our research show the negative impact the absence of voice has on their life opportunities. The quotes from the teachers point to both the benefits of recognizing the children's voice, but also the challenges of teaching self-advocacy. In this final section, we focus on the role educational institutions can play in fostering voice for all. This means acknowledging that educational institutions cannot encourage children's voices without first enabling teachers to have a voice as well. Ultimately, we envisage a system where children and adults participate equally to determine valuable functionings and capabilities.

In putting forward a different approach to listening to children with disabilities and SEN, we agree with Biggeri *et al.*, (2006) that 'children are subjects of capabilities' and as such they should be consulted, guided and educated on what constitutes well-being. Yet, to achieve this in schools attention must shift from a preoccupation with individual capabilities and collective responsibilities to one that also pays attention to individual responsibilities and collective capabilities (Ballet *et al.*, 2007). It is at the interface between these two dynamic spheres that educational provision should work because it is through this dynamic and challenging situation that individual and collective resources can be converted into functionings and capabilities for both the children and their teachers.

If it is right to assume that the primary role of teachers is that of converting different types of resources into capabilities for the children, it is also right to acknowledge that teachers should be given the time and opportunity to convert their knowledge and experience into valuable functioning and capabilities for the children. This is to claim that the capabilities offered to the children, including that of voice, are dependent on the capability set offered to teachers.

Usually the question of how to provide teachers with the knowledge, skills and understanding required is framed within a human capital approach. Such an approach, as Robeyns (2006: 73) claims, 'is *entirely* instrumental: it values education, skills and knowledge *only* in so far as they contribute (directly or indirectly) to expected economic productivity' (emphasis in the original). As enhancing the opportunity for voices to be heard and acted upon is not directly productive, a human capital approach alone is necessary but not sufficient to provide children and their teachers with what they need to enhance their well-being.

We espouse the idea that a focus on establishing educational institutions which provide spaces for democratic dialogue in which teachers and children can deliberate on what they have reason to value, is a system that is more conducive to enhancing those freedoms and opportunities to be and do. Such views are not new in the field of inclusive education. For over three decades, there has been an increase in research on establishing and developing educational systems which recognize the right to all to participate fully in their education (Vitello and Mithaug, 1998; Tilstone and Rose, 2003; Armstrong *et al.*, 2010). However, the inclusion movement has been criticized for not having produced clear ways of evaluating the impact of theory onto practice (Hansen, 2012; Hodkinson, 2012). It is now under threat by a resurgence of the medical/deficit model which will restore the view that disability is something to be cured (Runswick-Cole, 2011). Such a model, which is grounded in the view that 'experts' know what is best for children with SEN and disabilities, will be most likely to disregard children's voices.

Conclusion

We acknowledge that more has to be done to prove the validity of listening to children as those who, with all the limitations of their differences and age, still hold the key to developing educational provision which is effective. The capability approach offers, in the first instance, a new conceptual space in which to argue this case. More, however, needs to be done in operationalizing the capability approach in relation to disability and, more specifically, the education of children with SEN and disabilities. To date only a handful of researchers have attempted to fully address this issue, and empirical research in this field remains limited. We do not hide the shortcomings of our own engagement so far, but we acknowledge the potential of the capability approach as an innovative lens through which all children can be supported in living flourishing lives.

Note

1   See for example, Hart (2012), Burchardt (2009).

References

Armstrong, A., Armstrong, D. & Spandagou, I. (2010) *Inclusive Education: International Policy and Practice*. London: Sage.

Arnot, M. & Reay, D. (2007) 'A sociology of pedagogic voice: power, inequality and pupils consultation', *Discourse: Studies in the Cultural Politics of Education*, 28(3), 311–325.

Ballet, J., Dubois, J. & Mahieu, O. (2007) 'Responsibility for each other's freedom: agency as the source of collective capability', *Journal of Human Development*, 8(2), 185–201.

Barton, L. (2005) 'Emancipatory research and disabled people: some observations and questions', *Educational Review*, 57(3), 317–327.

Bernstein, B. (1990) *Class, Codes and Control: The Structuring of Pedagogical Discourse*. London: Routledge.

Biggeri, M., Libanora, R., Mariani, S. & Menchini, L. (2006) 'Children conceptualising their capabilities: results of a survey conducted during the first Children's World Congress on child labour', *Journal of Human Development*, 7(1), 59–83.

Biggeri, M., Bellanca, N., Tanzj, L. & Bonfanti, S. (2010) Sulle politiche per le persone con disabilità: Il progetto di vita e la strategia a mosaico, in Biggeri, M. & Bellanca, N. (eds) *Dalla Relazione di Cura alla Relazione di Prossimità: L'Approcccio della Capability alle Persone con Disabilita*. Napoli: Liguori.

Booth, T. (2002) 'Inclusion and exclusion in the city: concepts and contexts', in Potts, P. & Booth, T. (eds) *Inclusion in the city*. London: Routledge.

Brighouse, H. (2003) 'How should children be heard?' *Arizona Law Review*, 45, 691.

Burchardt, T. (2009) 'Agency goals, adaptation and capability sets', *Journal of Human Development and Capabilities*, 10(1), 3–19.

DCSF (Department for Children, Schools and Families) (2004) *Every Child Matters*. London: DCSF.

Deuchar, R. (2009) 'Seen and heard and then not heard: Scottish pupils' experience of democratic education practice during the transition from primary to secondary school', *Oxford Review of Education*, 35(1), 23–40.

Devecchi, C. (2010) *Which Justice for Children with Special Educational Needs and Disabilities? The Application of Sen's Capability Approach to the Analysis of UK School Workforce Reform Policies*. Amman: Human Rights and Human Development, University of Jordan.

DfES (Department for Education and Skills) (2001) *Special Educational Needs Code of Practice*. London: DfES.

Dowse, L. (2009) 'It's like being in a zoo': researching with people with intellectual disabilities', *Journal of Research in Special Educational Needs*, 9(3), 141–153.

Drèze, J. & Sen, A. (2002) *India: Development and Participation*. Oxford: Oxford University Press.

Durkheim, E. (1956) *Education and Sociology*. Glencoe: Free Press.

Edwards, M. (1996) 'Institutionalising children's participation in development', *PLA Notes*, 45, 47–51.

Fielding, M. (2001) 'Beyond the rhetoric of student voice: new departures or new constraints in the transformation of 21st century schooling?' *Forum for Promoting 3–19 Comprehensive Education*, 43(2), 100–109.

Fielding, M. (2007) 'Beyond "voice": new roles, relations, and contexts in researching with young people', *Discourse: Studies in the Cultural Politics of Education*, 28(3), 301–310.

Florian, L., Dee, L. & Devecchi, C. (2008) 'How can the capability approach contribute to understanding provision for people with learning difficulties?' *Prospero*, 14(1), 24–33.

Hansen, J.H. (2012) Limits to inclusion, *International Journal of Inclusive Education*, 16(1), 89–98.

Hart, C.S. (2012) *Aspirations, Education and Social Justice: Applying Sen & Bourdieu.* London: Bloomsbury.

Hodkinson, A. (2012) 'Illusionary inclusion – what went wrong with New Labour's landmark educational policy?' *British Journal of Special Education*, 39(1), 4–11.

Horgan, G. (2003) 'Educable: disabled young people challenge the education system', in Shevlin, M. & Rose, R. (eds) *Encouraging Voices: Respecting the Insights of Young People Who Have Been Marginalised.* Dublin: National Disability Authority, 100–120.

Ignafieff, M. (2001) *Human Rights as Politics and Idolatry.* Princeton, NJ: Princeton University Press.

Kittay, E.F. (2005) 'Equality, dependency and disability', in Lyons, M.A. & Waldron, F. (eds) *Perspectives on Equality: The Second Seamus Heaney Lectures.* Dublin: The Liffey Press, 95–122.

Lansdown, G. (2005) *The Evolving Capacities of Children: Implications for the Exercise of Rights.* Florence: UNICEF Innocenti Research Centre.

Lawson, H. (2010) 'Beyond tokenism? Participation and "voice" for pupils with significant learning difficulties', in Rose, R. (ed.) *Confronting Obstacles to Inclusion: International Responses to Developing Inclusive Education.* London: Routledge, 137–152

MacConville, R. (2007) *Looking at Inclusion: Listening to the Voices of Young People.* London: Paul Chapman.

Munby, S. (1995) 'Assessment and pastoral care, sense, sensitivity and standards', in Best, R., Lang, C., Lodge, C. & Watkins, C. (eds) *Pastoral Care and Personal Social Education.* London: Cassell, 141–154.

Nussbaum, M.C. (2000) *Women and Human Development: The Capabilities Approach.* Cambridge: Cambridge University Press.

Nussbaum, M. C. (2001) *Women and Human Development: The Capabilities Approach.* Cambridge: Cambridge University Press.

Nussbaum, M. (2006) *Frontiers of Justice: Disability, Nationality, Species Membership.* Cambridge, MA: The Belknap Press.

Nussbaum, M.C. (2009) 'The capabilities of people with cognitive disabilities', *Metaphilosophy*, 40(3–4): 331–351.

O'Leary, K. (2003) 'Living in the real world', in Shevlin, M. & Rose, R. (eds) *Encouraging Voices: Respecting the Insights of Young People Who Have Been Marginalised.* Dublin: National Disability Authority, 277–279.

Oireachtas (2004) *The Education of Persons with Special Educational Needs (EPSEN) Act.* Dublin: The Stationery Office.

Paige-Smith, A. & Rix, J. (2011) 'Researching early intervention and young children's perspectives – developing and using a 'listening to children approach', *British Journal of Special Education*, 38(1), 28–36.

Rawls, J. (1971) *A Theory of Justice*. Cambridge, MA: The Belknap Press.

Riddell, S., Baron, S., Stalker, K. & Wilkinson, H. (1997) 'The concept of the learning society for adults with learning difficulties: human and social capital perspectives', *Journal of Education Policy*, 12(6), 473–483.

Robeyns, I. (2006) 'Three models of education: rights, capabilities and human capital', *Theory and Research in Education*, 4(1), 69–84.

Rose, R. & Shevlin, M. (2004) 'Encouraging voices: listening to young people who have been marginalised', *Support for Learning*, 19(4), 155–161.

Runswick-Cole, K. (2011) 'Time to end the bias towards inclusive education?', *British Journal of Special Education*, 38(3), 112–119.

Sen, A. (1992) *Inequality Reexamined*. Oxford: Clarendon Press.

Sen, A. (1999) *Development as Freedom*. Oxford: Oxford University Press.

Sen, A. (2004) 'Elements of a theory of human rights', *Philosophy & Public Affairs*, 32(4), 315–356.

Sen, A. (2009) *The Idea of Justice*. London: Allen Lane.

Shevlin, M. & Rose, R. (2003) *Encouraging Voices*. Dublin: National Disability Authority.

Terzi, L. (2005) 'Equality, Capability and justice in education: towards a principled framework for a just distribution of educational resources to disabled learners', 5th international conference on the capability approach: 'Knowledge and Public Action', Paris, 11–14 September.

Tilstone, C. & Rose, R. (eds) (2003) *Strategies to Promote Inclusive Practice*. London: Routledge.

United Nations General Assembly (1989) *The Convention on the Rights of the Child*. New York: United Nations.

Unterhalter, E. (2003) 'The capabilities approach and gender education: an examination of South African complexities', *Theory and Research in Education*, 1(1), 7–22.

Vitello, S. & Mithaug, D. (1998) *Inclusive Schooling: National and International Perspectives*. Mahwah, NJ: Lawrence Erlbaum Associates.

Vorhaus, J. (2005) 'Citizenship, competence and profound disability', *Journal of Philosophy of Education*, 39(3), 461–475.

Vorhaus, J. (2007) 'Disability, dependency and indebtedness?', *Journal of Philosophy of Education*, 41(1): 29–44.

Walker, M. (2010) 'Capabilities and social justice in education', in Otto, H-U. & Ziegler, H. (eds. *Education, Welfare and the Capability Approach. A European Perspective*. Opladen: Barbara Budrich Publishers, 155–70.

Wehmeyer, M.L., Agran, M. & Hughes, C. (1998) *Teaching Self Determination to Students with Disabilities*. Baltimore, MD: Paul Brookes.

8

Evaluating Children's Capabilities Enhancement in Schools

John Schischka

Introduction

This chapter begins the with the background to the development of Choice Foundation StandTall (CFST) which is a New Zealand-based non-governmental organization (NGO) aiming to enhance opportunities for children attending schools in low-income areas who, because of their families' circumstances, lack the resources to achieve their potential. The introduction includes a summary of the results of the first two years of a participatory appraisal study carried out with a group of 12- and 13-year-old children taking part in the programmes on CFST. The next section develops the need for better ways of appraising children-focused development endeavours such as CFST by reviewing some of the literature from philosophy and education. In the next section there is an analysis of the capability literature in relation to children and how this relates to the work of CFST. Following this, there is an outline of the participatory appraisal methods used in this study. A summary of the findings is presented in the penultimate section based on the transcripts of the focus group interviews with the children, their teachers and their parents and caregivers. In the final section the chapter concludes with comments on the benefits of appraising programmes such as CFST through the lens of the capability approach (CA).

The need to improve the prospects for children from low-income areas is compelling. Ortiz *et al.* (2012: 1) note that 'the consequences of poverty and inequality are very significant for children. Children experience poverty differently from adults; they have specific and different needs. While an adult may fall into poverty temporarily, falling into poverty in childhood can last a lifetime – rarely does a child get a second chance at an education or a healthy start in life'. The OECD (2009) as cited in Infometrics (2011: ii) states that there is a need to 'design interventions for children that reinforce positive development across their life cycle and across a range of well-being outcomes' and to 'create clear, achievable targets for child well-being outcomes'. CFST is one programme established in 2009 specifically as an intervention to achieve such improvement in the well-being of children living in poverty. CFST as an organisation,

> works with children in schools who show great potential at school but because of their environment and circumstances do not have access to the necessary resources to meet this potential. The programme aims to provide these children with the necessary skills, inspiration and opportunities to meet their goals in life and become successful at whatever they want to be.
>
> CFST, 2013

While there is anecdotal evidence that such a programme is successful in terms of its stated mission, 'to enhance the capabilities of children and youth in low decile schools' (CFST, 2013), there remains the question of how best to systematically evaluate the outcomes of such a programme.

The CFST aims to utilize the theoretical framework of the capability approach (CA) in the development and appraisal of its programmes in school (CFST, 2013). A CA-based participatory appraisal methodology has been used with groups of children shortly after they were selected for the programme, and then for the next two years while they were active. The CA offers the opportunity for more fully appraising the evolving development of the children involved. This is part of a longitudinal study and the interviews will be repeated at regular intervals throughout the course of the children's involvement with CFST in order to ascertain how their experiences are matching up with their expectations and changes that are occurring for them. The comments cover the children's expectations as well as their motivations for applying to be a CFST cadet, and how they expected to be different in a year's time, along with changes, resulting from their participation, they expected for their family and friends. Analysis of the transcripts of the focus groups conducted in this study reveals potential for significant outcomes from the programmes of CFST, particularly recognizing the evolving nature of the capabilities of the children involved. The predominant feeling among participants in all five school groups is that they are involved in a programme for children to help them follow their dreams and to be inspired by other people who are successful.

The need to develop better ways of appraising CFST

A range of approaches are possible in analysing programmes such as CFST. There could be an attempt to appraise the changes that result from such a programme in monetary terms, such as the future government expenditure that would be saved from avoidable expenditure on public health, welfare, remedial education, crime and justice. However, these savings cannot always be easily linked to positive results from one such programme. Furthermore, such potential savings from future outcomes are often in the long term and not of immediate use to the stakeholders in proving the programme's worth. Similarly, it could be possible to attempt to appraise the benefits by determining if there have been significant improvements in the academic performance of children taking part. Relying solely on quantitative analysis using monetary measures or academic performance does not allow for the children themselves to be at the centre of the evaluation or for them to have time to reflect on the nature of the changes going on for them while they are participating in CFST. Moreover, while such an evaluation may be useful from an educational perspective, once again, this method would involve long-term appraisal that would not suit the time frame of many potential funders who are often looking for short-term ways of showing a programme's success.

Philosopher Onora O'Neill (2001: 131) discusses what she calls the 'audit agenda' which she argues seeks to improve accountability by continuous and exhaustive scrutiny of how organizations are achieving their goals. O'Neill summarizes the differences between the new systems of this 'audit culture' and older systems of control and accountability. She notes that older systems of accountability were usually qualitative, normally in-house and locally centred. She also sees them as being based on a high degree of trust, and allowing organizations a significant amount of individual self-governance. O'Neill compares these systems with what she terms the 'new systems of accountability' which are numerically based, external to the organization being evaluated, and are often carried out from a distance. She also observes that they demonstrate little trust in those being evaluated, they fail to allow institutional autonomy, and are most often completed by looking at what activities an organization has carried out in the past.

In appraising development initiatives such as CFST it can be argued that excessive focus on the quantitative analysis of programmes could produce 'perverse incentives', whereby some indicators that are easy to measure become the measures by which success is judged. It might be easy to measure the amount of money spent in particular development programmes but it is much more difficult to quantify the real changes that occurred in people's lives during their participation. To overcome the limitations of over-reliance on the 'audit agenda' mentioned above, O'Neill (2002) proposes instead a new form of 'intelligent accountability' in which participants in programmes provide an explanation of what they have done, including achievements and problems encountered, rather than relying on producing a set of quantitative indicators that ignore the narrative behind what these numbers may represent.

The research conducted with the participants in CFST contributes to the development of this 'intelligent accountability'. There are indeed many aspects of successful development programmes, such as increases in self-confidence and social inclusion, 'that have to be accounted for' and which are better appraised using an explicitly subjective qualitative research method. While quantitative measures are certainly an important part of allowing those involved in development initiatives to be accountable, there is also a definite call for these to be supplemented by qualitative measures.

If better methods of appraisal are to be developed, to allow for this 'intelligent accountability' and to allow for an enabling environment whereby children are active agents for change in development programmes such as CFST, then it is valuable to examine what exactly is meant by the term 'development'. Insight into the processes occurring in the individuals taking part in development initiatives can be gained by looking at the writings of the Brazilian educationalist Paulo Freire. In his famous book, *Pedagogy of the Oppressed*, Freire (1996) outlines the need for a process of conscientization to take place in education. He outlines a traditional view of education, what he calls the 'banking' method (1996: 54), and contrasts this with a more progressive view of education, what he calls 'problem-solving' education (1996: 60). It is possible to compare this 'banking' method of education with traditional development practices and the 'problem-solving' method of education with more participatory development programmes.

Freire espouses 'problem-solving education' which could be seen to be the basis for having the children involved in such initiatives as CFST as active participants in the ongoing evaluation and development of the programme. He advocates that students involved in any kind of education should be seen foremost as cognizant individuals and that education involves contemplating the dilemmas of humans in worldly interactions and that students should be 'thinking fellow explorers' in conversation with their instructors. In this way Freire believes that students will act in response to challenges that relate to real issues in their world. Similarly, sound evaluation and development of child-focused development initiatives such as CFST should start with a recognition of the children's background and what they have to contribute with what they already know, rather than treating them as if they are totally ignorant 'blank sheets' upon which the all-knowing 'outside expert' can place the blueprint of a new plan.

There are consequences for children involved in this kind of problem-solving education. Freire argues that it will lead to a much less fatalistic perception of their situation (Freire, 1996: 60), and the problem-posing method presents this very situation to them as a problem. By being active participants Freire determined that the students could develop a deepened awareness of their situation which could be transformed and through this transformation and ongoing investigation, they could come to feel in command of their lives. It is this conscientization process that has considerable importance for those involved in enlightened development opportunities, and which CFST aims to promote for the young people involved. The behavioural changes in this conscientization process occurring within the recipients of programmes could be regarded as central to the appraisal of any such programme.

The need to find ways to include children in the appraisal of programmes in which they are involved has become clear in recent literature specifically related to research involving children. McLeod (2008: 25) notes that 'we should listen to children because it makes our work with them more effective. The most compelling reason for professionals to take notice of what children say is perhaps the most pragmatic one: we waste our time if we do not.' It has been less clear how to operationalize this process of inclusion of children's views within regular evaluation of the programmes in which they are involved.

The CA and improving ways of developing and appraising poverty alleviation initiatives involving children

The CA relates poverty as capability deprivation which prevents people from achieving their full potential simply through lack of opportunity, resources, health or education. Sen (1999: 85) calls for poverty alleviation programmes 'focusing directly on the substantive freedoms of the individuals involved' and for a 'general approach that concentrates on the capabilities of people to do things, and the freedom to lead lives, that they have reason to value'. The CFST programme aims to promote the capabilities of the children involved and particularly to increase the choices and opportunities they have to lead lives that they have reason to value.

There has been a paucity of studies relating the CA in determining children's perspectives in poverty alleviation programmes. Biggeri *et al.* (2006: 60) stress the importance of 'seeing the child as a subject having identifiable capabilities and considering children not simply as recipients of freedom, but as participants in the process of identifying a set of core capabilities'. They also observe that 'The capability approach per se is a powerful tool for understanding a child's well-being since we are forced to think about the complexities that characterize a child's life' (p. 77). Other researchers have noted the importance of childhood experiences in establishing future prospects in adult life. Bornstein (1989) (quoted in Yacub 2008: 440) states that 'some of the evidence shows how favourable development in childhood leads into a good start in early adulthood. People have "sensitive periods" when the development of a particular characteristic is most receptive to influence by environmental factors'. Yacub (2008: 444) puts this concept into a capability perspective by arguing that 'functionings at earlier ages are correlated with functionings at later ages'. Furthermore, Yacub (2008: 450) advocates prioritizing poverty alleviating measures to these 'sensitive periods' such as childhood, 'when the worst damage from poverty can be avoided, when the most gains in functionings can be obtained, and fastest returns accrue'. Other researchers working with children have noted the importance of placing children who are in poverty alleviation programmes at the centre of the programmes' evaluation and of recognizing their abilities to achieve change for themselves and for others in their lives, similar to major proponents of the CA. Nieuwenhuys (2004: 206) notes the need to 'take issue with treating children as passive recipients of expert knowledge and stress the need to acknowledge their *agency . . .*'. In addition, Sen (1999: 11) argues that

> with adequate social opportunities, individuals can effectively shape their own destiny and help each other. They need not be seen primarily as passive recipients of the benefits of cunning development programs. There is indeed a strong rationale for recognizing the positive role of free and sustainable agency.

The need to involve children as active participants in programmes aimed at improving their opportunities in life (such as CFST) is recognized as having an intrinsic value and not only for the benefit of the potential adults they will become and the society they will contribute to in the future. Comim (2011: 338) notes that 'children are not simply "becomings" they are also "beings" with values, personalities, imagination, feelings and dreams. And they need to be considered as such by having their views considered as standards for assessing and monitoring their development'. Similarly, when appraising CFST activities and other development initiatives involving children there is a need to recognize that 'conceptualizing children as active agents and co-producers of their capabilities enables fresh insights into how capabilities can initially be built and subsequently assessed' (Comim *et al.*, 2011: 5).

Methodology

The use of focus groups with children

The study used CA-based participatory appraisal similar to those developed in previous studies in Samoa and Christchurch (Schischka, 2005), and with groups of parents of pre-school children in Vanuatu (see Swain *et al.*, 2008). The focus groups allowed for evaluation of the programme's progress in terms of criteria that are especially relevant to the participants in the programmes. The use of focus groups when conducting research with children is well established in the literature. Hennessey and Heary (2005: 237) note 'a considerable rise in the number of publications where focus groups were used with children and teenagers' and that 'focus groups are a versatile method of gathering qualitative data with children from as young as eight years old through to adolescence' (p. 250). There are a wide range of methodologies that are possible to use with children, such as art, photography journaling and other written responses. Freeman and Mathison (2009: 103) note that focus groups offer the opportunity to 'engage children with a common set of activities, or bring together participants who have had a common experience or life situation [and] are suitable for children of all ages'. Mauthner (1997) argued that focus groups are suitable for investigating the perspectives of children as they constitute a safe peer environment for children and replicate the kind of group work that children are familiar with in the classroom setting. Indeed, focus groups can help to rectify the power imbalance between child and adult that may exist in a one-to-one interview. Levine and Zimmerman (1996) state that focus groups involving children allow the participants to be the experts sharing their experiences with a group of their peers rather than being individually questioned by an outside adult expert. Hennessy and Heary (2005) note that children may be more inclined to give their opinion when they hear others do so and they can be prompted to remember events via the input of their contemporaries in a group discussion. Also, the context of a group discussion can provide a much richer dialogue than relying solely on individual interviews.

While there are a number of advantages to focus group interviews with children, it is also necessary to be aware of potential disadvantages. Hennessy and Heary (2005) point out that there is the possibility of group dynamics resulting in intimidation of some participants, or that shy children may be unwilling to contribute in the presence of others who are more articulate. Consequently there is great importance placed on the role of the moderator in effectively managing the focus group to ensure that all participants can express their views. Westcott and Littleton (2005) point to the challenges of interviewing children and highlight what they describe as the 'myth ... that interviewing [children] is an easy research method' (p. 141). They outline a host of issues including arranging access, obtaining consent from children and their parents or caregivers, confidentiality and ethical dilemmas. But despite these challenges they argue that 'children's perspectives are central to research, policy and practice' and that 'far from being passive recipients of the adult's utterances, they are actively making sense of the interview situation for themselves'.

Outline of focus groups used

In developing the focus group methodology for this study, close reference was made to the guidelines developed by experienced researchers in working with children. Westcott *et al.* (2002), as reported in Westcott and Littleton (2005: 151) reviewed the style of questioning appropriate for children from a range of studies. Among their guidelines the following were incorporated into the construction of the discussion guide for the interviews.

Open-ended question forms (for example, the 'Wh' questions such as 'what?') encourage much longer responses from children with more detailed replies, than focused or specific questions. Closed-ended questions that require single-word responses from children such as 'yes' and 'no' should be avoided. Such guidelines are useful in many research interview situations, not only with children. However, it is particularly important when interviewing young people where there are considerable prospects for a perceived and real power imbalance between the adult interviewer and the children. Similarly, during the course of the interviews care was taken to put into practice the recommendations of Westcott and Littleton (2005) and McLeod (2008), who note that interviewers should resist the temptation to interrupt children being interviewed, and should be prepared to tolerate long pauses and not expect questions to lead the respondents to a desired response.

Focus group interviews were conducted in five South Auckland schools with five groups of six participants selected to be CFST children. The five schools selected by CFST Charitable Trust are all located in the poorest part of Auckland, New Zealand's largest city, which has a population of 1 million. The schools are all ranked as either decile 1, 2 or 3 where a decile ranking of 1 is the poorest income area and decile 10 is the richest, based on the income of the parents of the students at the school according to census data. The focus group interviews were carried out at the beginning of the first year of the programme and were then repeated twice in that year and then three times in the second year, so as to ascertain the main trends in the perspectives of the participants. The interviews were scheduled at times and locations selected as appropriate by the schools so as to minimize the impact on the activities of the students. Separate groups of teachers, parents and caregivers were interviewed to determine their views on what was happening for the children in the CFST programmes.

Interview procedure

The interviews generally began with an introduction by the programme director of CFST Charitable Trust who then left so that the participants could feel free to express their opinions. Before the focus group interviews began, the children and their parents/caregivers had signed forms giving their consent to participation. At the beginning of the interview the participants were given a brief overview of the aims of the evaluation and were informed that their participation was entirely voluntary, that they could leave at any time and that their anonymity was guaranteed. All the participants present at the start of the interviews stayed to the end and generally they all contributed well to the discussions, although there was some initial shyness demonstrated and at times there were long silences.

Analysis of the focus group interviews

A summary discussion of the main themes that came up in the different focus groups in the community is given in the following sections. To gain an understanding of the expectations of the children when they were first selected for the programme, the first two questions were asked.

Could you please tell us what StandTall is?

The comments from the initial question indicate that the reputation of CFST has been firmly established with some reference to the CFST expo held earlier in the year to raise awareness of what would be involved. Many reported that they thought the programme would develop leadership and help them to learn how to achieve goals. Some talked about the anticipation they had regarding social contacts while others focused on particular activities like camping. A common feeling was that CFST would involve meeting inspirational people and having experiences that would allow them to have a more successful life.

What are you going to do on the programme?

Many participants reported being clear about what to expect from their involvement in CFST. The most common expectations related to going on camp (which was the first major activity) and the prospects of meeting famous television and sporting personalities. Particular outdoor activities were also keenly anticipated such as abseiling, rock climbing and kayaking. Some were looking forward to having fun and socializing with other students.

Is there any activity that you are particularly looking forward to?

This question (and the other ones that followed) was asked in the first focus group and again at the final focus group at the end of the second year, to ascertain what changes, if any, may have occurred during this time in the views of the children. The answers to each question are reported here in two parts, (a) before the children started and (b) after the students had been participating for some time. Initially, going on camp and the opportunity to meet famous people were the two most popular activities, with training with national sports teams also important.

What was your favourite StandTall activity and why?

The camp was overwhelmingly the most popular activity with all children. They particularly enjoyed the chance to try new things which took them out of their usual experiences, built their confidence and gave them opportunities to make new friends among other children. Although some reported that they found some of the activities physically challenging it was apparent that they had all realized the considerable gains they had made in confidence during the camp. A visit to some local fashion studios was also very popular, generally owing to the opportunity it offered for them to develop new skills. A farm visit was also mentioned favourably for the encounters with the various animals. The visits to the TV studios, the Westin Hotel and the All Blacks training session were popular generally because of the opportunities available to participate in activities. Others talked about the visits to city tertiary institutions (to look at future study options), work experience sites and the careers expo as being important for them in giving them ideas about what they could do in the future and how they could achieve their goals. The community project (which involved the potentially unappealing activity of clearing rubbish from Eastern Beach) was actually mentioned as enjoyable owing to the chance to work together with other students and to give something back.

What do you hope to learn or gain from StandTall?

The children reported diverse expectations about what they hoped to gain or learn. While there was no one dominating hope, some of the main themes in their comments revolved around anticipated increases in confidence, willingness to take risks and being able to face their fears. Some made mention of specific skills they hoped to develop such as kayaking and public speaking. A predominant feeling remembered by the children when applying was that they saw participating in CFST as a means to follow their dreams and achieve their goals. Related to this was their intention to become more confident, be a role model for others and to try new experiences and activities. When the children looked forward one year and described how they imagined they would be different after significant time involved in CFST, the predominant response was the belief that they would be less shy, be more able to talk in public and more willing to be adventurous and take risks. Other common sentiments centred on being able to share with others such as family and friends, to give and receive support and encouragement, achieve goals and be a better role model.

What have you gained from the StandTall activities?

Underpinning all the discussion of how the children thought they had benefited from involvement in CFST was increased self-confidence and self-belief. While some students reported expecting to be more confident in the focus groups at the beginning of the first year, it was apparent from the end of year interviews that this gain in confidence was much greater than they had expected and that it was now manifest to them in a number of concrete ways – from greater willingness to speak out, to increased ability to take leadership roles, to increased independence.

The children reported a wide range of personal benefits as a result of their participation in StandTall activities across the previous year. Common gains they felt they had made revolved around self-respect and relations with others, including trust and the ability to work as part of a team. A number also talked about how they could see benefits flowing on to other aspects of their lives at school and at home, such as willingness to cooperate, contribute and to take leadership roles as well as to concentrate in school work. They also talked positively of increased willingness to try new experiences. The children talked readily about how various activities during the year and the final CFST prizegiving held at the end of the year had enabled them to take social risks by speaking publicly in front of their peers and others as well as being more willing to join in and offer their thoughts in group activities. Related to this was the view among a number of children that their belief in themselves and their abilities had increased considerably in the course of the year. These reflections by the children were reflected in the comments of the various school staff, CFST coordinators and parents/caregivers.

From a practical perspective the children talked about the knowledge they had gained that would set them up for the future. They could give many examples of skills they had gained such as public speaking and relating to others that they could use in other situations and would be useful in their future prospects. The knowledge they had gained was of considerable importance in helping them decide what careers they might want to pursue. Some talked enthusiastically about careers that they now thought possible for them because of the visits they had made to tertiary institutions. It was apparent that for most of them it was the first time they had had the chance to visit such places of higher learning, to talk with people who taught and studied there. One example cited by a number of students was a meeting with a law lecturer at Auckland University of Technology. They were not only informed about the courses that were available but were also clearly impressed about her life story, about her early challenges in her studies and how her early life was not that dissimilar to their own. Others talked in similar ways about what they had learned from teachers in fashion design and mechanical engineering. Visits to workplaces such as the Westin Hotel and the New Zealand Air Force also produced many favourable comments from the children, especially concerning future employment opportunities that they would never have considered before. In contrast, a few said the visits to workplaces and tertiary education institutes had not changed what they wanted to do. Seeing people from similar backgrounds to their own, studying and working in a variety of areas, meant that they were now more determined than ever to pursue their goals. The importance of these initial experiences with work and study provided by CFST is reflected in the literature. Legum and Hoare (2004: 154) note that 'as students begin to connect their academic accomplishments with the expectations of the world of work, they are more likely to understand the significance of remaining in school and may make more prudent decisions concerning their short- and long-term futures'. A common comment from the children was that the various work experiences and visits to tertiary institutions and workplaces had made them realize not only what they might want to do in their future careers but also what they needed to do at high school and in the future to accomplish these career goals.

When asked about the most difficult thing they had done in CFST, most mentioned social skill activities such as giving speeches, although they also commented on how this had become easier for them during the course of the year with the opportunities they had in the programme. Others talked about the physical challenges they had undertaken at camp such as abseiling and hiking. A common theme in this discussion on mental and physical challenges revolved around how they had come to realize the importance of perseverance and how they had become aware of how they had improved at activities over time.

Another aspect discussed was the benefits of both mentoring and being mentored by fellow students. Year 8 students in their second year of CFST activities were required to meet regularly with Year 7 students. There was an overwhelmingly favourable response from the younger students regarding their experiences of being mentored by the Year 8 students who had been through the Year 7 programme last year. They particularly enjoyed the support, the questions and the advice they received. Developing communication skills, leadership abilities and sharing knowledge were common benefits the Year 8 leaders saw resulting from their time mentoring the Year 7 children. The importance of the opportunities for peer and community support offered by CFST is reflected in the literature on children's educational achievement. In a major best evidence synthesis study for the New Zealand Ministry of Education, Biddulph *et al.* (2003: 45) report on community and family influences on children's achievement in New Zealand and comment that:

> ambient positive peer influences for learning include a) positive role models and supportive social contexts for learning, b) 'safety nets' for intellectual and emotional risk-taking, c) understanding to enable children to cope, communicate and otherwise realise their potential as learners and people, and d) settings for sharing educational resources and cultural capital.

Downey (2008: 61) discusses the benefits to older students when they are given the opportunity to work with younger students. She notes that at-risk students tend to experience educational resilience when they have opportunities to develop skills in communicating, coping with stress, managing conflict, problem-solving, decision-making and critical thinking. From the camps at the beginning, through the ongoing mentoring and cooperative excursions as well as the concluding prizegiving event, it was apparent that the CFST programme provided many such opportunities for the children involved to experience the positive influences of peer support and learning.

There was discussion about the gains that could be made for the children's friends and families because the children were participating in CFST. There was some concern expressed by a number of participants that their friends (and sometimes members of their families) would be jealous of them being chosen for CFST and the experiences they would have. However, most saw positive impacts on those around them – many reporting that their family were very proud and supported them. A number talked about the possibility that they would be able to be role models to siblings and friends who may be able to follow in taking more risks.

Conclusion

In conclusion, the children talked about what they had learned about the challenges of balancing the CFST activities with their normal school routines. While they sometimes found keeping up with both difficult, a number talked about how they had learned some valuable lessons about managing their time and about what they could achieve if they were motivated. Such ongoing awareness of what is happening for the children is vital for them if they are to fully realize the benefits of programmes such as CFST. Many of the easily quantifiable outcomes from such programmes operating with children are best determined in the long term, such as higher achievement in secondary education or improved participation in secondary education. However, relying solely on this long-term analysis does not allow for the voice of the children to be heard. This long-term time frame also does not suit the funding providers who often want much shorter-term feedback. Using an ongoing CA based participatory methodology of monitoring a programme such as CFST will allow for a much enhanced and more immediate view of what the children see for themselves is happening while they are taking part.

The interviews with participants in CFST revealed significant gains in terms of skills and opportunities for the children selected. Discussions with the teachers and parents/caregivers of these children indicated that already they show some signs of increased confidence and willingness to engage in learning opportunities. However, it is apparent that these gains cannot be adequately appraised by looking only at measures such as monetary gains or improvements in academic performance. Many anticipated an increase in confidence and looked forward to new experiences, and from the focus groups at the end of the second year it was apparent that the CFST programme provided both. The social context in which the children developed competencies challenged and supported them in this development over a wide range of activities and social situations. It helped to develop capabilities and learning opportunities for the children which may be useful to them for their future lives. As CFST uses both peer and adult mentors, the children see people they value and look up to and model these competencies, leading to an increase in the likelihood that they too will develop and use them over a wide range of situations and into the future. It is also important that focus groups place the children at the centre of the evaluation process and that they provide the means by which the children can reflect on what is changing for them and what they have achieved in the CFST programme.

The transcripts indicated that participatory evaluation using the CA is effective in assessing capability development from a child's perspective. James (1999: 246), writing about psychological research with children, notes that,

> recognizing children as people with abilities and capabilities different from, rather than simply less than, adults may persuade us to be more adventurous in our methodology to find ways in which we can engage children in our research so our research *on* childhood can be effected through research *with* children.

James no doubt intends the term *capabilities* here in its general English definition rather than the specific meaning in Sen's CA in evaluating the benefits of development programmes aimed at enhancing the choices and opportunities for children, such as CFST. However, it is argued here that it is essential to consider the *capabilities* of the children in the sense of the word discussed in the CA. As discussed in earlier chapters, according to Sen (1992: 40), a person's capability 'represents the various combinations of functionings (beings and doings) that the person can achieve'. Functionings are what Sen (1999: 75) calls 'the various things a person may value being and doing'. Ballet *et al.* (2011) outline the case for the development of a wider theoretical and policy basis to better encapsulate what they term children's 'evolving capabilities'. In order to achieve this they advocate for enhanced opportunities for children to participate in programmes and policies that are aimed at enhancing these evolving capabilities. The methodology developed in this study with CFST offered the opportunity to ascertain the valued functionings of the children participating and how they perceived their capabilities changing as their involvement continued. There remains the difficulty of summing up all the opportunities resulting for the children involved in CFST after only two years of the programme. While some more qualitative benefits such as increased confidence, increased awareness of future career and work options are apparent, it is also clear that many of the more quantifiable results of the programme such as enhanced performance in secondary education qualifications and higher participation in post-compulsory education can only be determined in future by comparison of these children with their peers in such activities. There is the opportunity to track these 30 children as they progress through high school and possibly on into post-compulsory education to ascertain changes in their long-term outcomes. In the meantime it is argued here that there are clear benefits of using an ongoing capability-based participatory evaluation of the programmes with the children so that they have the opportunity to reflect and report on changes that are happening for them.

References

Ballet, J., Biggeri, M. & Comim, F. (2011) 'Children's agency and the capability approach: a conceptual framework' in Biggeri, M., Ballet, J. & Comim, F. (eds) *Children and the Capability Approach*, Palgrave Macmillan, Basingstoke.

Biddulph, F., Biddulph, J. & Biddulph, C. (2003) *The Complexity of Community and Family Influences on Children's Achievement in New Zealand: Best Evidence Synthesis*. A report prepared for the New Zealand Ministry of Education by Biddulph Educational Consultants, Ministry of Education, Wellington.

Biggeri, M., Libanora, R., Mariani, S. & Menchini, L. (2006) 'Children conceptualising their capabilities: results of a survey conducted during the first children's congress on child labour', *Journal of Human Development*, 7(1), pp. 59–83.

Bornstein, M. (1989) 'Sensitive periods in development: structural characteristics and causal interpretations', *Psychological Bulletin*, 105, pp. 179–197.

CFST (Choice Foundation StandTall) (2013) *About Us*, www.choicefoundation.org.nz/about-us, accessed 19 April 2013.

Comim, F. (2011) 'Developing children's capabilities: the role of emotion and parenting style' in Biggeri, M., Ballet, J. & Comim, F. (eds) *Children and the Capability Approach*, Palgrave Macmillan, Basingstoke.

Comim, F., Ballet, J., Biggeri, M. & Iervese, V. (2011) 'Theoretical foundations' in Biggeri, M., Ballet, J. & Comim, F. (eds) *Children and the Capability Approach*, Palgrave Macmillan, Basingstoke.

Downey, J.A. (2008) 'Recommendations for fostering educational resilience in the classroom', *Preventing School Failure*, 53(1), pp 53–64.

Freeman, M. & Mathison, S. (2009) *Researching Children's Experiences*, The Guilford Press, New York.

Freire, P. (1996) *Pedagogy of the Oppressed*, Penguin, London.

Hennessey, E. & Heary C. (2005) 'Exploring views through focus groups,' in Greene, S. & Hogan, D. (eds) *Researching Children's Experience Approaches and Methods*, Thousand Oaks, CA: Sage, 236–252.

Infometrics (2011) *1000 Days to Get it Right for Every Child: The Effectiveness of Public Investment in New Zealand Children*. Report prepared by Infometrics Ltd for Every Child Counts, Every Child Counts, Wellington.

James, A. (1999) 'Researching children's social competence: methods and models, in Woodhead, M., Faulkner, D. & Littleton, K. (eds) *Making Sense of Social Development*, Routledge, London, 231–249.

Legum, H.L. & Hoare, C.H. (2004) 'Impact of a career intervention on at-risk middle school students' career maturity levels, academic achievement and self-esteem', *Professional School Counselling*, 8(2), pp. 148–155.

Levine, I.S. & Zimmerman, J.D. (1996) 'Using qualitative data to inform public policy: evaluating Choose to De-Fuse', *American Journal of Orthopsychiatry*, 66(3), pp. 363–77.

Mauthner M. (1997) 'Methodological aspects of collecting data from children: lessons from three research projects,' *Children and Society*, 11(1), pp. 16–28.

McLeod, A. (2008) *Listening to Children: A Practitioner's Guide*, Jessica Kingsley, London.

Nieuwenhuys, O. (2004) 'Participatory action research in the majority world', in Fraser, S., Lewis, V., Ding, S., Kellett, M. & Robinson, C. (eds) *Doing Research with Children and Young People*, Sage, London, 206–221.

OECD (2009) *Doing Better for Children*, OECD, Paris.

O'Neill, O. (2001) *Autonomy and Trust in Bioethics* (the Gifford Lectures, University of Edinburgh 2001), Cambridge University Press, Cambridge.

O'Neill, O. (2002) *A Question of Trust* (BBC Reith Lectures 2002), Cambridge University Press, Cambridge.

Ortiz, I., Moreira Daniels, L. & Engilbertsdottir, S. (2012) *Child Poverty and Inequality: New Perspectives*, UNICEF, New York.

Schischka, J.A. (2005) *The capabilities approach in economic development*, PhD thesis, Lincoln University, Christchurch.

Sen, A.K. (1992) *Inequality Re-examined*, Clarendon Press, Oxford,

Sen, A.K. (1999) *Development as Freedom*, Alfred A. Knopf, New York.

Sen, A.K. 2005 'Human Rights and Capabilities' *Journal of Human Development* Vol. 6 pp151–166.

Swain, P., James, J. & Schischka, J. (2008) *Janis Blong Toktok: Pri-Skul Asosiesen Blong Vanuatu and the role of New Zealand Volunteers*, Volunteer Service Abroad, Wellington.

Westcott, H.L. & Littleton, K.S. (2005) 'Exploring meaning in interviews with children', in Greene, S. & Hogan, D. (eds) *Researching Children's Experience: Approaches and Methods*, London, Sage.

Westcott, H.L., Davies, G.M. & Bull, R.H.C (2002) *Children's Testimony: Psychological Research and Forensic Practice*, Chichester, Wiley.

Yacub, S. (2008) 'Capabilities over the life course: at what age does poverty damage most?' in Comim, F., Qizilbash, M. & Alkire, S. (eds) *The Capability Approach*, Cambridge, Cambridge University Press.

9

Agency, Participation and Transitions Beyond School

Caroline Sarojini Hart

Introduction

In this chapter, attention is focused on developing new understandings of the nature of transition in relation to the concepts of Amartya Sen's capability approach (1992, 1999a, 1999b).[1] The discussion draws on empirical data from two studies undertaken in Yorkshire in the UK. As discussed earlier in Chapter 1, the capability approach highlights that individuals with the same resources may have variable abilities to convert those resources into capabilities and ultimately ways of being and doing they have reason to value. There is a complex range of dimensions that may come together to generate conversion factors that have both positive and negative impacts on young people's aspirations. For instance, conversion factors linked to family circumstances, cultural practices or geographical circumstances may lead to a young person failing to realize an aspiration. In this chapter the nature of conversion factors is scrutinized in order to consider the positioning of individual conversion factors within broader transitional processes.

The empirical data are drawn from one study conducted in Bradford, West Yorkshire and a second study undertaken in Sheffield, South Yorkshire, in the North of England. The stimulus for the research was the UK government's widening participation policy which suggested that 'raising' young people's aspirations would lead to increased enrolment figures in higher education. In total over 1,000 young people aged 14–19 took part in the research aiming to explore the nature of young people's aspirations and their relationship to capabilities.[2] The Bradford study (Study 1) involved student focus groups, interviews and a survey to explore young people's aspirations and the factors that helped and hindered their achievement. Study 1 participants were drawn from a multicultural 11–18 comprehensive school in an area of high socioeconomic deprivation. The Sheffield study (Study 2) involved individual and group interviews with students, as well as a survey to further understanding of the factors influencing young people's decisions about higher education and other pathways beyond school and college.[3] In Study 2, young people were drawn from four schools and colleges from areas with both high and low participation in higher education and from a range of socioeconomic and cultural groups. In Sheffield many pupils attended schools only for 11–16-year-olds and if they wished to remain in education they had to choose between post-16 colleges and 'sixth forms' based in 11–18 schools. The colleges were situated in the northeast of the city and the latter were situated in the southwest of the city. The combined research findings from both studies help to extend understandings of the conversion factors influencing young people's pathways beyond school and college.

In light of reflections on the data from the two studies, a new conceptualization of 'transition' is developed in order to aid understanding of the dynamics of conversion factors regarding individuals' transitions beyond school and college. The analysis begins with some reflection on the conceptualization of the nature of aspirations and their relationship with capabilities.

Rethinking aspirations

Previous measures of aspiration have been linked to educational- and career-related achievements. Assumptions are made in government discourses about the possibility of ranking and raising aspirations, but aspirations can relate to many aspects of life and this was evident in both Study 1 and Study 2. For example in Study 1, examples of young people's aspirations included to 'find inner peace', to 'have a healthy social life', to 'become a proper baptized Sikh' and to, 'get married and have a family'. These contrasting and diverse aspirations resonate with Appadurai's view that 'aspirations are never simply individual. They are always formed in the interaction and in the thick of social life' (2004: 67). Earlier work by Hart (2004) has highlighted the crucial role of individual agency in the development and expression of aspirations. The degree of agency varies from high to low, influenced, for example, by individual levels of autonomy and social relations with others. From a capability perspective, it becomes apparent that aspirations are born from the 'capability to aspire' and individuals' abilities to develop this capability are variable (Hart, 2012a). Aspiration is a functioning but the freedom to aspire is a capability. Hart (2012a: 79) observes:

Aspirations may be related to any aspect of an individual's life and often aspirations cover multiple aspects of life experience … At the individual level, aspirations can be viewed as both goal-oriented and concerning the future of the self or the agency of the self in relation to goals concerning others. Understanding the nature of aspiring tells us more comprehensively about the freedom an individual has to develop capabilities and to choose to pursue a future they have reason to value.

A young person's interests and affiliations may influence their aspirations. For example, one young participant commented, 'I want to start Leeds [University] because it's got an Islamic society'. In this case, understanding the importance of religious faith to this individual helps to build a picture of how he is going about consideration of possible opportunities beyond school. For this young male it is not only the institution's reputation or the course that is of interest but the freedom to continue to pursue his faith.

Conversion factors

The process of converting resources, and other forms of capital,[4] into the 'capability to aspire' is subject to multiple conversion factors (Hart, 2010). Similarly, although two individuals may have the capability to aspire, they may exercise this capability to greater or lesser degrees, mediated by a range of variable conversion factors, such as family expectations. Hart has argued that an individual's 'aspiration set' is crucial in helping to shape an individual's 'capability set' and thus the real freedoms they have to pursue ways of being and doing that they have reason to value (Hart, 2012a: 80). There are many factors that affect an individual's 'capability to aspire' in the first place as well as their capability to transform aspirations into capabilities, that is real opportunities to pursue ways of being and doing that the individual has reason to value. These factors may collectively be referred to as 'conversion factors'. Thus a 'distillation' of aspirations into capabilities takes place followed by a second distillation of capabilities into functionings and this is illustrated in Figure 9.1.

Earlier work by Hart (2010, 2012a) has indicated that the transition from one stage of this model to the next occurs within wider social arrangements, and conversion factors are linked to different fields in which the individual is engaged. As Clark notes in Chapter 4, 'humans must be analysed as social beings rather than as autonomous choosers' and therefore we need to look at the social context of choice as well as the decisions individuals make. Those aspirations that are not

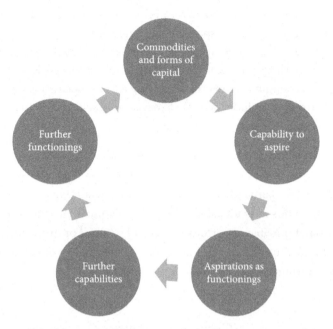

Figure 9.1 Model of aspiration formation and transformation to capability

converted immediately into capabilities may be converted at a later stage or they may be adapted into new aspirations (that are deemed more easily achievable or less threatening to others) by the individual. Many aspirations fall by the wayside as they are perceived to be unattainable by the individual. Relationships with and interventions by governments, local communities, families, schools and other networks may increase the conversion rate of aspirations into capabilities, that is from a dream to a tangible reality.

Conversion factors are generated, stabilized and destabilized through symbiotic relationships between social actors in a range of cultural and physical environments. Moreover, conversion factors are interrelated and are active in the processes of developing the capability to aspire through the conversion of i) resources to capabilities, ii) applying the capability to aspire to produce the functioning of aspiring (that is, having aspirations), iii) the transformation of aspirations into capabilities and iv) the conversion of capabilities into functionings. Understanding more about how conversion factors act to enhance or constrain the possibility of an individual transitioning from one stage of the model to the next is key. For example, understanding the transition of an individual with the *aspiration* to learn how to fly to an individual with the *capability*, i.e. real opportunity and freedom, to learn how to fly. In other words, the transition from someone with an aspiration, to someone with a freedom to do or be something they have reason to value. Similarly, there is an emphasis on understanding how the opportunity freedom to learn how to fly is 'converted' into the functioning of actually learning to fly, in other words, the transition from having capability to the related functioning.[5] It becomes apparent that individual conversion factors do not operate in isolation but rather they are integrally linked to processes whereby the individual interacts with, and makes meaning of, their environmental and social relations, as well as their own identities and biographies.[6] At any given point in time, an individual is likely to have resources, aspirations, functionings and capabilities, related to different goals, at different stages of the model shown in Figure 9.1. The discussion now turns to consider the nature of transition in more detail before exploring the empirical data further.

The nature of transition

Transition occurs in relation to some form of change of circumstances. 'Transit' suggests movement across time and space and some of this movement may occur rapidly, almost instantly, whereas other transitory changes may be so gradual they are almost imperceptible. Transition processes may occur consciously or unconsciously, deliberately or by default and may be associated with a range of positive and negative emotions. Life can be construed as constantly in flux on multiple planes. Changes may occur, for example, in relation to education, work, the individual's own sociobiological life course and the constellations of relationships they have with significant others. Change may be linked to interrelated individual, social and environmental processes, structures and systems. For example, where an individual's parents become elderly and frail, their relationship may experience a gradual transition from one where the parents are the dominant carers, providers and 'worriers' for their child (or adult offspring) to one where the roles are reversed.

In educational contexts the notion of transition is widely applied to the process of adjustment that pupils go through in moving from one stage of education or schooling to the next. Key points are identified across the course of young people's engagement in education where there is a particular focus on supporting transition, predominantly in terms of settling into the next stage of education and learning, linked to assessed competences and levels of achievement. Within special educational needs (SEN) and disability studies literature there has been increased interest in seeing the child as a whole person and taking account of the significant others and relationships these individuals form inside and outside of the education setting. There is some insightful work here that could be drawn upon in relation to children and young people of all abilities (Dee, 2006; Terzi, 2007;Trani *et al.*, 2012). For instance, Dee observes that 'transition has been largely synonymous with the period of leaving school' (2006: 3). Regarding transition planning for young people with special needs, Dee identifies three models of transition that can be related to different themes. One model relates to transition as a phase such that, for example, leaving school is not just an event but rather a phase that begins well before and finishes well after the moment of completion of school education. The second model relates to the degree of agency that may vary in different transition processes and for different individuals. A third model of transition relates to time, possibly in terms of the historical period or the individual's life course, or even a period of social change, for example, in terms of children's rights. All of these models have relevance for how we might think about all young people's transitions from school and college to the wider world.

In the UK, transition planning is emphasized in the move from preschool to the foundation year in primary school. It is also an area of emphasis in the transition from one year group to another throughout primary education and in the 'big' transition from primary to secondary school. Though practice varies widely, at the secondary level, attention is given to the transition between year groups, transition from Year 9 to Year 10 (14–15 years of age) when choices about GCSEs[7] are made, transition to sixth form/college, or out of education, and finally transition to higher education, work or further training. In England, SEN coordinators (SENCOS) have a particular responsibility for coordinating transitions for children identified as having SEN. This often involves multidisciplinary team working in partnership with parents. Dee observes, 'for young people with disabilities the process of leaving school and deciding what to do next is conducted largely in public . . . governed by administrative procedures . . . often recorded at formal meetings' (2006: 4). This formulation of transition may be supportive and helpful in many ways. However, it constructs transition as a linear, fixed process rather than the idiosyncratic, dynamic and evolving set of processes that became evident in Studies 1 and 2. The findings from the two studies showed evidence of the micro-complexities of psychosocial transition processes experienced by young people and the ways that this can affect the potential for them to develop their aspirations, capabilities and functionings.

So in thinking about young people approaching the end of compulsory schooling in England (and indeed elsewhere), the processes involved are broader that the geocultural shift of leaving school. There are multiple emotional, social and cognitive transitional processes that young people experience; from home and community to school; family, peer and power relationships; experiences of place, activity, nutrition and exercise. For example, William Bridges has conceptualized 'transition' as having three distinct phases starting, paradoxically, with 'ending', then entering a 'neutral' phase before moving onto 'new beginnings' (Bridges, 2004). In Bridges' model, 'transition' has been distinguished from 'change', with the former associated with personal psychological shifts and the latter with external contextual shifts. This approach has been widely applied in managing changes in the workplace. Essentially, structural, process-driven and organizational changes at work are viewed as external contextual changes. This model seems helpful in thinking about young people's experiences of transition. The human development needed to adapt to these new working conditions is referred to as the actual 'transition' and is seen as relating to the personal psychological process individuals go through in adapting to the changes in the environment around them. Thus there are likely to be behavioural, attitudinal, conceptual, physical and emotional responses to the change. These subtle and often hidden processes are largely underplayed in school plans, provision and wider support for young people and the psychology literature may be insightful in this respect. Hence psychosocial models of behaviour change are relevant in this context. For example, Prochaska and DiClemente's (1983) 'model of change', primarily developed to support clients experiencing drug- and alcohol-related problems, is insightful. Professionals working with clients experiencing drug- and alcohol-related problems use the model of change to work with individuals to move them through the stages of *precontemplation, contemplation, determination, action* and *maintenance*. In the case of substance use, precontemplation refers to the stage where individuals are not contemplating changing their behaviour. A shift to the second stage (contemplation) signals that the individual is now in a state of contemplating changing their substance use behaviour. At the next stage of the model (determination) the individual determines that they do wish to make a change in their behaviour and in the ensuing preparation stage they plan the changes and the support they will need to be successful. Attention is also paid by the client and professional to the possible 'cues' that may entice the individual back to their old behaviours and strategies and techniques are used to reduce the efficacy of such cues. The final stage in the model is maintenance, where the individual continually strives to maintain their new behaviour. A crucial aspect of Prochaska and DiClimente's model is that 'relapse' is an event that could occur at any stage in the model and this is readily apparent in relation to substance misuse.

The 'model of change' is helpful in thinking about the different stages that young people experience in deciding to, for example, start a new job or a new educational course after leaving school. It also highlights that 'success' is not guaranteed and there are many hurdles to overcome at each stage of thinking about and acting on the process of change from one set of circumstances to another, for instance, from living with parents and being in full-time education, to living independently. Relatively little attention is paid to these complex micro-processes of behavioural change that occur alongside the more explicit physical steps towards destinations beyond school and college, for example, in terms of completing application forms and stating preferences for particular courses of study. However, without sufficient personal resilience or external support the chances of 'relapse' or failure to achieve aspirations may be much more likely. So in thinking about young people's transitions, attention is drawn to the iterative nature and the deep psychological shifts that are required in order to move (psychosocially) from one set of circumstances to another. The phenomenon of transition is more than a logistical series of steps or the simple consequence of academic achievement or interview success.

Techniques of transition

Individuals in the two studies highlighted a range of ways in which they developed and utilized strategies to facilitate their transition beyond school or college. Thus a set of 'techniques of transition' was conceived based on the analysis of the findings from S1 and S2. These constructs are introduced and discussed further below.

Scoping

Young people in the study engaged in behaviour that can be interpreted as 'scoping' possible future opportunities. An analogy would be a lookout on a sailing ship, climbing to the crow's nest to see how the land lies in different directions. Based on the information that can be gathered individuals begin to make decisions about where they may wish, or be able, to travel. Regarding plans beyond school, different individuals adopted a variety of styles of scoping. For some the process was methodical, whereas for others it seemed more haphazard, chaotic or passive. The technique of scoping might be guided or intentional, but also individuals might stumble upon possible opportunities.

Mapping[8]

Appadurai (2004) describes a 'map of aspirations' and it is possible to conceive that in conjunction with scoping opportunities, individuals mentally 'map' out the possible range and breadth of opportunities they perceive that they have for the future. Application of this technique appears to be a fluid process with some opportunities fluctuating between those deemed possible and those seen as impossible. Research has shown that aspirations are 'dynamic and multidimensional' and may be related to numerous aspects of an individual's life (Hart, 2004, 2012a). At any given point in time, an individual is likely to have multiple aspirations at different stages of development, in transition to capability or in a dormant stage due to prioritizing or absence of the opportunity to fulfil a particular goal. Some aspirations are connected, even sequential, whilst others may conflict and undoubtedly many young people change their aspirations over time.

Aspirations are arguably linked to an individual's perception of opportunities. For example, the S1 study of young people in Bradford (Hart, 2004) showed that local employment trends influenced the aspirations of youth. Duflo (2012: 4, 52) has commented that 'the existence of a step that is too high to climb creates a rational temptation to hold back ... goals that are bite-sized and achievable may be necessary for people to get started'. Thus an individual's perceptions of what might be possible may have a strong influence on their attempts to map out particular futures. Metaphorically, some options will not even appear on the map for some individuals, not necessarily because they are not available, but because the individual does not perceive them to be. Similarly, others will map out perceived opportunities that onlookers might deem impossible to reach.

Planning

The third technique identified was 'planning'. The processes of scoping and mapping can help to identify the range, breadth and juxtaposition of an individual's different aspirations and possible opportunities. This evolving seascape may be punctuated by short, medium and longterm goals. These goals may seen more or less easily achievable. There was evidence in the empirical studies that the young people varied in their propensity to actively plan their futures and the steps needed to achieve particular aspirations. In some cases there was evidence that a young person was carefully seeking information about what would help them stage by stage and yet other individuals were much more ad hoc in their activities. Crucial information was often absent during critical stages of decision-making which meant goals became unexpectedly out of reach. Thus developing specific planning techniques and strategies may help enhance indviduals' agency and support their transition experiences.

Navigation

The fourth technique that emerged from reflection on the study data was 'navigation'. Continuing the analogy of the sailing ship, once an interesting destination, or set of destinations, has been sighted, then the individual has to navigate their way there, potentially having to overcome obstacles along the way. Some obstacles might be permanent and insurmountable but others might be manoeuvrable to some degree. For example, when a young person's parents say they will not allow their daughter to leave home to study at university this may, or may not, be a negotiable obstacle. It is possible that navigational techniques – for example, persuasive dialogue or a compromise to come home at weekends – might provide a way forward. Some individuals have more sophisticated navigational techniques than others and thus 'non-negotiables' are difficult to define. Individual resilience and confidence in dealing with adversity, for example, may help the individual to negotiate their way towards an end goal.

Agency and transition

There seemed to be particular types of features of young people's transition experiences that influenced their agency. These have been grouped conceptually under the headings of motivation, loci of control, synchronicity, transition platforms and 'binding constraints'.[9] A range of conversion factors contributed to each of these features and some examples are given below.

Motivation

Interestingly in both Studies 1 and 2, young people approaching the end of their schooling years indicated that lack of motivation was one of the key factors they felt would prevent them from achieving their aspirations. One of the young people described needing 'the right type of motivation' but in general motivation was seen as important in energizing processes of transition. The following extracts illustrate this further.

Tez: I know that my motivation is something I need. It plays a big part in wanting my aspirations so ... whenever I'm feeling down I just can't be bothered and I just think forget it, you know, it's too hard, why should I go on and there's nothing there to motivate me.

Paula: If I talk about it then it becomes more real and you want it more and more so you're willing to work more and more for it because you don't want to be stuck in a dead-end job and you know, so I think talking about it really does help because it makes you a lot more aware of what you want and how much work you've got to do to get it.

It emerged that individuals experienced what might be seen as 'negative' and 'positive' influences on their motivations. These might alternatively be seen as 'push' and 'pull' factors where negative forces push the individual away from one set of circumstances and positive forces 'pull' the individual towards a new set of circumstances. Paula illuminates the negative 'push' factors further. Regarding the council estate where she was brought up Paula, a white female from Study 2, commented,

I just know that I don't want to bring my children up on there and I want them to have a better life than what I've had. I don't want them to be stuck in a crappy little town and no money ... I don't know, I just want to get away from Bradford and it's a way of getting away from Bradford[10] with no money ... I just don't like Bradford. I think it's rubbish. I get bored, I'm bored in Bradford and I just ... I want to go away from it all. There's nowt keeping me here so why should I stay here?

Paula commented on the aspirations of her mother, and grandmother, which may be construed as positive motivational factors: 'me nan really wants me to do well. She's always wanted us all to do well, do you know. She's really for education ...'.

In this instance, Paula indicated that family factors had influenced her motivations towards particular goals. In other interviews the young participants indicated that significant others such as family, friends and teachers encouraged them in a particular direction. This highlights that motivation, in different forms, can play a crucial role in individual transition processes.

Loci of control

Whilst attempting to develop, express and realize individual aspirations, young people are often the subject of aspirations imposed externally by teachers, families and state institutions via policies, discourses and the dominant behaviours of peer groups. For example, we see this played out in relation to the UK's policies to widen participation in higher education, and more recently to raise the participation age to ensure young people stay in education or training beyond the age of 16 years.[11] These alternative aspirational agendas may be in tension with individual values and aspirations. In the following interview extract, Lucy (aged 18) describes how the careers adviser tried to direct her towards applying for higher education although she was actually interested in taking a 'gap' year after leaving school:

> I went to see her [the careers adviser] like a year ago. Well because I didn't actually fully know what I wanted to do I think I was a bit vague which didn't help but yeah she was, I was like wanting to talk about more about gap years and which internet sites were better to look at and she was like 'oh yes university sites, you should look at these' and I was like 'no I want to talk about gap years'.
>
> Lucy, white female, Study 2

In this second example, Amy describes how the careers adviser tried to persuade her to apply to study ecology at university when she was actually interested in other subjects:

> I just felt like she didn't help me in a way … I didn't get any information afterwards. Even though she said she'd get me information she didn't send it me and I mean I said about how I liked biology and things like that and chemistry and she said 'well I think you should do ecology' which is my worst subject ever and then I said 'oh no I hate it, I hate everything to do in geography and ecology I can't stand [it]' and then she kept pushing the idea of ecology.
>
> Amy, white female, Study 2

Family relationships also help to determine the loci of control. For example, Rani, an Asian female aged 17, indicated on the survey that her parents would 'probably' stop her from achieving her aspirations. In the interview she explained this related to:

> Living away from home. If the perfect course was away from home my parents might [say] 'no, you're not going to do that' and that might stop me achieving if that was the only actual course that I wanted to do … She [mother] come from back home and stuff – Pakistan. She's scared that I would become not more wiser but I'd know more about the world and I think she wants to restrict me from … because then she'd know that I would question why I'm at home and the rest aren't at home and why I wear what I wear and why I have to do some things that other people don't have to do. I don't think she wants that, I don't think she wants me questioning her, I think she just wants me to do what she says.

The transition process is likely to occur more smoothly where the locus of control rests with the young person themselves, rather than with others.

Synchronicity

There are often complex processes at play in the interactions between parents and their children regarding the young people's lives beyond school. These may lead, for example, to tension, conflict, negotiation, compromise and acceptance. It was evident in both the Bradford and Sheffield studies that family ties are strong for many young people and emotions and rationality play different parts in these processes. It became apparent from the interviews with young people that their parents also experienced transitional phases in relation to the aspirations and choices of their children. At times these transitions were in synchrony with the young people, with parents 'getting on board' with young people's plans. At other times there was significant dissonance. For example, Rani explained:

> *Rani:* I'd seriously consider moving away but I don't think my mum would be too happy with that.
>
> *CH:*[12] Right, why not?
>
> *Rani:* I don't have a clue. I always thought that she was all right with it, my parents were actually all right with that but obviously not. Recently when it's actually come to I'm looking at universities now and looking at courses, it's actually come to the point it's sort of like 'oh, no, you're not going away from home'. I think it's just hit her.

In William Bridges' (2004) terms, Rani's mother has not moved into the first stage of transition which is 'ending' and she is still committed to maintaining the status quo. If Rani were to move away from the family home the impact would involve transitions for all the individuals involved. A lack of synchronicity can therefore act as a barrier to transition for many young people.

Transition platforms

In considering how to achieve their aspirations, young people in Study 2 illustrated a range of ways in which they identified what might be termed 'transition platforms' in the transition process. These might be features of life that remain stable or new support systems that come into place as the individual moves into the changed set of circumstances. Platforms may be designed or identified by the young people themselves, they could be put in place by others or might spontaneously occur and be utilized by the individual. They might include family, community, affiliation with a particular group (for instance, a faith-based society, a sports club or a social networking site such as Facebook). Some platforms are 'rocks' with high levels of stability; others may appear to have stability but are actually subject to uncertainty, volatility, erosion, disturbance and fragmentation. For example, staff attrition, a change of headship, a poor Ofsted report and examination irregularities are just a few examples of factors that may reduce the stability of school-based platforms. In relation to the 'traditional' role of transition planning in schools, new support systems might be offered by school staff, for example, through arranging a buddy system for new students with older peers. The 'platforms' can be seen as points of 'safety' during periods of change and psychosocial transition, where the familiar becomes unfamiliar and the unknown has to be accommodated within variably negotiable existing structures. In the interviews with young people in Study 1, religion appeared to be a strong platform for many young people. In Study 2, Helen explained that she was applying for a higher education place at her local university because she knew the bus routes and how to get there. In this case the familiarity of place and routine provided the platforms. Many young people in both studies commented that they would like the professionals who offered them careers advice to be familiar, trusted adults; if this were to be the case, they could act as a 'platform' to support individual transitions. In England in recent years there have been changes to the careers service leading to lowly-qualified personnel without personal knowledge of the young people for whom advice is provided. They are often only available by telephone or email, thus weakening the potential to support young people.

Binding constraints

The 2010 *Regional Human Development Report* for Latin America and the Caribbean identified, 'binding constraints' as those factors associated with one generation that negatively influence the achievements of the next generation (Lopez-Calva and Soloaga 2010: 21). For example, when Tez (Asian female, Study 2) was asked about what she thought her mother would want her to do when she left school, she replied:

> probably stay at home, cooking and cleaning, get married at 18, 19, I don't know. I think it would be ... for my mum it would be more like arranged marriage and my father, if my mum said that's how it is then I think my father would go along with it.

In particular this was related to the perceptions of other family members such as parents, extended family and older siblings in terms of what was possible for themselves. It may be argued that this sociocultural habit then in turn influences the horizons of younger generations in terms of their beliefs about what may be possible for them to achieve. It may be that tension and resistance serve to lower young people's motivation. In this sense young people's transitions are to some extent dependent on the transitions of their parents. Although the emphases of support mechanisms tend to centre on the young person, in fact there is an impetus for adjustments to occur on both sides of any relationship the young person is in, and where transition is occurring, as discussed in Rani's case earlier. Drawing on William Bridges' transition model, Tez's mother is not prepared to 'lose' the state of being she is currently in, namely adhering to her perceived cultural norms. As she has not moved into a 'neutral' phase, if her daughter aspires to do anything other than maintain the cultural traditions of her family she will experience dissonance, tension and potentially conflict. The notion of binding constraints can also be applied to school and college environments and their cultures of channelling pupils through well-worn processes of applying to particular post-16 colleges or automatically applying for university rather than exploring other options.

In Helen's case (Study 2), she had quite negative feelings towards the way she felt her teachers at her 11–16 school had perceived her. She felt that her aspirations were influenced significantly by the contrasting support and 'faith' that she experienced, first in the 11–16 setting and then later at Sherwood College. Helen vividly describes the transition in her construction of self:

CH: How do you think you were viewed by teachers at [your 11–16 school] in terms of where you were gonna end up if you like?

H: Sort of like working class, you know you just and everybody, a lot of people from Sheffield are working class but some have got that spark or whatever they can go on to you know make Sheffield look more intelligent or whatever than it is, instead of just becoming a cleaner or whatever, but I felt working class, like as soon as I leave that's it. I've done my time in forced education and have no interest in going any further than that. They just don't have any faith in me ... It's sort of like not worth me thinking about applying to go to college to then even dare to think about going to university.

Helen said that the key time when young people need their teachers' support and 'faith' is in Years 10 and 11 because that was seen as the crucial turning point in terms of whether individuals would stay in education and 'go any further'. Helen continued, 'there's nowt stopping anybody like me going, you just need to know how to get there'. However, at her 11–16 school, Croft Corner, Helen did not feel she was getting any help in developing this knowledge of 'how to get there'. In the light of these examples, the following section gives further consideration to the role of professionals in supporting young people in their transitions beyond school and college and the potential to enhance individuals' capabilities in this respect.

The role of professionals

Educational professionals have the potential to provide stability, familiarity and support to young people, as they plan their futures in the crucial period towards the end of school and college. They are also powerfully positioned in terms of helping young people to develop the skills they may need in order to scope, map, plan and navigate towards their goals. However, there is also a possibility that schools and colleges can become sites of 'binding constraints'. In terms of young people's experiences of support from professionals in the decision about what to do after leaving the 11–16 schools in the Sheffield study, the evidence was mixed. In Study 2, overall, there was a lack of evidence of organized activities to help individuals explore different post-16 education and training opportunities and decisions seemed to be made based on limited information about one or two colleges provided in the school setting. For example, Helen commented that her 11–16 school made no arrangements for pupils to visit post-16 institutions where they could apply to continue their studies. She described her careers adviser as, 'horrible' and said that the main focus in school was preparing students for an interview with the principal of the local sixth-form college. She felt the emphasis was on getting them to that particular college and said, 'nothing really emphasized on the importance of picking courses that are right for you'.

It was apparent from the young people's narratives that the quality and consistency of professional support available through their schools and colleges varied enormously. Although there were some positive comments made, many of the participants described difficulties with gaining the kind of support that they felt was important. It was evident from the Bradford and Sheffield data that there were instances where school and careers staff portrayed narrow views in terms of their aspired trajectories for pupils.

For instance, one young male in Study 2 reported how students at his 11–16 school were encouraged to submit their applications to one particular school sixth form and that prior to his application he had only heard of one other place he could apply to. He commented, 'I didn't know about Queen Elizabeth's and Speedwell [sixth forms] and all these [other places] until after I'd applied for them and by then when I found out it were too late then.'

However, school-based professionals were not viewed as monolithic by the young people in either of the two studies. There was an interesting distinction made between the role of form tutors and the role of subject teachers by some of the young people interviewed in the Sheffield study. In England, school pupils are divided into 'tutor groups' of around 25–30 individuals. Tutors are usually responsible for taking a register at the start of the school day and have pastoral responsibility for their tutor group, usually with some time set aside each week. One female described her form tutor as 'quite narrow minded and focused on her thing. She won't like listen to anyone else'. Another individual described their tutor, saying she was, 'a maths teacher so she doesn't really have a clue what I'm doing'. On the other hand, subject tutors were seen as generally more accessible. For example, Helen (Study 2) commented, 'I see my art teachers like, all day, every day and we've sort of like got a personal thing going and they know what I'm doing so they can ... just better that way'.

Helen's experience at Sherwood College was completely different from her 11–16 setting and the support from staff was a huge boost to her confidence and self-belief. She commented, 'I'm going to university from thinking that nobody cared about what I were gonna do with my future'. Looking back to her time at Croft Corner, Helen said she had not thought about university as an option then, 'not in a million years' did she think she would apply for higher education. She reflected:

> I feel like I am going to university to be a university student and then graduate from being somebody that I now see nobody would take notice of, nobody had faith in, to me getting on to the highest of education I could get into.

At the time of the fieldwork, Connexions were providing careers support and guidance to young people in schools and colleges in Sheffield. However, some research participants saw these advisers as someone to go to when there was a specific problem to address rather than someone to mentor, bounce ideas around and to support individual reflection on possible aspirations and their feasibility. For example, Lee (white male, Study 2) commented,

> the only time I've ever been to Connexions [careers] is like when the teacher says 'right we want everyone to have an interview'. Do you see what I mean? And that's the only time I've seen them. I've never really had any problem that I need to go and see a Connexions adviser.

Access to Connexions advisers was seen as generally limited and not necessarily timely in terms of planning for the future. There was generally no prior relationship between these professionals and the young people, and they were usually perceived as someone to go to if you had a problem rather than as part of an ongoing support or a 'platform' in transition.

The role of families

Alongside transitions related to education, many young people who were interviewed in the two studies described significant transitional experiences linked to their home lives. For example, Amy (white female, Study 2) commented:

> I live with my mum but my mum and my dad got divorced and then my mum remarried to my step-dad who has three children of his own and they used to live with us but now they don't, they live with their mother but we have to pay their maintenance still so the amount of money that we pay maintenance is basically what my parents would use [to pay] for me to go to uni, and my brothers and sisters . . .

Here the constitution of the family has completely changed and one of the impacts identified relates to the possibility of financial support for Amy to go away from home to study at university. Other young people described the physical as well as psychological transitions they made on a regular basis due to living between two parental homes following the breakdown of their parents' relationship. For example, Hanna (white female, Study 2) commented:

> . . . when I'm at my mum's I'm more focused and I'm more like . . . and I do my work because I've got my own room at my mum's and it's a big room and I've got lots of space to do my work and it's not all crowded and it's all organized but when I'm at my dad's I share and it's like the kitchen's a bigger place and then there's our living room and that's really busy and then there's their living room and that's just busy as well and everywhere is really busy because there's so many of us.

Thus, as highlighted elsewhere, families have key roles to play in supporting young people's transitions, with the potential for both positive and negative impacts (Comim, 2011).

Discussion

The interviews with young people revealed that it was common for individuals to hop from one possible career trajectory to another but without necessarily having in-depth knowledge of the roles they were considering. For example, Paula (white female) commented,

> I wanted to teach forever and I wanted to be a doctor but then I'm rubbish at science and now I want to be a solicitor but law's just gone wrong so now I think I want to be a teacher again and just do performing arts.

One young person explained, 'I don't know, I think everyone changes their mind a little bit. I think you get a bit more of a reality check as you get older'. Individuals construct reality in different ways based on contrasting perceptions of whether they feel particular futures are feasible and hence the notion of a 'reality check'. There is a suggestion that there are boundaries between what is, and is not, possible for a given individual, and over time one becomes more knowledgeable about where those boundaries might lie. Another way of looking at this is to consider the roles that different 'players' may have in shifting the socially constructed boundaries of what may be possible. These players might include family members, professionals (e.g., teachers, careers advisers, employers) along with the young people themselves. An individual's capability to navigate transitions will depend on themselves but also their wider support networks and relationships. It was apparent from the young people's narratives that professional roles as 'players' were significant, both positively and negatively, in how young people perceived their options for the future.

The analysis of the data illuminated the way that individuals experience a range of 'steps' in relation to processes of psychosocial transitions. In the beginning the impetus for change may be internally or externally driven and each new scenario will engender different feelings, thoughts and experiences. There will be different sources of motivation in moving towards a different state of being in relation to the particular transition. These motives may be conscious, unconscious, positive, negative, intrinsic or extrinsic. The individual undergoes processes of navigating shifts from one state to another and may look for, or be offered, 'platforms' to help support and scaffold their experience. Where difficulties are encountered, again there will be psychosocial impacts which may be met with resilience, renewed faith, or, at the other end of the spectrum, loss of self-belief and a sense of defeat. David Bridges writes about the pluralistic reasons why individuals might 'adapt' their preferences in terms of the being and doings they have reason to value (Bridges, 2006). The reasons relate to individual, social and environmental factors. Any of these can culminate in the 'reality check' referred to by one of the young research participants.

Concluding remarks

Presently government evaluation of school success at individual and institutional levels is focused on achievement, for example, higher education admissions or the national floor targets in primary education (Shepherd, 2013). The emphasis is on getting 'there', in terms of a particular quality benchmark, and not on the individual's negotiation of transition processes related to converting resources to aspirations, then capabilities and finally functionings.

At any one point in time, young people may experience an eclectic mix of transitional experiences, some gradual, some abrupt, some planned by themselves, some planned by others and some not planned at all. The conversion factors acting on an individual's capability to aspire and their capability to realize aspirations as functionings are crucial in developing human flourishing among children and young people. The analysis of the two studies presented here suggests that the mechanisms of conversion factors seem to be linked to the broader processes of transition. Therefore, developing policies and practices that encourage and support positive conversion factors and help to reduce constraints is important. Public and democratic deliberation, including young people, may help to identify factors that help and hinder the creation of flourishing contexts for capability expansion.

In thinking about how we support children and young people as they grow and develop through schooling there are positive steps that can help them to develop agency and empowerment in relation to the experience of transitions. Understanding the processes that are occurring and developing the skills to scope, map, plan and navigate through different stages of these transition processes are important. Similarly, the capacities to identify opportunities for transition, decision-making, accelerating, decelerating and even neutralizing transition processes are also significant. This might all be encapsulated by the ethos of Amartya Sen's capability approach where individuals are seen to flourish where they have the freedom to choose ways of being and doing they have reason to value (1992). A thick description of transitional states of being and doing is needed in order to highlight the dynamic multi-dimensional context in which the individual chooses the beings and doings they wish to pursue. Possible combinations of functionings are mediated by synchronous and asynchronous configurations of 'conversion factors' that shape the degree to which the individual is able to convert resources and other forms of capital into aspirations, capabilities and, ultimately, functionings. These conversion factors shape the pathways of transition vectors which are variably within the individual's control.

The multi-layered structures and configurations of social relations that influence transition vectors include, for example, relations with family, friends, peers, teachers and significant others in the community. The skills of the individual in working with these relationships will in turn influence their psychosocial experiences of transition. Thus, understanding the structure of transition (e.g., the social relations), the processes of transition (e.g., the nature of relationships, as for example, nurturing, conflicting, coercive) and the individual's experiences of transition (e.g., positive psychological experience, adapting to new space, negative experience, lowering self-esteem and confidence) can all contribute significantly to our insights into the complex nature of transition and its role in relation to young people's capabilities.

Notes

1   Amartya Sen's capability approach is distinguished from other interpretations of the approach as concepts are defined differently, notably in Nussbaum's work. See Hart (2010, 2012a & 2012b) and Nussbaum (2000, 2011) for further discussion.
2   Where interview data are reported throughout this chapter the young people are all aged 17 or 18.
3   Further details about the studies have been reported elsewhere, see Hart (2010 & 2012a).
4   Earlier work by Hart (2012a) has shown how Pierre Bourdieu's forms of capital contribute 'resources' in addition to those more usually included in assessments of individual assets and endowments.
5   Although not all capabilities will be converted to functionings.
6   Robeyns (2005) and Hart (2012a) offer further discussion of the nature and role of conversion factors. Hart draws on Pierre Bourdieu's concepts of 'field', 'capital' and 'habitus' in order to give a deeper sociological understanding of conversion factors relative to earlier models.
7   GCSE stands for General Certificate of Secondary Education and is the term used to refer to the examination(s) generally taken at 16 at the end of Year 11 in England.
8   I am indebted to Arun Appadurai (2004) for drawing my attention to the notion of 'mapping' aspirations although I did not come across his work until some time after developing my own conceptualization of the nature of aspirations (Hart, 2004). I think

the strands of thought are complementary and address slightly different issues and therefore recommend readers who are interested to consider Appadurai's work further.

9   This term is drawn from the *Human Development Report for Latin America and the Caribbean* 2010 (Lopez-Calva and Soloaga) and I am indebted to the authors.

10 Paula is referring to applying for a higher education place.

11 By 2015 the coalition aims to require all young people in England to remain in education or training up until the age of 18 (an extension from the compulsory leaving age of 16 which has been in place over recent decades). The training may be part-time and could be work-based but nonetheless the government is extending its reach in terms of overseeing the lives of 16–18-year-olds.

12 CH refers to the interviewer, Caroline Hart.

References

Appadurai, A. (2004) The capacity to aspire. culture and the terms of recognition, in Rao, V. & Walton, M. (eds) *Culture and Public Action* (Stanford, CA, Stanford University Press).

Bridges, D. (2006) Adaptive preference, justice and identity in the context of widening participation in higher education, *Ethics and Education*, 1(1), pp. 15–28.

Bridges, W. (2004) *Transitions: Making Sense of Life's Changes* (New York, Addison-Wesley).

Comim, F. (2011) Developing Children's Capabilities: The Role of Emotions and Parenting Style in Biggeri, M., Ballet, J. & Comim, F. (eds) *Children and the Capability Approach* (Basingstoke, Palgrave).

Dee, L. (2006) *Improving Transition Planning for Young People with Special Needs* (Maidenhead, Open University Press).

Duflo, E. (2012) *Hope as capability*, Tanner Lecture 2, Harvard University, May 2012.

Hart, C.S. (2004) *A study of students' perceptions of their aspirations and needs in relation to Aimhigher widening participation policy*, MPhil (University of Cambridge, library copy).

Hart, C.S. (2010) Aspirations re-examined: a capability approach to widening participation in higher education, PhD thesis (University of Cambridge).

Hart, C.S. (2012a) *Aspirations, Education and Social Justice: Applying Sen and Bourdieu* (London, Bloomsbury).

Hart, C.S. (2012b) The capability approach and education, *Cambridge Journal of Education*, 42(3), pp. 275–282.

Lopez-Calva, L.F. & Soloaga, I. (eds) (2010) *Regional Human Development Report for Latin America and the Caribbean: Acting on the Future – Breaking the Intergenerational Transmission of Inequality* (New York, UNDP).

Nussbaum, M.C. (2000) *Women and Human Development. The Capabilities Approach* (Cambridge, Cambridge University Press).

Nussbaum, M.C. (2011) *Creating Capabilities: The Human Development Approach* (Cambridge, MA, Harvard University Press).

Prochaska, J. & DiClemente, C. (1983) Stages and processes of self-change in smoking: toward an integrative model of change, *Journal of Consulting and Clinical Psychology*, 5, pp. 390–395.

Robeyns, I. (2005) The Capability Approach: A Theoretical Survey, *Journal of Human Development*, 6(1), pp. 93–114.

Sen, A. (1992) *Inequality Re-Examined*, (Oxford, Clarendon Press).

Sen, A. (1999a) *Commodities and Capabilities* (Oxford, Oxford University Press).

Sen, A. (1999b) *Development as Freedom* (Oxford, Oxford University Press).

Shepherd, J. (2013) Tougher targets mean hundreds more primary schools risk failure, *Guardian*, 5 March, www.guardian.co.uk

Terzi, L. (2007) The capability to be educated, in Walker, M. & Unterhalter, E. (eds) *Amartya Sen's Capability Approach and Social Justice in Education* (Basingstoke, Palgrave Macmillan).

Trani, J-F., Bakhshi, P. & Nandipati, A. (2012) Delivering' education; maintaining inequality: the case of children with disabilities in Afghanistan, *Cambridge Journal of Education*, 42(3), pp. 345–366.

10

School Enrolment and Child Labour

Zina Nimeh and Robert Bauchmüller

Introduction

At the beginning of the new millennium Jordan had shown a noticeable increase in its public expenditure on education compared to the 1970s (2008); an expenditure of 6.4 per cent of its gross domestic product (GDP) on public education was more than the Middle East and North Africa (MENA) average (5.3 per cent). The growth in public investment in education had been accompanied by a growth in net enrolment rates. In 2003, all children at school age were enrolled, grade repetition stood at 0.5 per cent and nearly all children reached Grade 5, the best performance of any country in the MENA region. However, secondary net enrolment rates in Jordan, 87.4 per cent, are lower than the top group of MENA countries. In 2003, 9.7 per cent of 15-year-old children were still not literate. About 61 per cent of children out of school in 2006 were girls (UNESCO, 2009).

There are many children between ages 5 and 16 in Jordan who work in addition to attending school, or who work in place of attending school (NCFA, 2007). Official figures on the incidence of child labour in Jordan are difficult to come by, however there have been several attempts in the past few years to draw attention to this problem (see Al-Rousan, 2000; Gharaibeh and Hoeman, 2003; Hawamdeh and Spencer, 2001). Official figures put the rate of labour among children at 1.9 per cent (DOS-ILO, 2009).

By many accounts, Jordan has shown a strong record of extending school education and reducing child labour as compared to other countries in the MENA region and the rest of the developing world. However, there are still significant numbers of disadvantaged children in Jordan who are deprived from achieving their full educational potential. We wanted to examine whether underperformance in both records was concentrated in specific clusters of disadvantaging factors. Survey data for the years 1996 and 2003 allows us to shed more light on the factors that are related to lower school enrolment at the compulsory age period 6 to 15 years and a higher incidence of paid child labour for the ages 10 to 17. In this empirical study, conducted in 2011, we were interested in going beyond the aggregate, to capture some of the underlying household determinants of not attending school in Jordan and to see if the results are comparable with generic findings that link child labour and school enrolment. We present the Jordanian case along with a discussion of the literature, followed by our empirical results, and then we conclude by recommending future steps for the research agenda pertaining to children.

Literature review on child labour and schooling

An encompassing definition of child labour is given by the International Labour Organization (ILO) as work that deprives children of their childhood, potential and their dignity. It is work that is mentally, physically, socially or morally harmful to children's development; interferes with their schooling by depriving them of the opportunity to attend school; obliges them to leave school prematurely; or requires them to attempt to combine school attendance with excessively long and heavy work (ILO, 2004). UNICEF expands the ILO definition by emphasizing the importance of domestic work by children, that is, in addition to economic work (Chaubey *et al.*, 2007).

Poverty is regarded as the major cause of child labour (Siddiqi and Patrinos, 1995), and various empirical studies make that link (see, for example, Asogwa, 1986; Banerjee, 1991; Meenakshi *et al.*, 1985). Patrinos and Psacharopoulos (1999) found evidence that children who work formally in the labour market often contribute a significant share of total family income. But the relationship between poverty and child labour has also been put into question by some recent studies; in particular, labour markets and education provision have been identified as imperfect for those who are persistently poor, lowering the opportunity for upward social mobility (Basu and Chau, 2004; Ranjan, 1999). Imperfections in the market could also lead to what is called the 'wealth paradox' where the children of land-rich households are more likely to work and also less likely to be in school than the children of land-poor households. It is a market imperfection because what ought to happen is that landowners would hire adult workers and send their children to school (Bhalotra and Heady, 2001). This would not be easy to capture in the Jordanian case as agriculture comprised only about 3 per cent of GDP in 2006 (MoA Jordan, 2007). Additionally, the Jordanian Law of Labour does not cover children working in family projects and agricultural activities (Al-Rousan, 2000).

Additionally, literature on child labour describes how it entails a trade-off between immediate benefits (increased current income) and the extent to which it interferes with the accumulation of the child's human capital and potential long-run costs (lower future earnings potential). Psacharopoulos (1996) found that a working child reduces his or her educational attainment relative to a control group of non-working children. Moreover, child labour in the place of educational attainment should not be considered a single 'one-off' event since it marks the entire life span and future generations (Biggeri *et al.*, 2003).

Grootaert and Kanbur (1994) provide a compact theoretical framework for studying the child labour/schooling decision and its determinants. Households take decisions on allocating the non-leisure time of their members to work (helping at home and income-earning at the market) and to schooling. However, the majority of research has focused on decisions to send children to school rather than on child labour.

The time allocation of children is determined by the number of children that in turn is related to fertility, and the household structure. Some found that household-size effects are smaller in rural areas, when social infrastructures are bigger and more inclusive and when extended family systems allow more fostering possibilities (Lloyd, 1994). At later moments of demographic transitions larger household sizes tend to have stronger impacts on the availability of household resources. While family size is important, it is also important to take the order and activities of siblings into consideration. Empirical evidence suggests that having a greater number of younger siblings implies less schooling, and more child labour (Patrinos and Psacharopoulos, 1997).

A large family size is hypothesized to lower the probability of a child enrolling in school, in particular for poor families (Patrinos and Psacharopoulos, 1997). Subsidies and scholarships for children, breaking the impact of household-size effects, increase the likelihood of school attendance. If capital markets fail for poor households, parents cannot borrow against future earnings from their children and thus under-invest in their childrens' education (Jacoby and Skoufias, 1997).

Child labour is often a household strategy to manage income risks through mitigating and coping with income losses such as failing harvests and sudden unemployment.[1] A diversification of income-generating activities assures more constant income streams. This implies that the introduction of child labour legislation, prohibiting such diversification mechanisms, might in the short-run cause households to encounter severe income loss, which tends to hurt the poorest households the most. More stable parental work patterns and income streams reduce the need for child labour (Kruger *et al.*, 2012).

A fundamental question with respect to the education decision is whether it is worth the individual and correspondingly the whole society investing more into education. Is the rate of return on the investment sufficiently positive? Heckman and Masterov have argued that early skill acquisitions are essential for later skill acquisitions, making investments in the human capital of children the investments with the highest returns of all (Heckman, 2006). Even if the returns for the private household appear negative, a society might benefit at large from the social returns from better educated households. Haveman and Wolfe (2001) list a number of social returns of education such as, for instance, better social cohesion, crime reduction and faster technological change. Esping-Andersen (2005) makes a strong case for making such benefits available to all those who are truly needy of better quality investment in their early childhood so as to reap higher returns for the receiving child and the society as a whole.

Parental education and higher household incomes are strong determinants of school enrolment. More educated parents are more able to identify the best human capital investments for their child and higher incomes make such investments more affordable. At the same time, school enrolment depends on the quality of the provided education. Low quality of schooling may also lead a household to substitute work for school (Bonnet, 1993; Lavy, 1996). Restrictions on the capital market may induce parents to reduce their investment in the human capital of their children (Cigno and Rosati, 2002; Edmonds and Pavcnik, 2005). If parents perceive learning on the job as a better training with better rewards in the labour market they will not send their children to school but let them gain work experience instead. Mingat and Tan (1996) show that at times it might be a rational decision to not invest in education.

The capability approach as a framework has also been very useful in understanding the well-being of children, and the importance of education. Applying the capability framework to children, Biggeri (2003) argues that the role of children's education in changing the conversion factors which turn commodities into functionings and capabilities is important; additionally, children's capabilities play a central role in this development since individual capabilities are the outcome of a cumulative path-dependent process that involves different generations of human beings.

Robeyns (2006) makes the argument that the intrinsic aim of educational policy should be to expand people's capabilities. The capability approach advances both intrinsic and instrumental values for education. Education and being knowledgeable allows one to flourish and that is arguably a valuable capability. To be well-educated is instrumentally important for the expansion of other capabilities. It is necessary to also keep in mind the concept of agency when we talk about valuable capabilities, as agency is what is being done in line with what a person perceives to be of value (Sen, 1985: 206). Additionally, it is valid to argue that we need to also consider other capabilities, and not just focus on educational deprivation (see, for example, Ballet *et al.*, 2006). The work of Biggeri *et al.* (2006) shows that the three most important capabilities for children themselves were education (73 per cent), love and care (52 per cent), and life and physical health (35 per cent). A study by Andresen and Fegter (2009) showed that children aged 6–13 found that education and care are among those things that are decisive for a good life.

The value of considering the issue of child labour from a capability perspective is not just that it looks at their well-being today but also their 'well-becoming' in the future and not just in education but in the multidimensional capability space (Biggeri *et al.*, 2011).

Schooling and child labour: The case of Jordan

Demographics

Although Jordan is a relatively small country, it has experienced a steady and fast increase in its population. Jordan's population grew significantly in the years after the Second World War, from 0.6 million in 1952 to 6.1 million in 2010 (Department of Statistics, Jordan, 2010). Jordanian society transformed profoundly upon the arrival of hundreds of thousands of Palestinian refugees during the Israeli-Arab Wars of 1948 and 1967, and the annexation of the West Bank to the kingdom in 1950.

The remarkable growth rate has always been a concern for policy-makers in the country, as it posed a challenge for the balance between natural resources (especially food, water and energy) and population. The increase in population is also an impediment to efforts to improve quality of life, especially when the population in question is relatively young (Mufti, 1999), with the latest official records of 2010 putting 37.3 per cent of the population under the age of 15 (DOS, 2010).

According to the United Nations Relief and Works Agency for Palestinian Refugees (UNRWA, 2008), 1.7 of the 5.5 million people in Jordan are registered refugees. Most Palestinian refugees in Jordan have full Jordanian citizenship,[2] however they are still labelled as 'refugees' whether they themselves were refugees or are descendants of refugees. When the 1990 Gulf crisis occurred, another wave of immigration took place in just a few months, and following 2004, Jordan saw a rapid increase in its population due to the heavy migration of Iraqi refugees. Exact figures are still not available. However, the UNHCR estimates that 500,000–700,000 Iraqi refugees now live in Jordan (Human Rights First, 2007).

Education

Education was given considerable attention early on in the Jordanian constitution of 1952. Article 6ii states that the government shall ensure work and education[3] within the limits of its possibility, and it shall ensure a state of tranquillity and equal opportunities[4] to all Jordanians. Article 20 states that elementary education shall be compulsory for Jordanians and free of charge in government schools.

Education in Jordan is free and compulsory for children from the age of 6 to 15. The education cycle is divided into two parts: a 10-year basic cycle became compulsory for all 6–15-year-olds and continued to be provided for free in public schools; the two years of secondary education are not compulsory but are also provided for free to all students who wish to continue beyond the basic cycle. Secondary education can take the form of academic or vocational education. Another educational provider in Jordan is the UNRWA. In Jordan, UNRWA runs 172 schools providing basic education from first to tenth grade, for more than 122,000 students. The UNRWA schools follow the national curriculum taught at government schools, in addition to early exposure to concepts of human rights (UNRWA, 2011).

As a country, Jordan has gone through several changes in its education system over the last three decades. The first attempt at major educational reform began in 1973 so as to correct the imbalance that existed between labour supply and demand, but the resulting reforms were modest and had a limited impact (Bint-Talal, 2004). The mid-1980s saw a larger, more comprehensive review and assessment of the educational system (Fafo, 1996). Finally, the Education Reform Program was initiated under the 'Human Resources Development Sector Investment Loan' (HRDSIL) project with World Bank assistance (WBOED, 2000). This project presented a shift in the investment of the bank in Jordan from the area of infrastructure to education. A follow up project (HRDSIL II), in 1997, aimed to improve the quality of Jordan's education provision, as well as to enhance the institutional capacity and delivery of education (Muta and Sasaki, 2007; World Bank, 2003). However, the results were less than what was initially expected, a main shortcoming being low education quality (WBOED, 2000). In 2003–2008, a new wave of educational reforms started with the 'Education Reform for a Knowledge Economy' project (HRDSIL III) that was initiated as a large multi-donor support project and aimed at 'transforming the administration and delivery of public primary and secondary schools with enhanced teaching and learning to produce graduates with skills necessary for the knowledge economy' (SJE, 2009).

Perhaps as a result of all these reforms, Jordan ranked as 49th among 125 countries in the 'Education For All' Development Index (EDI)[5] in 2004, earning it a classification of a medium EDI (EFA, 2009). According to the National Council for Family Affairs (NCFA) report of 2006, Jordan is close to achieving universal primary education, with the primary-level enrolment remaining steady at well over 90 per cent over the last decade. School dropout rates are low in the initial grades, but begin to rise slowly in Grade 4, and more sharply at the secondary level, and are higher among boys (NCFA, 2007). As for the literacy rate in 2004, Jordan achieved one of the highest levels in the region (DOS, 2006).

Table 10.1 shows our calculations for non-enrolment rates, which are within the range of the different percentages that are given for Jordan, confirming the

Table 10.1 Jordan's non-enrolment rates for children at compulsory schooling age

	% of not enrolled children at ages 6–15	
	1996	**2003**
Total	2.4	0.6
Male	2.3	0.6
Female	2.5	0.7
Capital	1.9	0.2
North	2.3	0.7
Middle	3.0	0.8
South	3.0	1.4
Non-refugee	2.4	0.8
1948–1967	2.4	0.4
Gaza	0.5	0.0
Male Headed HH	2.4	0.6
Female Headed HH	2.0	0.9

Source: Authors' calculations based on 1996 (JLCS) and 2003 (JMHS) surveys

Table 10.2 Reasons for not enrolling or dropping out of school

	Adults answering the question about themselves	Parents answering the question about their children
1. Disability or illness	1.5	4.1
2. Family poverty	7.3	12.0
3. Family disintegration	0.6	–
4. School not available nearby	6.8	–
5. Transportation not available	0.3	–
*6. Left school for marriage**	9.2	3.3
7. Care for family members	5.2	1.0
8. No interest in school	12.7	39.3
9. Repeated failure	18.7	26.6
10. Work to support family	18.2	2.9
11. High costs of schooling	5.5	1.0
*12. Having children**	0.3	–
13. Bad treatment at school	0.3	–
*14. Social restrictions**	10.9	7.7
15. Other undisclosed reason	2.6	2.1
Total	100.0	**100.0**
Observations	24,324	109

Source: Authors' calculations based on 2003 JHMS data

Note: * applicable mainly to females

trend of improving enrolment rates. Table 10.2 shows two results, the first is the response to different options about why adults have not attended or have dropped out of school, and the second shows the responses of the parents whose children are not currently in school. We found that the response frequency on the options of no interest in school and repeated failure is high in both groups. In the case of the adults explaining about themselves, reasons are work to support family, poverty and social restrictions, which are applicable mainly to girls. As for the parents who were answering for their children, poverty makes a higher percentage as well as family restrictions. Labour accounts only for 2.9 per cent as opposed to the 18.2 per cent for adults; this could be due to the fact that parents might be reluctant to say that the reason their children are currently not in school is due to being employed.

Child labour

When children are involved in child labour, when they work too early and undertake hazardous tasks, it can have adverse effects on their well-being. Studies have shown that a consequence of suffering bad health during childhood can be adverse effects on later health outcomes and productivity (Roggero *et al.*, 2007). The problem of child labour thus extends beyond protecting the rights of children to considering the potential for a loss of productivity in the economy of the future.

According to Jordanian Labour Law,[6] the minimum working age is set at 16 years and no one below the age of 18 is allowed to be employed in dangerous, exhausting or health-hazardous occupations. The includes operating machinery and working in extreme conditions. In 2006, the minimum wage in Jordan was raised from 96 Jordanian dinars to 110 Jordanian dinars per month; this is equivalent to US$155, which comes to US$5.15 a day. Additionally, Jordan ratified the ILO convention No. 138 in 1998 (ILOLEX, 2009), the Convention on the Rights of Children in 1999[7] (with reservations on three articles),[8] and the ILO convention No. 182 in 2000 (ILOLEX, 2009).[9]

A recent report of UNICEF and the National Council for Family Affairs (NCFA) in Jordan (NCFA, 2007) concluded that the problem of child labour became visible only in the last decade; however, the severity of the problem is not known as there is under-reporting of child labour in the informal and agricultural sectors as well as family businesses and domestic work, which is not recognized by law.

There are more girls in agricultural work and more boys in the industrial and commercial sectors (NCFA, 2007). Most are working because they are pressured to do so in order to improve the income of their families (AFP, 2008). The Jordanian Department of Statistics and the ILO (DOS-ILO) published the results of a survey conducted in between 2007 and 2008 which aimed at getting an approximation of labour among children between 5–17 across the country (DOS-ILO, 2009). The study concluded that child labourers make up approximately 1.9 per cent of the total population between 5–17, a number which according to this publication is much lower than countries similar to Jordan. The study also confirmed that child labour among girls is mainly in agriculture, while for boys it is in the industrial and commercial sectors; the study had no indication on domestic work for girls.

The Jordanian NCFA estimates the number of working children to be above 32,000 and rising (NCFA, 2007), the DOS-ILO study puts it at 33,190 (DOS-ILO, 2009), while others estimate the number as significantly higher, between 100,000 and 120,000 (Hawamdeh and Spencer, 2001). Given that the group aged up to 19 years has a population size of about 2.7 million (UNPP, 2008, 2005 figures), this boils down to a child labour rate of roughly 1.2 to 4.5 per cent. Table 10.3 shows

Table 10.3 Child labour incidence in Jordan

	% doing child labour		
	1996 (15–17 yrs)	2003 (15–17 yrs)	2003 (10–17 yrs)
Total	6.9	4.1	1.9
Male	12.3	7.2	3.5
Female	1.1	0.6	0.2
Capital	6.6	5.3	2.5
North	6.6	5.0	2.5
Middle	8.0	2.3	0.9
South	6.3	1.4	0.6
Non-refugee	5.6	2.6	1.4
1948–1967	8.4	6.2	2.6
Gaza	9.6	10.6	4.4
Male-headed HH	7.1	4.0	1.9
Female-headed HH	4.8	4.4	2.1

Source: Authors' calculations based on 1996 (JLCS) and 2003 (JMHS) surveys

our calculations for child labour incidence in Jordan, which is consistent with the secondary literature. For 1996 we only have data available for the group 15–17.

Household determinants of schooling and child labour

Dataset

Our study is based on two household surveys, the 1996 Jordan Living Conditions Survey (JLCS) and the 2003 Jordan Multi-purpose Household Survey (JMHS). The surveys were an adaptation of the existing Scandinavian Living Conditions Surveys to Jordan.[10] Stemming from the philosophy that many of our living conditions are influenced by our direct environment, through the household, the family, the community and society, the living conditions' unit of analysis is both the individual and the household.[11] For the 1996 survey, a response rate of 94.7 per cent resulted in information on about 5,919 households with 36,126 observations and 5,501 observations for the randomly selected person section (Fafo, 1996). The 2003 JMHS had a sample of 9,711 households with 57,761 observations and 6,405 observations for the randomly selected person section.

The 1996 data provides information on currently not enrolled children and dropout adults as well as the reasons for not being enrolled or dropping out, which include poverty or having to work. As compared to the 2003 data, which covers employment from the age of 10, the 1996 data is more limited with respect to information on educational attainment and child labour, covering employment only as of the age 15.

Methodology

We use a population logistic model to estimate the impact of a set of individual, household and geographic characteristics on two binary dependent variables. The parameters of binary-choice models are estimated by maximum likelihood techniques. Our two dependent variables are i) the likelihood to engage in child labour at the age 10–17 (estimation model I) and ii) the likelihood of dropping out of school during compulsory schooling age of 6–15 (model II). Using those indicators, we identify children who experience child labour and deprivation of schooling, and also the variations among different household types to which these children belong. This includes, for example, income quintiles, region within Jordan,[12] refugee status, gender of household heads and employment status, among other indicators (see, for example, Cigno *et al.*, 2003).

Estimation results

In Table 10.4 we provide estimation results for models I and II. Most of the included risk factors predict, with at least 90 per cent confidence, part of the probability to do child labour. As for model I, the biggest risk factor predicting child labour is the share of non-enrolled children at compulsory schooling age. The odds of boys doing child labour are higher than the odds of girls doing child labour, which can be explained principally due to a cultural factor, where boys are the ones who would go out to find work and support the family. A noteworthy finding is that being born later in the child sequence increases the likelihood of labour for that child. As expected, when the household head (HH) has a paid job and higher educational attainments the child is less likely to do child labour. Higher levels of education of the HH appears to decrease the likelihood of child labour; children in households where that HH holds a university degree are 91 per cent less likely to participate in child labour than those who live in households where the HH has low education.

Children in the northern and southern regions of Jordan are much less likely to do child labour than those who live in Amman, the middle region showing the

Table 10.4 Logistic regression results, 2003

Estimated OLS model	I	II
Explanatory variables	Child aged 10–17 doing child labour	Child aged 6–15 not going to school
Gender	19.51***	0.67
(boy = 1, girl = 0)	[8.31]	[0.17]
Child's birth order among siblings	1.19***	0.69***
(higher values for being born later)	[0.07]	[0.07]
HH-head: employment status	0.76	0.56
(employed = 1, unemployed = 0)	[0.24]	[0.23]
HH-head: education level 2	0.40***	0.72
(basic education; baseline = below	[0.12]	[0.23]
basic education)		
HH-head: education level 3	0.19***	0.80
(high school)	[0.11]	[0.40]
HH-head: education level 4	0.09**	0.89
(university)	[0.09]	[0.44]
HH-head's spouse educated above	1.00	0.54
basic education	[0.00]	[0.24]
(yes = 1, no = 0)		
HH-head's health	1.00	0.56
(chronic disease = 1, healthy = 0)	[0.24]	[0.21]
HH-head's health insurance	0.52***	1.11
(insured = 1, uninsured = 0)	[0.13]	[0.36]
HH sub-region location: middle/central	1.38	2.24
(baseline = Amman)	[0.40]	[1.28]
HH sub-region location: north	0.33***	1.89
(baseline = Amman)	[0.11]	[1.09]
HH sub-region location: south	0.22***	4.40***
(baselin e= Amman)	[0.11]	[2.49]
HH-head: refugee of 1948 or 1967	2.71***	0.93
(baseline = non-refugee)	[0.76]	[0.33]
HH-head: refugee from Gaza	1.52	1.00
	[1.08]	[0.00]
HH income: 2nd income quintile	1.80	0.90
	[0.70]	[0.35]
HH income: 3rd income quintile	2.47**	1.00
	[0.96]	[0.40]
HH income: 4th income quintile	2.27**	0.66
	[0.89]	[0.29]
HH income: 5th income quintile	2.62**	0.39*
	[1.08]	[0.22]
HH crowding: 2 hh members per room	3.18**	0.78
(baseline = 1 hh member)	[1.55]	[0.23]

Table 10.4 *continued*

HH crowding: 3 hh members per room	5.80*** [2.90]	0.71 [0.39]
HH crowding: 4 hh members per room	5.65*** [3.12]	2.28 [1.34]
HH ownership *(owned = 1, not owned = 0)*	1.61* [0.41]	1.29 [0.38]
HH workforce *(share of working adults aged 18 and above)*	7.57*** [4.21]	2.02 [1.56]
Observations	6617	11281

Note: * significant at 10 per cent level; ** at 5 per cent level; *** at 1 per cent level; standard errors in brackets

highest incidence of child labour. This could be explained by the fact that Amman is the most urban and highly populated area, so there are more labour market opportunities existing there, thus creating a pull factor for child labour. Children in refugee households are as likely to do child labour as in non-refugee households, which is a curious finding and is worth investigating further. However, one explanation could be that citizens from Gaza do not have networks for allocating children to labour opportunities, especially as the majority of them reside in refugee camps, but again this particular point warrants further investigation.

Higher household incomes are associated with higher child labour incidences. This finding is surprising at first, but we must realize that we are looking at total household income, so the income that the child is bringing home is included in the calculation. Household ownership, which is an indicator of household wealth, is marginally significant in predicting higher child labour incidences. While this finding requires further investigation, one plausible explanation is the need for liquidity, since home ownership normally requires house-related payments and so can reduce available household cash. A better indicator of the deprivation situation of the household is to look at overcrowding, and here we see that when the number of household members per room is higher, when there are two, three or four household members per room, a child is four times as likely to do child labour as in the case of one household member per room.

Once income and household density are included in the model, the employment and health status of the HH does not change the probability of doing child labour. Health insurance for the HH usually reflects working in the private sector or in a public sector job such as a public administrator or in the armed forces. Children in such insured households are half as likely to do child labour. Doing child labour is also strongly related to the share of working adults in the family. This might be explained in part by family-related business activities, or family networks.

As for model II, boys and girls are equally likely to not attend schools. Being born later in the child row is related to a lower probability of not attending a school, which could reflect the positive trend in enrolment.

The geographic location of households does not make a significant difference in the likelihood of non-attendance, once all other covariates are considered constant, except for the South which shows substantially higher rates of non-enrolment. Children from any refugee household are similarly as likely not to attend school compared to other households' children. This could be explained by the strong presence of the UNRWA educational programmes in the refugee camps.

There are no significant differences between income groups in the non-attendance of schools, only children from the top income quintile show a lower likeliness to be not enrolled.

The p-values associated with the Pearson's chi-squared likelihood ratios indicate the goodness of fit of the chosen model specification (Kohler and Kreuter, 2005). For both models the p-values of the chi-squared likelihood ratios are statistically significant. About 26 per cent of the variance in the incidence of child labour and respectively 6 per cent of the variance in the non-attendance of schools can be explained by the two estimated models. This indicates that that there are still unaccounted factors, such as for example the child's relative productivity potential in both schooling and child labour, which could be more relevant in explaining our outcomes than the factors that we can account for so far.

Both estimation models essentially indicate the effects of risk factors that we have previously anticipated. However, we need to point out that we cannot make causal inferences from our estimation models. Some endogenous process might also cause effects from the dependent variable on the risk factors themselves. We see this for instance for income: as child labour contributes to household incomes, a higher income is strongly related to the occurrence of child labour, but at the same time more household income decreases the need to allocate child labour. However, we cannot differentiate the one from the other effect without any source of exogenous information about the availability of income. While this is also the case for making some causal claims on the effects of the other risk factors, we cannot expect such bias to be substantial, beyond the reverse links between household resources and child outcomes.

If a child has a paid job and/or stays at home instead of going to school there are more resources available for parents to have more children. Even though this link is unlikely to be strong, in theory it could cause an endogeneity problem. As mentioned before, income and the variables related to household resources, such as owning the house, health insurance status, income earners and room density might be endogenously affected, in particular by child labour that directly increases such resources.

Conclusions and recommendations

In this study, we have highlighted the schooling and child labour situation of children in Jordan, looking in more detail at reasons behind not attending school, factors associated with non-enrolment in school, and child labour. Although Jordan has seen a gradual improvement in its child protection legislation in the last three decades, the results demonstrate that economic hardship in Jordan contributes to the persistent problem of child labour and thus school dropout. While education can be considered a catalyst for fighting child labour, from reviewing the literature we can conclude that given Jordan's substantive population growth, new legislation has not enabled sufficient provisions to be made as yet. The availability and quality of schools cannot match the growing needs to meet full enrolment and completion of compulsory schooling in Jordan. Our regression estimates show that girls are less likely to be involved in child labour than boys, but this does not take into consideration that girls are involved in housework. Children born later in the child order, who live in households with more members per room and whose family were refugees from 1948 or 1967 are more likely to do child labour. Living in households in the northern or southern region makes it less likely for child labour to occur, compared with the middle region and Amman.

A consistent finding of empirical studies of child labour is that the child's age and gender, education and employment of the parents, and rural versus urban residency are robust predictors of child labour.[13] The dearth of direct data on child labour has led many researchers to focus on the determinants of school attendance, even though it is recognized that school attendance is not the 'inverse' of child labour. Nevertheless, much of this literature views schooling as the most important means of drawing children away from the labour market (Siddiqi and Patrinos, 1995), and this also applies to this study.

Due to data limitations, we are not able to specifically address the gaps of knowledge that pertain to the constraints affecting children themselves, which results in them dropping out of school or into child labour. Child research in

Jordan for the most part has focused on the society and the household as units of analysis pertaining to the child and the capability approach has much to offer in focusing analysis at the individual level. In this study we also focus on child labour and schooling, however it is worth mentioning that schooling and child work are not all aspects of child well-being, for example, excluding adverse effects of household size on child's health, intelligence, physical development (see, for example, King, 1987). This leads us to our recommendation for what should come next as far as child research in Jordan is concerned.

Understanding the determinants of child labour is one thing, but it also important to consider the total well-being of the child and here we strongly believe that the capability approach can provide the appropriate framework for further development in the topic. By doing so we are not only concerned with child well-being but also with child well-becoming, and the expansion of children's future capabilities (see, for example, Biggeri *et al.*, 2011). The capability approach would serve as a starting point to conduct a data-driven initiative that would enable us to go beyond first evidence correlations to develop estimation models of the child labour decision which capture the household's behaviour, taking into account the well-being and well-becoming of the child. This would enable us to investigate, in the Jordanian context, the elements of freedom and agency, and shift from the focus on deprivation to the more inclusive idea of capability deprivation. Doing so will enable a deeper understanding into why child labour persists despite continued efforts to curtail it. In such an analysis focus must be placed on the issues of dropping out of school due to lack of interest and repeated failure, as well as societal restrictions (especially as they pertain to gender differences), and this must in turn be linked to an assessment of the quality of education. Additionally, we support the view that children should not be seen as passive recipients of their own well-being, but rather as active contributors to it, and therefore their perspectives on deprivation and well-being need to be taken into consideration, both on a reseach level and a policy level.

Most MENA countries including Jordan have achieved universal primary enrolment and significant secondary enrolment rates. Nonetheless, the number of out-of-school children is expected to grow by over 40 per cent, with disproportionate shares among the rural poor and girls by 2015 (Tzannatos, 2000: 12). Thus when child labour, due to its variety of economic or social explanations, prevents the child from achieving an education (Basu and Van, 1988), we must not ignore the fact that this child is being denied a universal human right, and is becoming deprived of a valuable capability not just today but for the future.

Notes

1 Child labour might (partially) substitute work of siblings or parents if the child's income elasticity is sufficiently higher. This might in particular be true for the poorest households who are living at subsistence levels. There, children often engage in the same occupations as their parents. If households discriminate their choices with respect to the child's gender, specialization with respect to activities can occur. That is, for instance, the case when boys are favoured with respect to school investments if their labour market returns are considered higher those those for girls, for example, because girls often marry at an earlier age.

2 With the exception of about 120,000 refugees originally from the Gaza Strip, which up to 1967 was administered by Egypt. They are eligible for temporary Jordanian passports, which do not entitle them to full citizenship rights such as the right to vote, employment with the government and medical access.

3 The 'duty bearer' for education in Jordan is the Ministry of Education which was established in 1956, and is currently operating under the Education Law (3) of the year 1994.

4 The Education Law stipulates no discrimination in education among the genders, where it is explicitly stated in Article 2 of the Law that law applies to both genders.

5 The EDI composite index incorporates four quantifiable 'Education For All' (EFA) goals – universal primary education, as measured by the total primary net enrolment ration; adult literacy, as measured by the adult literacy rate; gender parity, as measured by the gender-specific EFA index; and quality of education, as measured by the survival rate to Grade 5.

6 Labour Law No. 8 of the year 1996 issued in accordance with a resolution of the Minister of Labour published in the Official Gazette (issue 4181) on 1 February 1997.

7 Law in accordance with a resolution of the Minister of Labour published in the Official Gazette (issue 4787) on 16 October 2006.

8 The articles were Article 14, the child's right to freedom of religion, Article 20, related to foster care and Article 21, related to adoption procedures.

9 The ILO Convention No. 138, adopted in 1973, sets 15 as the minimum age for work in developed countries, but permitting work at the age of 14 for apprentices and vocational trainees. Over 130 countries have ratified this convention, yet little progress in reducing child labour had been made. In 1989, the United Nations General Assembly adopted the *Convention on the Rights of the Child*, which is now ratified by 193 countries. In addition, in 1999, the Worst Forms of Child Labour Convention No. 182 was adopted at the International Labour Conference in Geneva by delegates of the 175 ILO member countries (see ILO, 2004).

10 At the time of writing this chapter, the 2003 survey is the most recent multidimensional household survey that has been done in Jordan following the Scandinavian Living Conditions Approach.

11 Both surveys have been collected by the Jordan Department of Statistics in cooperation with the Norwegian Fafo Institute for Applied International Studies under advice of UNICEF-Jordan, Canada International Development Research Centre and Canada International Development Agency.

12 Jordan is divided into four regions (and 12 governorates): capital region (Amman), middle/central region (Balqa, Zarqa, and Madaba), north region (Irbid, Mafraq, Jerash, Ajlun) and south region (Karak, Tafileh, Ma'an, Aqaba).

13 Reviews of the child labour literature can be found in ILO (1986) and Grootaert and Kanbur (1994).

References

Agence France-Presse (2008) *Jordan to Tackle Child Labor Problem*. Amman: Agence France-Presse.

Al-Rousan, S. (2000, September 4–8) Child labour in Jordan, paper presented at the *IAOS Conference on Statistics, Development and Human Rights*, Montreux, Switzerland.

Andresen, S. & Fegter, S. (2009) *Spielräume sozial benachteiligter Kinder* [*Scope of Socially Disadvantaged Children*]. Germany: Bielefeld University.

Asogwa, S.E. (1986) Sociomedical aspects of child labour in Nigeria, *Journal of Occupational Medicine*, 28: 46–48.

Ballet, J., Bhukuth, A. & Radja, K. (2006) Child labour, human rights and the capability approach, paper presented at the *International Conference of the Human Development and Capability Association*, Groningen, September.

Banerjee, S.R. (1991) Child labor in suburban areas of Calcutta, West Bengal. *Indian Pediatrics*, 28(9): 1039–1044.

Basu, K. & Chau, N. (2004) Exploitation of child labor and the dynamics of debt bondage, *Journal of Economic Growth*, 9(2): 209–238.

Basu, K. & Van, P.H. (1988) The economics of child labor, American Economic Association, *American Economic Review*, 88(3): 412–427.

Bhalotra, S. & Heady, C. (2001) Child farm labour: the wealth paradox, *The World Bank Social Protection Discussion Paper Series*, 125.

Biggeri, M. (2003, September 7–9) Children, child labour and the human capability approach, paper presented at the *3rd Conference on Capability Approach: From Sustainable Development to Sustainable Freedom*, September, University of Pavia, Italy.

Biggeri, M., Guarcello, L., Lyon, S. & Rosati, F.C. (2003) The puzzle of 'idle' children: neither in school nor performing economic activity: evidence from six countries, *Understanding Children's Work (UCW) Project Working Paper Series*.

Biggeri, M., Libanora, R., Mariani, S. & Menchini, L. (2006) Children conceptualizing their capabilities: results of a survey conducted during the first Children's World Congress on Child Labour, *Journal of Human Development*, 7(1): 59–83.

Biggeri, M., Bhukuth, A. & Ballet, J. (2011) Re-examining children's economic and non-economic activities using the capability approach, in M. Biggeri, J. Ballet & F. Comim (eds.) *Children and the Capability Approach: Studies in Childhood and Youth* (pp. 286–303). Basingstoke: Palgrave Macmillan.

Bint-Talal, B. (2004) *Rethinking an NGO: Development, Donors and the Civil Society in Jordan*, first edition. London: I.B. Tauris.

Bonnet, M. (1993) Child labour in Africa, *International Labour Review*, 132(3): 371–389.

Chaubey, J., Perisic, M., Perrault, N., Laryea-Adjei, G. & Khan, N. (2007) *Child, Labour, Education and Policy Options* (working papers). New York: UNICEF Division of Policy and Planning.

Cigno, A., Cuarcello, L., Noguchi, Y., Lyon, S. & Rosati, F.C. (2003) Child labour indicators used by the UCW Project: an explanatory note, *Understanding Children's Work Project Working Paper Series*, 43761.

Cigno, A. & Rosati, F. C. (2002) Why do Indian children work, and is it bad for them? *Pacific Economic Review*, 7(1).

DOS-ILO (2009) *Working Children in Jordan – Results of the Child Labour Survey* (in Arabic). Amman/Geneva: Jordanian Department of Statistics/International Labour Organization.

DOS (2006) *Jordan in Numbers*. Amman: Jordanian Department of Statistics.

DOS (2010) *Jordan in Numbers*. Amman: Jordanian Department of Statistics.

Edmonds, E. V, & Pavcnik, N. (2005) The effect of trade liberalization on child labor, *Journal of International Economics*, 65(2): 401–419.

Esping-Andersen, G. (2005) Children in the welfare state.: a social investment approach, *DemoSoc* working paper, 10, 1–33.

Fafo (1996) *Living Conditions in the Hashemite Kingdom of Jordan*. Jordan: Jordanian Department of Statistics/Fafo Research Institute.

Gharaibeh, M. & Hoeman, S. (2003) Health hazards and risks for abuse among child labor in Jordan, *International Pediatric Nursing*, 2: 140–147.

Grootaert, C. & Kanbur, R. (1994) *Child Labor: A Review*. Washington, DC: The World Bank.

Haveman, R. & Wolfe, B. (2001) Accounting for the social and non-market benefit of education, in HRDC/OECD (eds) *International Symposium Report: The Contribution of Human and Social Capital to Sustained Economic Growth and Well-Being*. Quebec: Human Resources Development Canada.

Hawamdeh, S. & Spencer, N. (2001) Work, family socioeconomic status, and growth among working boys in Jordan, *Archives of Disease in Childhood*, 84: 311–314.

Heckman, J.J. (2006. Skill formation and the economics of investing in disadvantaged children, *Science*, 312(5782): 1900–1902.

Human Rights First (2007) *Factsheet – Iraqi Refugees in Jordan and Syria*.

IBRD/WB. (2008). *MENA Development Report: The Road Not Traveled – Education Reform in the Middle East and Africa*. Washington, DC: International Bank for Reconstruction and Development; World Bank.

ILO (1986). *Annotated Bibliography on Child Labor.* Geneva: ILO.

ILO (2004) *Child Labour: A Textbook for University Students.* Geneva: ILO.

ILOLEX (2009). *Ratifications of the Fundamental Human Rights: Conventions by Country in Asia & Pacific.* Geneva: International Labour Organization, Information System on International Labour Standards.

Jacoby, H.G. & Skoufias, E. (1997) Risk, financial markets, and human capital in a developing country., *The Review of Economic Studies*, 64(3): 311–335.

King, E.M. (1987) The effect of family size on family welfare: what do we know? in D.G. Johnson & R.D.L. Madison (eds) *Population Growth and Economic Development: Issues and Evidence* (pp. 373–411). Wisconsin: University of Wisconsin Press.

Kohler, U. & Kreuter, F. (2005) *Data Analysis Using Stata.* College Station, TX: Stata Press.

Kruger, D., Soares, R.R. & Berthelon, M. (2012) Household choices of child labor and schooling: a simple model with application to Brazil, *Journal of Human Resources*, 47(1): 1–31.

Lavy, V.C. (1996) School supply constraints and children's eduational outcome in rural Ghana, *Journal of Development Economics*, 51(2): 219–314.

Lloyd, C.B. (1994) Investing in the next generation: the implications of high fertility at the level of the family, *New York Population Council Research Division Working Papers*, 63.

Meenakshi, N.M., Prabhu, S.V. & Mistry, H.N. (1985) Child labor in Bombay, *Child Abuse Negl*, 9: 107–111.

Mingat, A. & Tan, J.-P. (1996) The full social returns to education: estimates based on countries' economic growth performance, *HCD Working Paper*, 73.

MoA Jordan (2007) *Agricultural Sector Report 2007* (translated from Arabic). Amman: Jordanian Ministry of Agriculture.

Mufti, E. (1999) Social development and building the Arabic future: Jordan as a model, in K. Wazani (ed.) *Economic Reform and Human Development in Jordan* (pp. 139–151). Amman: The Abdul Hameed Shoman Foundation.

Muta, H. & Sasaki, R. (2007) *External Evaluation of the Second Human Resources Development Sector Investment.* Tokyo: Japan International Cooperation Agency JICA.

NCFA (2007) *Children in Jordan: Situation Analysis 2006/2007.* Amman: National Council for Family Affairs in Jordan/UNICEF.

Patrinos, H.A. & Psacharopoulos, G. (1997) Family size, schooling and child labor in Peru – an empirical analysis, *Journal of Population Economics*, 10: 387–405.

Patrinos, H.A., & Psacharopoulos, G. (1999) Educational performance and child labor in Paraguay, *International Journal of Educational Development*, 15(1): 47–60.

Psacharopoulos, G. (1996) Child labor versus educational attainment – some evidence from Latin America, *Journal of Population Economics*, 10, 377–386.

Ranjan, P. (1999) An Economic analysis of child labour, *Economic Letters*, 64(1): 99–105.

Robeyns, I. (2006) Three models of education: rights, capabilities and human capital, *Theory and Research in Education*, 4(69): 69–84.

Roggero, P., Mangiaterra, V., Bustreo, F. & Rosati, F.C. (2007) The health impact of child labor in developing countries: evidence from cross-country data, *American Journal of Public Health – Research and Practice*, 97(2).

Sen, A. (1985) Well-being, agency and freedom: the Dewey Lectures, *Journal of Philosophy*, 82(4): 169–221.

Siddiqi, F. & Patrinos, H.A. (1995) Child labor: issues, causes and interventions, *HCO Working Paper*, 56.

SJE (2009) Supporting Jordan's education portal, http://www.erfke.ca/, May 2009.

Tzannatos, Z. (2000) Social protection in the middle east and north africa: a review. Paper presented at the *Mediterranean Development Forum*, Cairo, March, 2000.

UNESCO (2009) *Education for All Global Monitoring Report – Overcoming Inequality: Why Governance Matters*. Paris: UNESCO.

UNPP (2008) *World Population Prospects*, retrieved August 11, 2009, from Population Division of the Department of Economic and Social Affairs of the United Nations Secretariat, http://esa.un.org/unpp.

UNRWA (2008) Jordan refugee camp profile, retrieved October 1 2008, from www.un.org/unrwa/english.html.

UNRWA (2011) Jordan newsroom features, retrieved November 7 2011 from www.unrwa.org/newsroom/features/jordan.

WBOED (2000) Partnership for education in Jordan, *Précis*, 193.

World Bank (2003) *Implementation Completion Report on a Loan in the Amount of $60 mil to the Hashemite Kingdom of Jordan, Report No: 25670-JO*. Washington, DC: World Bank.

11

Children's Autonomy in Conflict-affected Countries

Jérôme Ballet, Claudine Dumbi and Benoît Lallau

Introduction

Over the past 20 years or so, children in particular have fallen victim to structural adjustments in some developing countries (Cornia *et al.*, 1987; Cagatay *et al.*, 1995). In addition to the 'adjustments' imposed by international organizations, some countries have also sunk into economic crises and violent civil conflicts. The Democratic Republic of Congo (DRC) is one such country.

The DRC is currently undergoing a major social breakdown, a crisis of social capital (Luzolele, 2002), and this opens the way for reconstruction, which is often being undertaken by religious movements. The State's failure to act and the lack of governmental social capital are partly compensated for by an 'NGO-ization' of society, especially in Kinshasa (Giovannoni *et al.*, 2004). Such NGO-ization is reflected by the considerable expansion of religious movements, including fundamentalist Christian movements and, more specifically, neo-Pentecostal and apocalyptic movements.

Not only are Congolese children the main victims of the ongoing social breakdown in the country, they are also being targeted by the social reconstruction driven by neo-Pentecostal Churches. Children are the victims both of street violence (cf. Muwalawala's description, 1994) and of violence inflicted upon them as a result of accusations of witchcraft (Madundu Tumwaka, 2002). Such intergenerational social breakdown is occurring in an ambivalent context where children are not only victims but also agents. They find that they are in a situation of autonomy and sometimes of significant power. In this context, the development of children's agency appears very problematical, and it is this duality of children's agency that we explore in this chapter. We draw our conclusion on the basis of an empirical investigation in Kinshasa, led by qualitative interviews with children accused of sorcery.

Firstly, we describe the conceptual and methodological foundations of our analysis. We focus in particular on the question of agency and of children's agency in particular. Secondly, we describe the Congolese context, highlighting the aspect of social breakdown. Thirdly, we discuss children's agency, the role children play in this context and the violence of which they are victims, but also how, in spite of themselves, they are involved in perpetuating violence. Finally, we draw some conclusions about children's agency.

Conceptual and methodological roots of the analysis

Several authors have highlighted the difficulties of applying the capability approach to children's issues (see in particular Biggeri *et al.*, 2011). Biggeri *et al.* (2010) and Ballet *et al.* (2011) suggest that the concept of evolving capabilities must be introduced into the capability approach in order to take into account the changes in the capabilities of children over time. Their evolving capabilities reflect developing capabilities and agency, starting from a position in which children have only weak autonomy to one in which they exercise greater autonomy (Ballet *et al.* 2010). Children can develop agency at any time in their life, but of course it reflects their age. Even in dramatic circumstances, such as surviving in the street, children can develop agency. For instance, Horna Padrón and Ballet (2011) show in the case of street boys in Peru, that children do develop some forms of agency and do not define themselves purely and simply as street children. Anich *et al.* (2011) underline children's capacity to identify relevant capabilities according to their age, even in street situations. As underlined by Bellanca *et al.* (2011), people, and notably children, may have a limited capability set, but can develop exaptation, i.e. creative adaptation.

Then, even in a context of dis-capability (Bellanca *et al.*, 2011), following Giddens (1979) we consider agency to be 'the capacity for autonomous action by the actors' – i.e. the capacity of these actors not only to act, but also to project themselves in their action. Such a definition opens numerous avenues, which can be organized around the concepts of autonomy and of resilience, at both the individual and collective levels.

From freedom to autonomy

Giddens' definition relates back to Amartya Sen's thinking about the 'real freedoms' of individuals. Sen distinguishes between *well-being freedom* and *agency freedom*; the latter making it possible to apprehend the individual according to his or her ability to conceive goals, undertakings or values, that is, to exercise free will. Despite focusing on the general goals which the individual has a reason to value, Sen pays little attention to the processes involved in forming these values and undertakings, and therefore to what really constitutes the basis of the capacity of people to act. However, it would seem to be essential to contextualize this capacity for agency, both in order to understand the circumstances under which it develops, and to analyse its effects.

One way of going beyond the limitations of this freedom of the agent involves the concept of autonomy, as it is used in the work of Elster, as freedom to do otherwise: 'I do in fact suggest that the degree of freedom depends on the number and importance of the things that one (i) is free to do and (ii) autonomously wants to do' (Elster, 1983: 128). From this perspective, agency is related to the capacity to actually act as much as to the capacity to decide one's actions in an autonomous manner, that is, the freedom to do otherwise; here Giddens' concept of the 'capacity for autonomous action' takes on its full meaning, particularly in situations described as 'survival situations'. This concept relates back also to those of creative adaptation used by Bellanca *et al.* (2011) in the case disabled people.

In our study, the capacity for agency thus opens a dual perspective. On the one hand it stresses the capacity of children to act in a given context, here in a context of survival. On the other, it calls into question the capacity of these children to act otherwise.

From survival to resilience

Individuals in a situation of great precariousness, such as the 'deprived Kinois' must, indeed, adapt to the high risks that they face and to the strict constraints that the environment brings to bear on them. This idea of the capacity to adapt to a difficult situation refers to the concept of adaptive preferences and to the related concept of resignation, but also refers to the capacities of individuals to react, even when they are in very difficult situations; this means that the notion of resilience can usefully be invoked.

Individual resilience usually corresponds to the capacity to deal with a critical situation, to resist it and survive it. More precisely, it can be evaluated as a state (to succeed in returning to the initial situation in terms of agency), or as an adaptive process, to employ the strategies required to reconquer one's agency and anticipate future crises, and to aspire to a potential improvement in one's situation, that is, to project oneself outside the situation in which one finds oneself after the crisis: 'A resilient individual is an individual who is aware of the risks s/he runs and his or her ability to act on his or her potentialities in the context of preventative and offensive strategies' (Rousseau, 2005: 151–152). Two elements emerge from such a definition of the resilient person. On the one hand, 'awareness' of one's own situation, of one's means of action, and here we encounter again the question of aspirations. On the other hand, that of having 'possibilities of acting' and of devising 'strategies'. The question of agency is thus focused on concrete practices which will make it possible to survive, or better. As a process, resilience is expressed through the choices the individual makes, and can be assessed via an analysis of the strategies for managing the risks adopted, and in particular of their defensive aspect (tending to preserve the existing situation) or their more offensive aspect (trying to modify, or even break away from the current situation). Low resilience often leads to prioritization of defensive strategies, intended to protect what can be saved, by emergency management tinged with fatalism and passivity, and thus to difficulty in 'projecting oneself', to use Giddens' definition.

The question asked in our study therefore concerns the degree to which the capacity for agency produced by children allows them to escape from their situation, namely, to be resilient.

Methodological options

These theoretical considerations underlie our fieldwork. It involves analysing the capacity for autonomous action of children in the particular context of the social disintegration currently taking place in the DRC.

We then go on to analyse the violence encountered by children accused of sorcery, and the agency they have developed in this context, on the basis of the existing literature, and of a qualitative survey we carried out in Kinshasa. Our survey focused on 31 so-called *child sorcerers*. Our methodology highlights two main aspects. Firstly, it is not easy to meet children accused of sorcery, as most of them live on the streets. Any long-term survey work carried out on the streets is difficult, and can even be dangerous, for adults but also and especially for children. A compromise solution involves interviewing street children at child reception centres (22 out of the 31 interviews), that is, centres that give accommodation to children. This makes it possible to conduct interviews in complete safety for both parties, and to meet children who need time before they can report their experience and story. Even in this case, it is not easy because most of them go back to the street at one moment or another.

Secondly, the children's experience is recorded using an interview guide based on a kind of 'life story' approach that makes it possible both to get beyond the children's hesitations or reservations, and to get a better picture of the mechanisms at work in 'child sorcery'. Interviews were done by a member of the research team working in reception centres.

This survey of a sample of 31 'child sorcerers' makes no claims to be representative, particularly because there are no reliable statistics about the reference population. Our aim is, rather, to provide some evidence about the nature and extent of the problem, and to identify the main issues at stake. To do this, we also draw on the literature on sorcery and witchcraft, and on our previous studies of the 'multicrisis' in DRC (Lallau, 2007; Lallau and Dumbi, 2007).

Social breakdown and emergence of the new sorcery

The DRC is undergoing what is now commonly described as a multicrisis. This refers not only to economic and social dimensions, but also to the imaginary or invisible sphere, as opposed to the real or visible. The world of magic or witchcraft is currently undergoing massive changes. Sorcery, which was traditionally viewed as something practised by adults and even mainly elderly people, now places children at the core of the system (De Boeck, 2000). This change is linked to the current economic situation in the DRC, where the bulk of the population is struggling to survive, whilst an elite grows ever richer.

Logic of survival and disintegration of social ties

The level of poverty in Kinshasa is such that half of the city's population eats only once a day, and a quarter of the population has only one meal every two days (Tollens, 2003). This observation itself reflects an extreme struggle for survival. It should also be pointed out that feeding one's children decently is an important reason for pride (De Herdt, 2001). Under these conditions, poverty is not simply a matter of material destitution: it also strikes a profound blow at self-esteem, which inevitably impacts on social ties (Falangani, 2002).

Adapting to this multicrisis is based on an 'ethics of practice' (De Villers and Monnier, 2002: 31) based on *mayele*. *Mayele* (or resourcefulness) equates to '*inventiveness mingled with intelligence, cunning and determination*'. It is intended to ensure survival (Trefon, 2004: 15) through one's own ability to adapt on an ad hoc basis, but also, when this is possible, by devising longer-term projects. *Mayele* legitimates all the means used to survive, including 'corruption, robbery, extortion, collusion, fraud, counterfeiting and prostitution' (Trefon, 2004: 23). Everyone strives to survive, taking advantage of all the opportunities that arise from the surrounding disorder (Nzeza Bilakila, 2004), without either questioning the circumstances that are responsible for their situation, or considering the side-effects on the community as a whole. As Trefon puts it, society falls prey to itself.

All in all, this approach penalizes most those who have the greatest difficulty in surviving, that is, those whose social capital ordinarily constitutes their main endowment (Lallau and Dumbi, 2007). The logic of survival feeds on and, in return, contributes to further social breakdown by destroying old solidarities and social rules, and by weakening family ties. The family thus comes to be a place of tensions and jealousy, conflicts between more or less 'fortunate' relatives, between generations, and between the sexes. Family becomes a place where neither confidence nor sharing can be taken for granted any more (Luzolele, 2002). Young unmarried mothers find it difficult to find a place (De Herdt, 2003), and the place of children is profoundly modified. '*Mwana na mwana na tata naye*' (Each child is his own father), as the saying goes in Kinshasa. Children become responsible for themselves at a very early age, because their parents cannot afford to send them to school or feed them properly. This early 'autonomization' not only prevents the accumulation of human capital by the rising generation (due to their failure to attend school), it also harms the intergenerational dimension of social capital. Parental authority is weakened, as is the sort of 'old-age insurance' that large families have always represented. Early autonomization can also fuel accusations of sorcery levelled against children.

The emergence of new forms of sorcery

Alongside the growing influence of NGOs and charities, accusations of sorcery have also been increasing steadily over the past 20 years or so (Douglas, 1999) and are one aspect of economies in crisis. Sorcery is a way of mediating and imagining the world (Ruel, 1997) and it gives rise to multiple interpretations. In the DRC, for instance, international NGOs now report that children are increasingly being accused of sorcery (Aguilar Molina, 2006; Human Rights Watch, 2006). There have been countless accusations, and they are now swelling the numbers of children on the streets – some 20,000 to 25,000 according to Pirot (2004). They are known as *Sparrows*, *Bana Shege* or *Bana Imbwa*, depending on their age, and contribute to making the phenomenon of street children commonplace.

Fisiy and Geschiere (1991) have attempted to explain the capacities for modernization of the language on sorcery or witchcraft in Africa. They point out the ambivalence of messages based on envy that underpins the notion of jealousy as much as that of success. This language emphasizes the unfairness or injustice of the inequalities of wealth and power, and also suggests that sorcery can enable people to accumulate this wealth and power. Individuals thus become caught up in this ambivalence, torn between denouncing others and resorting to sorcery themselves.

Language invoking sorcery and witchcraft obviously reflects the current economic changes in Africa, as well as the resulting social tensions. Comaroff and Comaroff (1999) stress the growing place of the economy in witchcraft-related explanations and imagery. There are numerous links between sorcery and the economy, thus forming an economy of the occult. These links range from real transactions (for example, the removal and sale of organs), to relationships in the 'alternative world', which show clear signs of some kind of economic power struggle. The most widely cited example is that of individuals under a spell who, in their sleep, are forced to go and plough someone else's imaginary fields or invisible plantations for the benefit of the latter or of a third party. Economic relationships in the world of sorcery can take multiple forms (for example, the ousting of a rival, exploitation of the labour force), but are always closely connected with the development of a society where inequalities are becoming increasingly blatant, and where a small elite class is growing richer while the vast majority of the population is barely able to survive.

These mutations of sorcery are not incompatible with accusations of child sorcery. On the contrary, as Englund (2007) notes in the case of Malawi, children who are too tired to perform their domestic chores or to do their homework are asked what they were doing during the night. When the woman of the household is not the child's biological mother, this questioning often involves violent methods.

Accusations in the context of family breakdown

Family breakdown often lies behind accusations of sorcery. Twenty-one of the children interviewed belonged to reconstituted families, in 13 cases as a result of the death of one or both parents. Furthermore, 20 out of the 31 children thought that they really did constitute a threat to their family. These accounts or testimonies confirm the destruction of solidarity both between generations and within reconstituted families. They back up, and indeed radicalize, the findings of studies carried out in Brazil, Kenya and India showing that a child's social value is extremely relative, and depends on the make-up of the family. Families often make heroic efforts to support their children in situations of extreme economic stress. But some are led to make selective choices that may affect the survival prospects of some family members, especially children (Scheper-Hughes, 1992; Last, 1994). Our survey reveals that children in a household including at least one non-biological parent are more likely to be accused of sorcery than children living with both their birth parents. This can be viewed as the consequence of a selective choice in a situation of survival. In a context in which family survival is not guaranteed, adults regard a non-biological child as just another useless mouth to feed. Madungu Tumwaka (2002) confirms this clearly in the survey he has carried out among a sample of 350 children accused of sorcery: 80 per cent of them were living in families of which the head of the household was not their biological parent.

The increase in the number of female children accused

It is worth noting that the numbers of girl children being accused is increasing. Out of the 31 children interviewed, 14 were girls. Our survey is certainly not representative, but we never at any time specifically set out to contact girls rather than boys, and there is an increasing proportion of girls among children accused of sorcery. By way of illustration, Monzenu (2001) reported that 400 girls aged between 6 and 12 had been accused in Bagira (Bukavu). Girls are usually exploited for household activities, and take over numerous domestic chores with a view to giving the mother or stepmother some spare time (Elson, 1982; Kabeer, 1994). For this reason, there are generally fewer girls than boys among street children (Lalor, 1999). However, the increasing feminization of street children, which had been a predominantly male phenomenon, is a sign of a deep social crisis. As Marguerat (2003) points out, families now prefer to get rid of girls instead of exploiting them domestically, as had usually been the case hitherto.

The rationalization of misfortune

The prevalence of magico-religious beliefs suggests ways of avoiding misfortune, as well as of rationalizing hardship or unlucky strokes of fate (Lallau and Dumbi 2007). The magico-religious system, which is fundamentally based on uncertainty, systematically provides a *post-factum* explanation (Desjeux, 1987). Once again, it is often the most vulnerable children, above all, who are usually viewed as the culprits to blame for the misfortunes that occur (De Boeck, 2004). Such a projection of sorcery onto children seems to be a paradigmatic inversion of group solidarity, as has been widely proposed by the micro-sociological theories of sorcery (Englund, 2007).

Sorcery accusations are often levelled in the wake of family misfortunes, or events considered to be misfortunes. Sorcery accusations are used to rationalize events *post-factum*, in an attempt to create certainty when uncertainty prevails. Out of the 31 children interviewed 16 were in such a situation. For example, one child commented, 'My mother died when I was two years old. My father did not want to stay with me because I was often ill. He told me I was cursed by my mother. He and his wife thought I was a sorcerer' (Nsiala Nsimba Reagan). 'My father beat me, accusing me of sorcery because he could not find a job' (Patrick Musungani Gemuso). Eight of the children had been accused on the basis of physical and psychological symptoms. These findings highlight the interweaving of old and new forms of witchcraft 'imagery'. Distinctive signs, which often are recognizable from birth or at an early age, constitute a central element in certain older forms of witchcraft imagery (Evans-Pritchard, 1937). The new forms of witchcraft imageries open up a wider sphere of recognition since the economic dimension, especially enrichment, often manifests itself in adulthood. In a good many cases, these new forms of sorcery are combined with older forms. Certain Churches even make considerable use of the children's physical and psychological features, which they regard as being an indication that they are sorcerers. Some of the leaflets distributed by such Churches are quite eloquent about this, providing such extensive descriptions of physical and psychological symptoms of sorcery that all sorts of accusations are possible. For example, they suggest that a child's good behaviour or restlessness, docility or stubbornness, cleverness or stupidity, are all possible signs indicating whether a child is a sorcerer or not. The range of distinctive signs is so wide that no child can be sure of escaping classification as a sorcerer.

Children as agents and victims

As Ballet *et al.* (2011) underline, formal and informal social norms in different cultures and societies affect children's capabilities. The social breakdown currently occurring in the DRC is radically changing the place of children, opening new capacities for child agency while the new logic being constructed is also producing victims. Then, the changing context and social norms simultaneously open new opportunities and create capability deprivation. In such a context, we highlight the ambiguity of children's agency.

Children as social actors of the crisis

The dislocation of intergenerational solidarity is occurring in an ambivalent context, in which children are indeed victims, but in which they also acquire autonomy and sometimes considerable power. They are not only victims in this transformation, they are also actors. The place that children are forced to occupy has to be viewed in the context of the society they inhabit, and the idea of a vulnerable and dependent child victim derived from a western vision should be open to discussion (Edwards, 1996). If we adopt a more 'flexible' vision of the place of children, one related to the society they inhabit, it is undeniable that in recent decades some countries have seen a structural disintegration of intergenerational relationships that has radically altered the place of children.

De Boeck (2000) identifies four main things that highlight a significant change in the place of children in the DRC. Firstly, children are not solely victims, they also have the power to kill. The child soldiers, the *kadogo*, who entered Kinshasa bearing arms when Kabila seized power in 1997, led to a radical revolution of the traditional image of children. Even in this situation, these children could in fact be victims, but despite this they took on an image of gun-toting power.

Secondly, the massive migration of teenagers into the Angolan province of Lunda Norte in pursuit of the wealth accruing from the mining of diamonds has led to an unprecedented breakdown between generations. Some of these teenagers came back home with far greater financial clout than their parents. They had become *mwana ya kilo*, 'heavy children'. Children are always expected to make a financial contribution to the family purse in developing countries, and they often contribute between 15 to 40 per cent of the family income (Save the Children Fund, 1995). However, what is involved here is no longer a useful financial contribution, but financial power that can become social power, and which plays an essential role in the redistribution of wealth within the family. This new social role triggers numerous family conflicts and constitutes fertile ground for accusations of sorcery. The acquisition of diamonds by means of sorcery becomes symptomatic of the social upheaval induced by this new social configuration (De Boeck,1999a, 1999b). Thirdly, children have become essential social agents in popular urban culture, in both popular music and in the media. This culture transmits an image of the 'bewitched' child to adults. Child-spirits or child sorcerers often appear in television series and on the radio (Biaya, 2000). Fourthly, the children themselves exploit this status, which may have been conferred on them, to acquire independence and demand their freedom. They themselves may claim to be sorcerers, and accuse someone of having bewitched them in order to settle old scores with this person.

This mutation involves an unprecedented ambiguity concerning child autonomy and vulnerability. Children acquire autonomy as a result of the power that money gives them, and go on to exploit this new autonomy. Thus, they are indeed agents in bringing this shift about. At the same time, this autonomy is an open door towards making the child more vulnerable to devastating consequences, because the power acquired is readily attributed to sorcery, leading to a terrible retribution for the children accused.

Children victims of accusations and violence

Children accused of sorcery are victims of violence both from family members, and from the Churches that propose deliverance. First, children accused of sorcery are frequently subjected to physical violence, and are thrown out of the family home or forced to run away. Out of the 31 children interviewed, 26 declared that they had suffered physical violence from family members. 'If you don't leave the house, you will be poisoned or burnt' (Blanche Nsona, 8 years old). 'My 5-year-old little brother could not stand up under torture. So he confessed to get some peace' (Tatukila Thamba, 19 years old). Numerous cases of deaths following ill-treatment of children accused of sorcery have been reported (Delanaye, 2001). Madungu Tumwaka (2002) reports a similar situation, and his survey further highlights the fact that violence is not limited to family members. When children are accused of sorcery, their neighbours, friends and teachers at school also indulge in regular acts of violence and humiliation.

Second, children are subjected to violent treatment organized by churches intent on delivering them from the evil. Kinshasa is characterized by an explosion in the number of churches (2,498 in 2000 according to Malandi, 2000). The neo-Pentecostal movement is highly represented, especially through Revival Churches (Mvuezolo Bazonzi, 2006). This context tends to favour or legitimate sorcery accusations, and the different Churches try to outdo each other in order to attract believers. As pointed out by Comaroff and Comaroff (1999: 291), 'Pentecostalism meets neoliberal enterprise: the chapel is, literally, a storefront in a shopping precinct'. Religion has carved out its own niche in the free market economy, and competition drives some Churches to indulge in radical practices.

Be this as it may, this movement triggers a change in social relationships and, in its own way, plays a part in the reconstruction of social capital (Musenge Mwanza, 2005).

Several studies have revealed the violent treatment meted out to children accused of sorcery (see De Boeck, 2000, for instance). Our survey testifies to sometimes extremely violent practices which result in the death of some children:

> The healing ceremonies took place in revival churches. A pastor burnt my body with candles. A prophet mother covered my body with some red sheet. In yet another church, tree sap was poured into my eyes. This made my eyes sting a lot. The healer then said that sorcery had gone. It was so painful.
>
> Glodi Mbete, 11 years old

> My aunts Emilie and Dinzolele took us to Pastor Okono in Kingasani. He made us drink some kind of strange water which was supposed to chase away evil spirits – or so he said. I went there along with my brothers and sisters Estella, Christelle, Dieudonné, Véronique, Tipy, Luyeye and Putu. When I drank that water, I vomited black. They all died, except Putu and me.
>
> Fabrice Khasa

Both agent and victim: From confession to the interiorization of the accusations

Out of the 31 children surveyed, 15 confessed they were or had been sorcerers. These confessions are often an opportunity for children to indict adults. Out of the 15 confessing children, 14 claimed that they had been bewitched by a close relative. 'I was bewitched by my grandmother (my father's mother). One day she gave me bananas (bitabe). She came back in the night and asked me to give her my mother' (Mayi L'Or, 7 years old). Confession thus proves to be both a method of 'deliverance' for children, and an indictment of adults.

Another phenomenon is that a child who lives with the wife of their father, or in a family member's house, is made to believe and say that he is a sorcerer, as the child is unaware and does not know what it means. However, they bring the child to the church and make him or her say publicly '*Naza ndoki. Ngai mutu naliaki maman na biso*', that is, 'I am a sorcerer, I am the one who ate (killed) my mother'. Sometimes they can even show him or her on television. Naively a child is happy to say these words without knowing the consequences of them. After this confirmation by the child himself, he will be evicted at home and rejected by society.

Confessions may in fact have various facets. But most of the time, there are strategic confessions by which children exploit the fear of adults, and seize the opportunity to take revenge on them. There also are non-autonomous confessions, which reconstruct reality after the children have been subjected to various supposed therapies. In very many cases, confessions help to redistribute suffering and violence among adults. They very frequently lead to real violence against the adults accused, and in some cases to their death. The path of violence thus comes full circle, from an adult to a child and then on to yet another adult. In line with Geschiere (1998), we can suggest that the new forms of witchcraft imagery should not simply be interpreted as a new capitalist version of sorcery, as they remain tightly linked to the notion of close relationships, especially within the family circle. To paraphrase Geschiere, any form of therapy requires, first and foremost, a journey into the heart of families.

As far as our survey is concerned however, religious therapy proves perverse in that it does not deliver children, but rather imprisons them. Out of the 15 children who confessed, 13 declared that they had been 'cured', whereas the others did not think they had yet been cured. In all cases, the accusation had been totally internalized, so that deliverance could only be achieved by accepting the accusation of sorcery. Deliverance is only temporary, and the accusations themselves are very rarely challenged. The 'healing' process is one of inactivation rather than of elimination. It strengthens the new imagery of witchcraft, and keeps it going for generations to come.

Conclusion: Agency and resilience in the Congolese context

New forms of witchcraft imagery are developing within a context marked by a twofold process of the destruction and reconstruction of social capital. On the one hand, many factors are contributing to the destruction of social capital (for example, civil war, economic crisis, AIDS and so on). On the other hand, factors that contribute to the reconstruction of social capital depend to a great extent on the role of Churches, especially those that are called sects. Reconstruction of this type is somewhat ambivalent: it allows the population to forge new bonds, but at the cost of legitimating child abuse. The reconstruction of intragenerational social capital occurs via intergenerational violence. The backlash of this reconstruction takes the form of a vicious circle of violence involving the children's confessions, with violence being transferred to adults and redistributed amongst them, and the children being impregnated with violence for the rest of their lives.

This is a very high price to pay for such a reconstruction, probably because social issues have also entered the market-place where the imagery of relationships has a market price, that is, the price that has to be paid for 'healing'. Such a price is not only a question of money: it should also be viewed in terms of the number of human lives it claims, or at least in terms of lasting losses of the capacity to act autonomously. In addition, the brunt of the human cost of such a 'survival reconstruction' process is primarily borne by children, whose resilience or indeed very existence is compromised.

In such a context, children develop an agency, which is certainly limited, but in which rest problems. It tends to have the effect of reinforcing the current intergenerational breakdown between children and adults. In addition, even though the children do develop a real capacity for action, their capacity to act contributes to exacerbating the social disruption and in some cases is targeted against adults. We cannot strictly call this 'agency' in Giddens' sense of the term. The context in which these children find themselves allows them little capacity to act otherwise.

Can we, therefore, speak of resilience in the children we met? First of all, we can consider that resilience is present, as a state, if we find the capacities for autonomous action that gave rise to the accusations of witchcraft. However, we are forced to admit that several months or even many years later the children we met were still in a situation of vulnerability. Firstly because the accusations, or at least the suspicions, persist even after religious therapy. Then also because these children, even after receiving 'therapy', are often driven out of the home, and so forced to confront the 'permanent shock' of the life of street children. Those that we met in a child reception centre seemed to have recovered a greater degree of agency, in particular displaying a capacity to formulate projects for the future ('I want to be a doctor', 'teacher', etc.). However, none of them had returned to 'life before'. Their resilience is therefore expressed by adapting to this new situation in a process rendered insecure by the multicrisis context in the DRC.

References

Aguilar Molina, J. (2006) *The Invention of Child Witches in the Democratic Republic of Congo: Social Cleansing, Religious Commerce and the Difficulties of being a Parent in an Urban Culture*, Save the Children, London.

Anich, R., Biggeri, M., Libanora, R. & Mariani, S. (2011), 'Street children in Kampala and NGO's actions: understanding capabilities deprivation and expansion', in

Biggeri, M., Ballet, J., & Comin, F. (eds) *Children and the Capability Approach*, Palgrave Macmillan, Basingstoke, pp. 107–136.

Ballet, J., Biggeri, M., & Comim, F. (2010) 'Children's autonomy, education and capabilities', in Lebmann, O. Hans-Uwe O. & Ziegler, H. (eds) *Closing the Capability Gap: Renegotiating Social Justice for the Young*, Barbara Budrich Publishers, Opladen-Deutschland, Heidelberg, pp. 165–177.

Ballet, J., Biggeri, M. & Comim, F. (2011), 'Children's agency and the capability approach: a conceptual framework', in Biggeri M., Ballet J. & Comin F. (eds) *Children and the Capability Approach*, Palgrave Macmillan, Basingstoke, p. 45.

Bellanca, N., Biggeri, M. & Marchetta, F. (2011) An extension of the capability approach: toward a theory of discapability, *ALTER, European Journal of Disability Research*, 5: 15–176.

Biaya, T.K. (2000) Jeunes et culture de la rue en Afrique urbaine, *Politique Africaine*, 80, December: 12–31.

Biggeri, M., Ballet, J. & Comim F. (2010) 'The capability approach and research on children: capability approach and children's issues', in Andresen, S., Diehm, I., Sander, U. & Ziegler, H. (eds) *Children and the Good Life: New Challenges for Research on Children*, Springer, pp. 75–89

Biggeri, M., Ballet, J. & Comim, F. (2011) *Children and the Capability Approach*, Palgrave-Macmillan, Basingtoke.

Cagatay, N., Elson, D. & Grown, C. (1995) 'Introduction: gender adjustment and macroeconomics', *World Development*, 23: 238–253.

Comaroff, J. & Comarroff, J. (1999) 'Occult economies and the violence of abstraction: notes from the South African postcolony', *American Ethnologist*, 26(2): 279–303.

Cornia, G., Jolly, R. & Stewart, F. (1987) *Adjustment With A Human Face*, Oxford University Press, Oxford.

De Boeck, F. (1999a) 'Domesticating diamonds and dollars: identity, expenditure and sharing in South-Western Zaïre (1984–1997)', in Meyer, B. and Geschiere, P. (eds) *Globalization and Identity: Dialectics of Flow and Closure*, Blackwell, Oxford.

De Boeck, F. (1999b) 'Dogs breaking their Leash: globalization and shiffting gender categories in the diamond traffic between Angola and DR Congo (1984–1997)', in De Lame, D. & Zabus, C. (eds) *Changements au féminin en Afrique noire. Anthropologie et littérature*, vol.1, Musée Royal de l'Afrique central/L'Harmattan, Tervuren/Paris.

De Boeck, F. (2000) 'Le deuxième monde et les enfants sorciers', *Politique Africaine*, 80: 32–57.

De Boeck, F. (2004) 'Etre Shege à Kinshasa: Les enfants, la rue et le monde occulte', in Trefon, T. (ed.), *Ordre et désordre à Kinshasa: Réponses populaires à la faillite de l'Etat*, ASDOC/L'Harmattan, Cahiers Africains, Bruxelles/Paris p. 173–192.

De Herdt, T. (2001) 'Social policy and the ability to appear in public without shame: some lessons from a food relief programme in Kinshasa', paper presented at the Conference Justice and Poverty: Examining Sen's Capability Approach, Cambridge, 5–7 June.

De Herdt, T. (2003) 'Poor parents, their daughter, her child and her lover, Understanding changes in household size and composition in Kinshasa', working paper, Institute of Development Policy and Management, University of Antwerp, July.

De Villers, G. & Monnier, P. (eds) (2002) *Kinshasa: Manières de Vivre*, Cahiers Africains, 49–50.

Delanaye (2001) *Les chrétiens face aux accusations de la sorcellerie*, Le Senevé, Kinshasa.

Desjeux, D. (1987) *Stratégies paysannes en Afrique noire, le Congo, Essai sur la gestion de l'incertitude*, L'Harmattan, Paris.

Douglas, M. (1999) 'Sorcery accusations unleashed: the lele revisited, 1987', *Africa*, 69(2).

Edwards, M. (1996) 'New approaches to children and development: introduction and overview', *Journal of International Development*, 8(6): 813–827.

Elson, D. (1982) 'The differentiation of children's labour in the capitalist labour market', *Development and Change*, 13: 479–497.

Englund, H. (2007) 'Witchcraft and the limits of mass mediation in Malawi', *Journal of the Royal Anthropoligical Institute*, 13: 295–311.

Evans-Pritchard, E.E. (1937) *Witchcraft, Oracles and Magic among the Azande*, Clarendon Press, Oxford.

Falangani, Mvondo Pashi (2002) 'Paupérisation de familles petites-bourgeoises et transformation des valeurs en période de crise', in De Villers, G. & Monnier P. (eds) pp. 113–140.

Fisiy, C.F. and Geschiere, P. (1991) 'Sorcery, witchcraft and accumulation: regional variations in South and West Cameroon', *Critique of Anthropology*, 11(3): 251–278.

Geschiere, P. (1998) 'Globalization and the power of indeterminate meaning: witchcraft and spirit in Africa and East Asia', *Development and Change*, 29: 811–837.

Giddens, A. (1979) *Central Problems in Social Theory: Action, Structure and Contradiction in Social Analysis*, California University Press, Berkeley, CA.

Giovannoni, M., Trefon, T., Kasongo-Banga, J. & Mwema, C. (2004) 'Agir à la place-et en dépit-de l'Etat: ONG et associations de la société civile à Kinshasa', in Trefon, T. (ed.), *Ordre et désordre à Kinshasa: Réponses populaires à la faillite de l'Etat*, ASDOC/L'Harmattan, Cahiers Africains, Bruxelles/Paris, pp. 119–134.

Horna Padrón, M. & Ballet, J. (2011) 'Child agency and identity: the case of children peruvian children in a transitional situation', in Biggeri, M., Ballet, J. & Comin, F. (eds) *Children and the Capability Approach*, Palgrave-MacMillan, Basingstoke, pp. 162–174.

Human Rights Watch (2006) *Quel avenir? Les enfants de la rue en République démocratique du Congo*, Human Rights Watch, New York.

Kabeer, N. (1994) *Reversed Realities: Gender Hierarchies in Development Thought*, Verso, London.

Lallau, B. (2007) 'Capacités et gestion de l'incertitude: essai sur les stratégies des maraîchers de Kinshasa, République Démocratique du Congo', *Journal of Human Development*, 8(1): 153–173.

Lallau, B. & Dumbi, C. (2007) 'L'éthique du mayélé: les fins et les moyens de la "débrouille" dans la filière maraîchère de Kinshasa', *Mondes en Développement*, 137(Mars): 67–80.

Lalor, K.J. (1999) 'Street children: a comparative perspective', *Child Abuse and Neglect*, 23(8): 759–770.

Last, M. (1994) 'Putting children first', *Disasters*, 18: 192–202.

Luzolele, Lola Nkakala, L. (2002) *Congo-Kinshasa: Combattre la pauvreté en situation de post-conflit. Synergie entre l'Etat, le marché et le capital social*, L'Harmattan, Collection Etudes Africaines, Paris.

Madungu Tumwaka, P. (2002) 'La violence faite à l'enfant dit sorcier à Kinshasa', 11ᵉ Colloque de l'AIDELF (Enfants d'aujourd'hui: Diversité des contextes, pluralité des parcours), Dakar, 10–13 December.

Malandi, K. (2000) *Guide pour l'option religieuse ou chrétienne pour la ville de Kinshasa*, Working paper, Kinshasa

Marguerat, Y. (2003) 'Malheur à la ville dont le prince est un enfant (de la rue): un essai de synthèse sur la dynamique sociale du monde des enfants de la rue', in Marguerat, Y. (dir.) *Garçons et filles des rues dans la ville africaine: diversité et dynamique des marginalités juvéniles à Abidjan, Nairobi, Antananarivo: rapport de l'équipe de recherche Dynamique du Monde des Jeunes de la Rue: recherches comparatives sur l'évolution de la marginalité juvénile en Afrique et à Madagascar*, EHESS, Paris.

Monzenu, M. (2001) 'Tu me verras le soir', *Afrique-espoir*, 16: 25–26.

Musenge Mwanza, G. (2005) 'Evangélisation à Kinshasa: une stratégie d'exploitation ou l'expression d'une foi ardente', Centre d'Etudes Politiques, Université de Kinshasa, February.

Muwalawala, Kipanda (1994) 'Les formes d'oppression subies par les enfants de la rue à Kinshasa', in Marjuvia (coll.), *A l'écoute des enfants de la rue en Afrique noire*, Fayard, Collection Les Enfants du Fleuve, Paris, pp. 361–375.

Mvuezolo Bazonzi, J. (2006) *Les églises du réveil de Kinshasa à l'ombre du mouvement néopentecôtiste mondiale: entre nivellement et déconstruction culturels*, Centre d'Etudes Politiques, Université de Kinshasa.

Nzeza Bilakila, A. (2004), 'La coop à Kinshasa: survie et marchandage', In Trefon, T. (ed.) *Ordre et désordre à Kinshasa: Réponses populaires à la faillite de l'Etat*, ASDOC/L'Harmattan, Cahiers Africains, Bruxelles/Paris, pp. 33–46.

Pirot, B. (2004) *Enfants des rues d'Afrique centrale. Douala et Kinshasa. De l'analyse à l'action*, Karthala, Paris.

Rousseau, S. (2005) 'L'analyse de la vulnérabilité par l'approche des capabilités: Le cas des villages ruraux de Madagascar', PhD in Economics, University of Versailles Saint-Quentin-En Yvelines.

Ruel, M. (1997) *Belief, Ritual and Securing of Life: Reflexive Essays on a Bantu Religion*, E.J. Brill, Leiden.

Save the Children Fund (1995) *Towards a Children's Agenda: new Challenges for Social Development*, Save the Children Fund, London.

Scheper-Hughes, N. (1992) *Death Without Weeping: The Violence of Everyday Life in Brazil*, University of California Press, Berkeley, CA.

Tollens, E. (2003), *Sécurité alimentaire à Kinshasa: un face à face quotidien avec l'adversité*, Kotholieke Universiteit Leuven, faculté des Sciences Agronomiques et de la Biologie Appliquée, Working Paper no. 77, September.

Trefon, T. (2004) *Ordre et désordre à Kinshasa: Réponses populaires à la faillite de l'Etat*, ASDOC/L'Harmattan, Cahiers Africains, Bruxelles/Paris, pp. 61–62.

12

Youth Agency and Participation Outside the Classroom

Vittorio Iervese and Luisa Tuttolomondo

Introduction

According to Sen (1999) participation consists of the possibility for the individual to freely take decisions regarding his or her life and is therefore fundamental in human development processes. In this regard this chapter adopts a sociological perspective in order to provide Sen's capability approach (CA) with some multidisciplinary observations about the promotion of social participation among children and adolescents in the Occupied Palestinian Territories. With this aim, the chapter stems from recent literature on the sociology of childhood which considers children and adolescents as social actors able to exert agency on the society in which they live (James *et al.*, 1998; Corsaro, 2005; Tisdall *et al.*, 2006). Other references adopted regard the concept of promotion of social participation among children and adolescents (Baraldi and Iervese, 2012), meant as a methodology to foster in them the ability to behave and choose autonomously.

Starting from these assumptions, this chapter draws on data collected during research carried out in the framework of an international cooperation project called *The Rights of Minors in Palestine: Legal and Psychosocial Protection,* funded by the European Union and developed from 2008 to 2010 by the Italian NGO Oxfam Italy and the Palestinian NGO Defence for Children International (DCiP) Palestine. The project was aimed at promoting social participation and at raising children's rights awareness among Palestinian children and adolescents.

In the last 10 years Sen's CA as a theoretical framework, aiming to define and measure well-being, has spread consistently, thus being used in different fields regarding human development (Robeyns, 2006). Consequently, the application of the CA in so many different areas of research has led to the adoption of various and different methodologies, both quantitative and qualitative, and to the undertaking of a constant dialogue with many disciplines.

In this regard, the present chapter will be divided into two parts. Firstly, it will provide a brief description of some core concepts coming from the relatively recent sociology of childhood, for example related to, 'child agency' and 'child participation', in order to highlight some possible elements of difference and convergence with the fundamentals of Sen's CA. The aim is to understand whether the references to theories coming from this discipline can be applied within the capability framework and have the potential to be useful in fostering the development of CA studies dealing with children's well-being.

The same objective is pursued in the second part of the chapter. It shifts from the theoretical to the empirical field, providing a brief example of the possible implications and results coming from the application in practice of the theoretical tools and concepts discussed in the first part.

The child as a capable agent

Recently, within CA studies on children and the 'sociology of childhood' (SC), the child has started to be considered as a capable agent. Within the CA this has meant shifting the focus to the future realization of children's capabilities and increased interest in the development of capabilities during the present stage of childhood (Biggeri *et al.*, 2006; Bonvin and Galster, 2010; Babic, 2011; Ballet *et al.*, 2011). Within SC, considering the child as a capable agent means looking at him or her as competent in relationships with peers and adults and able to modify the social structures within which he or she finds themselves (Baraldi, 2001).

In both cases, on the one hand, the child is not considered as an isolated individual any more, but as a subject living within contexts of social interaction, of which he or she is an integral part. On the other hand the child is not a passive receiver, but a social actor that produces social practices and meanings that are able to have an impact on the social situation he or she experiences. In this sense, competence and individual skills are linked to the social conditions that allow them to be expressed and effective. Therefore, the individual is inscribed within a chain of relationships and social meanings that constitute the value and the opportunity of participating. These values and possibilities depend on a specific 'culture of childhood' made up in specific historical and cultural contexts. This is different from a 'culture of children' which is instead a product of the direct and active participation of children (James *et al.*, 1998; Iervese, 2006).

The mainstream culture of childhood follows a perspective that considers children according to an individualistic and biographic perspective. In other words, this culture is interested more in the 'becoming' rather than in the 'being' (this is evident overall in pedagogical psychology); the child is important because he or she will become an adult in the future.

Against this backdrop, an issue that has grown in importance over the last few decades is the debate on the autonomy of the child, understood as having the ability to make responsible choices, thereby demonstrating a capacity for self-realization.

Starting from these assumptions it is possible to point out two important elements for reflection upon the application of the CA to childhood. The first element concerns the awareness of the difference existing between the culture of childhood, created by adults, and that of the culture of children which is often ignored. Children's capabilities and functioning are observable only by enabling their self-expression.

A second relevant aspect to be considered concerns the dynamics of production and the observation of capabilities. The consideration of the child as a social actor allows a shift from the cognition of the individual to the social interactions that shape and give meaning to the contribution of every participant. In this sense, rather than through single performances, capabilities are expressed and defined by the social contexts of interaction and communication. Therefore, the next section follows this shift by suggesting consequent theoretical and methodological instruments.

Agency and interaction

The traditional concept of socialization evokes a view of the child as an incomplete, developing person; as a passive recipient of social interactions. The idea of agency, on the other hand, introduces a different conception: socialization takes place through children's participation (James *et al.*, 1998). Socialization is not the result of passive reception, but is determined by the capacity of children to extract meanings from social processes with which they come into contact.

The term 'agency', used in many psychosocial theories (Giddens, 1984; Bandura, 1989), generally refers to the ability and possibility for an individual to make choices and to act autonomously within a system of norms and constraints. Agency implies not only that the individual is endowed with a certain grade of competence but also the presence of favourable environmental conditions in order to express this competence.

Sen's CA draws a distinction between well-being freedom and agency freedom; the latter implying a person's capacity to exercise their own free will:

> the capability set would consist of the alternative functioning vectors that she can choose from. While the combination of a person's functionings reflects her actual achievements, the capability set reflects the freedom to achieve: the alternative functioning combinations from which this person can choose.

> Sen, 1999: 75

Given the lack of agency freedom during childhood, the interest of CA studies in this field has often focused on the analysis of children's functionings, considered as fundamental in determining the full development of their capabilities when adults.

In recent years, it has become clear within the CA that 'applying the capability approach to children therefore entails taking a stand with regard to their capacity for self-determination' (Ballet *et al.*, 2011). Therefore, it is possible to notice a fundamental convergence between the interpretation of agency in the most recent studies on children's capabilities (Biggeri *et al.*, 2006; Bonvin and Galster, 2010; Babic, 2011) and the one used within the SC. On the other hand, it is important to underline that SC looks at children as able to condition the actions of their interlocutors in communication with them, above all in interactions. In this sense, it is possible to understand agency as the capacity of children to shape one's own life and to influence the lives of others affecting their environment. This concept comes from the children's individual competences and awareness and pays attention to social interaction that allows finding out if and how some competences can be converted into capabilities.

How to observe agency

The CA asserts that the child's ability to convert resources and commodities into capabilities and functionings depends on individual and social conversion factors (Ballet *et al.*, 2011). Important *social conversion factors* can be observed in adult-children interactions, which break the common hierarchical 'generational order' (Alanen *et al.*, 2007).

For this purpose, we present data on interactions between adults and children, showing in which ways 1) adults' actions can promote opportunities for children's expression and 2) children can exploit this opportunity, projecting adults' subsequent actions and changing the structure of social relations with them. We aim to highlight empirical evidence of children's capabilities and functionings, on the one hand, and interactional facilitation of active participation as a powerful social conversion factor, on the other.

More specifically, attention is given to the turn-taking of children and their interlocutors in specific interaction sequences. Analysis of such sequences enables observation of: a) how the actions of children and adults are correlated, for example, how a certain kind of answer follows a certain kind of question; b) how each action of children and adults projects another one, making it relevant or probable, for example, that certain kinds of questions project certain responses. In particular, it is possible to observe: 1) value orientations (for example, the education and upbringing of children); 2) the definition of roles (for example, teacher and pupil) and the participants' scope for personal expression; 3) expectations about the results of the communication in terms of learning (cognitive expectations), compliance with rules (normative expectations) and the possibility for personal expression (affective expectations) (Baraldi, 2001).

This type of analysis makes it possible, therefore, to observe how the actions of children are coordinated with those of adults, and is useful for highlighting how children and adults are equally responsible and competent interlocutors in interaction. Secondly, this analysis positions interaction within a wider system of communication, such as an educational system. Finally, this type of analysis permits observation of capabilities in the interaction, that is, as a result of a participated social setting. Particularly in relation to the former point, the orientation of values emerging from communication is neither predetermined nor received equally to the those values that were transmitted, but is original and unexpected, because it is a spontaneous contribution from the participants.

The autonomy shown by children during interaction allows their action to be relevant for the society as a whole. Therefore, unlike education where the conformity of resultant communication does not allow the bringing about of any change to social life, in this case the action produced has public visibility, thus creating disturbances in the relationships among peers and with adults.

Approaching capabilities in practice: The promotion of agency and social participation in Palestine

The methodology and the theoretical assumptions shown in the previous paragraphs turned out to be very useful for the analysis of the participative workshops that took place within the framework of the project of international cooperation mentioned above, which was implemented from 2008 to 2010 in the Occupied Palestinian Territories. The project was aimed at contrasting the particular situation of rights violation affecting many Palestinian children and youths. Indeed, due to the regime of occupation inside the Territories they are often exposed to violence and also live in conditions of deprivation because of the economic difficulties of their families. All these factors prevent them from living in a comfortable environment, therefore undermining their well-being.

Among its many activities, the intervention concerned the establishment of participative workshops. The aim of these activities was to allow the children to develop children's rights awareness in an alternative context, but complementary to the school environment. About 40 participants among Palestinian children and adolescents usually attending DCiP centres were involved, coming from different social backgrounds (from middle class to low income) and cities (Nablus, Hebron, Bethlehem and Jerusalem).

The research, carried out between June and August 2009, adopted both quantitative and qualitative methods: five semi-structured questionnaires were completed by the social workers who facilitated the initiatives, seven video-observations of the participatory activities were made and two focus groups were carried out with the adolescents involved, with a total of 16 participants and a total of 16 hours of video-recording. Thanks to the data collected, the evaluative analysis can examine the participative processes carried out by the project and their coherence with the final objective of promoting social participation and children's rights awareness among children and adolescents. Moreover, the evaluative analysis highlights the added opportunities of using the promotion of social participation in children and in adolescents in order to raise their own rights' awareness and to improve their capabilities.

The activities were carried out at the DCiP centres of Nablus and Bethlehem, mainly during summer holidays. They consisted of: 1) municipal councils of adolescents (one for every participant's city of provenance), in charge of working out some initiatives regarding the rights of minors, and in particular the representations of childhood in the media, the rights of refugee children, identity and belonging, difficulties of movement due to the status of Occupation and the rights of female children; 2) meetings to discuss the rights of Palestinian children with the objective of drafting a document to modify the present law on the rights of minors and to be presented to the Palestinian Legislative Committee (PLC); 3) the involvement of both minors and members of some local community-based organizations (CBOs) in the process of working out a common strategy to guarantee the rights of minors inside the same organizations.

The general objective of these activities was not only the consultation but also the promotion of active participation between children and adults upon specific subjects. With this regard, a distinction has been made between consultation and participation, that is, between involvement in the decision-making tasks of adults and the taking of decisions: consultation offers children the opportunity to increase their capacity for personal expression and builds confidence in relations with adults, but only actual participation in decisions, together with intervention initiated by the children themselves, can be seen as participation created with and by children, making them feel influential (Holland and O'Neill 2006).

The collected data has been used firstly to look at the communicative processes carried out by the intervention, then to investigate the results; the meaning produced following the activities. In the first case, the video-observations allowed a detailed analysis of the forms and meanings circulating during the interaction among participants. In the second case, the two focus groups have been used to investigate the meanings produced by the intervention on the subjects of childhood, rights of minors and the opportunity to participate within society.

In order to better describe the observations from the analysis, some extracts from the conducted video-observations and focus groups are reported. Table 12.1

Table 12.1 Abbreviations and symbols used for transcription of collected materials

Abbreviation/symbol	Meaning
Att.	Activity
Foc.	Focus group
Op.	Operator
I	Interpreter
R	Researcher
Op/I	Operator and interpreter
G	Girl child
B	Boy child
A	Adult

provides a key to the main abbreviations and symbols used for the transcription of collected materials.

The analysis of the forms of communication has been carried out by taking into account the presence of the following elements in the communication: the typology of expectations produced during the interaction (what are the expectations towards the interaction and toward the participants?), the forms of the contribution (how is the participation of role and/or person structured?), the indicative values (which are the cultural meanings that drive the action of the participants) and the ways by which communication is structured (what are the relationships of symmetry/asymmetry among participants?). The observation of these features enables us to observe how the interaction is shaped by the contributions of the different participants and which meanings are produced. In other words, the analysis allows us to highlight the individual and social capabilities that are produced in a certain social setting.

One of the most striking elements coming from the analysis of the participative workshops is the spontaneity shown by children and adolescents during their participation in the activities. In fact, in all the three types of initiative observed, it is possible to notice their ease in taking the floor. This feature is mainly demonstrated by the frequent use of forms of *testimony*, where the personal experience of everyone becomes relevant and reveals itself to be the primary form of knowledge by which it is possible to give and understand opinions about the topic of children's rights:

(Att. 2)

Children take turns saying which points they want to insert on the brochure.

1(Op.): (Towards G2) Please explain the sixth point that is which problems we face because of the Occupation . . .

2(G2): Settlers arrive and then the soldiers, but they arrive to harm us instead of helping.

3(Op.): Are these things that happen every day to you?

4(Tutti): Yes, yes.

5(G2): When somebody goes to meet a friend he is always afraid of meeting the settlers.

6(G1): Yes, yes a friend of mine was walking and felt in danger because a soldier was watching him.

In this extract, for example, the daily experiences regarding the presence of settlers (the risk of being damaged or being observed by them), together with the feelings associated with them (fear of encounter, sense of insecurity), become a stimulus for discussion and a reason to participate in the activity. The personal story of every participant becomes an instrument to talk and think about a more general issue to the one of children's rights. This inductive dynamic, which goes from particular to general, also shows the participants' skills and competences in linking their personal experiences to the general context, identifying possible factors of risk, together with the ability to adopt strategies of prevention and adjusting to these factors. In this case, psychology uses the definition of 'coping strategy' to refer to those practices that lead to facing trauma or stressful situations (Holahan and Moos, 1994; Lazarus and Folkman, 1984). Every coping strategy implies a series of actions, cognitive, behavioural and intentional, aimed at controlling the negative impact of the stressful event and therefore can be interpreted as a dynamic process, as it is constituted of a series of reciprocal answers, by which the environment and the individual are reciprocally influenced. Therefore, coping strategies activate capabilities in response to problems, which in disadvantaged conditions are only observable through the examination of the daily practices of interaction.

However, in some cases adopting the form of personal testimony, rather than allowing the emergence of individual perspectives, moves collective identities into the foreground, conveyed by the use of an inclusive 'us' referring to the category of childhood or to belonging to an organization or other entity.

(Att. 6)

The presentation of the third group (South Hebron):

(B5): We offer psychosocial support but for cultural reasons not everyone refers to us. Some children for family reasons don't manage to attend the centre. We investigated these problems by organizing some seminars. The main problem is the closed mentality. The building of the centre is not that good, it lacks sufficient spaces. There is little contact with children. Why do volunteers work with us? They care about the centre. When there are problems within the family, children are the first suffering from that. Some of them come here to talk about it.

Presentation of the fourth group, Jaffa Cultural Centre, Balata refugee camp, Nablus

(G1): The centre teaches us which are our rights within the negative behaviours we are subjected to. I noticed that within the association children are thought to be able to think. With the other boys and girls we discovered this problem and we talked about it with the social workers but there are also problems of political divisions. In fact in the centre we can find the same problems we find outside it. These problems are visible to children, within the activities. Problems arrive inside the centre because the social workers come from outside.

In this extract we notice that the intervention of B5 and that of G1 are sharply in contrast in terms of a different use of 'us', that in both cases entail ethnocentric connotations. In the first case the use of the first person plural is referring to the association, as a whole, considered in its rescuing function towards a surrounding context which is not respectful of children's rights. In the second case, instead, 'us' refers to the category of children that are engaged in a permanent fight with an adult world that is unable to understand their values. Then, thanks to this contrast it is possible to observe the forms of awareness, analysis and self-organization adopted by the children themselves ('with the other boys and girls we discovered this problem and we talked about it with the social workers'). In this case their capabilities are expressed through the possibility of supporting and promoting the culture of children in spite of a culture of childhood that finds the causes of children's problems in the family and cultural system in general ('the main problem is the closed mentality'). Therefore, within the interaction, different orientations of values are opposed and determine the possibility of action from the single participants. In this way these create the appropriate conditions for the expression and valorization of the participants' competences.

Among these actions particular attention is paid to the discovery of the ways of conduct adopted by the social workers. Spanning from the activities of the municipal councils to the ones aimed at the elaboration of a draft document to modify the present Palestinian law for children's rights, the communicative approach they use is not always the same. Therefore, in some cases it is possible to notice the predominance of a promotional approach pointing to the participants' self-expression:

(Att. 1)

(G1): [towards the social worker] beyond the poster. I'll strangle you if [you] say we don't have enough money for these ideas we proposed! Let's start to talk about the logo. We have to remember we need a logo about refugees and not refugees without discriminations.

[They talk about their nail polish]

(Op.): So what do we have to write down on the poster?

(G2): We need to have four colours together: white, green, red, black, the colours of our flag or otherwise we can draw the shape of the Palestinian flag and write something in the middle or ...

(Op.): Or we can make a white frame and draw the words with four different colours!

(G1): Do we want to involve also the trendy kids with their underwear showing? Oops! I forgot there's a camera recording!

In this example, the seriousness and the commitment in the activity is interrupted by moments of conviviality and interpersonal communication (in this case the reference is to the nail polish and the telling of a joke) that appear as a simple digression from the main topic of conversation but actually confirm and project the affective expectations, therefore creating an atmosphere of intimacy and reciprocal trust. From this perspective, colloquial expressions such as 'I'll strangle you!' or the reference to 'the trendy kids with their underwear showing' are outside the norms of behaviour we would expect in more formal situations. The balance between entertainment and intimacy is typical of the communication in groups of adolescents (Baraldi and Rossi, 2002) and is also the most attractive form of communication for them. In this extract, the forms of interpersonal communication present specific objectives set out by adults. In this way the participants are put in the right conditions to participate as unique and specific persons, rather than as members of a group or with predetermined roles. It is exactly this combination that encourages the active and creative participation of the adolescents.

However, in the following case, communication seems to convey expectations of adjustment of the children to the social workers' requests. Their interventions during the interaction, in fact, appear to treat the adolescents' contribution as roles more than people.

(Att. 5)

The adolescents have to formulate the questions to be made in front of the Palestinian Legislative Council (Plc) during the next meeting

1(Op.): [Reformulating the question proposed by G2] The deficit is not only laws on children but also in other aspects. What do you think to do to fill this deficit as members of the Plc?

2(G4): Because you [the Plc] represent a State responsible for the children and their protection from the road to criminality, what have you already done until now to prevent children from taking the wrong direction? To allow them to use their time in a positive way?

3(Op.): We have to be more specific, we need to remember that we are talking to a Legislative Council, we have to ask them what they did in terms of infrastructure and recreational spaces for children.

In this case, adolescents are encouraged by the social worker to express the contents of their thoughts according to criteria that are considered to be more suitable for the situation, so producing normative expectations. On the one hand they are trying to obtain an alignment (Goffman, 1981) of the participants themselves, on the other they ignore the resources expressed in the conversation.

The analysis of the video-observations highlights the possibility of observing an oscillation on the side of communication between different forms of education. These are more oriented to role and to the creation of cognitive and normative expectations, and forms of promotion of participation defined by the testimony, where it is noticed that there is an orientation to person and the predominance of expectations of personal expression. Moreover, it is important to point out that the reproduction of one form rather than another inevitably influences the children's possibilities of taking part in the activity and of having an impact on the issues affecting them, the opportunity to make their participation effective, and thus distinguishing it from mere consultation (Hart, 1992).

The impact of the participative workshops on children's capabilities and agency

With the aim of investigating the impact produced by the promotional interventions examined so far, two focus groups were conducted with some of the children committed to the activities of the municipal councils and the activities for the elaboration of a draft document to modify the present Palestinian law for children's rights. In the first focus group, 11 adolescents, composed of five males and six females coming from Bethlehem, were involved. The second focus group saw the participation of five girls all coming from the district of Nablus. Due to the small number of participants, these focus groups do not have any comprehensive or representative value but they allowed us to obtain some significant data regarding the social consequences of the intervention. In this regard, a relevant element pointed out by the participants' answers concerns the idea of the effective success of the initiative in promoting the social participation of children and adolescents. In fact, they clearly demonstrate the perceived change produced by the intervention. They feel more aware of their rights and more prone to participate:

(Foc. 2)

(G4): Yes, sure. Without DCi we would know just the symbolic things we learn at school but here we have understood more. Thanks to DCi we believe we can change the society and improve the situation regarding children's rights.

(G6): Now we believe that even if I'm a child I can do many things, where there's the first step there are the others.

The merit of that is mainly attributed to the social workers' ability to create an atmosphere of trust towards themselves and towards the possibility of producing a change inside the surrounding reality, in particular in the field regarding the promotion of children's rights. Trust has to be considered as a sophisticated social device able to invest in the participants' interaction and agency and therefore able to support and free their hidden capabilities. Obviously, investing in trust can easily turn into delusion and consequently disillusion where the imagined scenarios are not realized. But this is a problem regarding the coherence that intervention and policies need to fulfil.

The right to participate is meant by the interviewees as a right referring to the ability and necessity of influencing and modifying some aspects of the general living conditions by exerting concrete, visible and active social action. In particular, among the fields of action is included the possibility for children and adolescents to be active promoters of their rights, by both becoming first guarantors of their respect and spreading their knowledge among other children:

(Foc. 2)

(G6): The first step we took consisted of participating when we entered here.

(G1): I came here when I felt something missing, I came to participate.

(Ric): Participate for what?

(G1): Firstly to know my rights, to understand the environment, to try to be active, to try to bring changes and be active in this city.

(Ric): Do you all agree?

[Everybody nods]

The acquisition of awareness of their own rights and the commitment in the promotion of them among other children and adolescents is one of the most evident effects of the communicative processes produced by the intervention. This effect can be described, following the terminology adopted in the framework of development cooperation, as a capacity-building stage, that is, 'a process of developing and strengthening the skills, instincts, abilities, processes and resources that organizations and communities need to survive, adapt, and thrive in the fast-changing world' (Philbin, 1996). In this way, the promotion of agency and participation becomes strictly linked to the strategies of the observation, support and development of capabilities.

A further consideration needs to be made regarding adolescents' ability to act autonomously and to exert their agency. From the opinions expressed during the focus groups, what stands out is the participants' perceptions of being able to express accurate judgements on the issues directly affecting them. In some cases they feel they have more complex and deeper insights compared to adults. For example, when dealing with the issue of abuse and violence suffered by children, adolescents work out explanations showing a more accurate perception of the problem.

However, children's active and visible participation is not automatically translated into innovation and change. On the contrary, children seem to carefully select resources and cultural orientations without any preclusion but on the basis of the value and potential they entail within their social horizon. During the focus groups, for example, the system of traditional values within Palestinian society is not criticized or challenged. The opinions expressed pointed out the belief that the commitment in encouraging the respect of rights of minors and above all in promoting social participation has to focus more on the institutional side than on breaking with certain social habits. This view ends up producing evident contradictions (for example, regarding a woman's position and her possibility of freely acting and choosing) but to be really understood it has to be linked to the analysis of communication. In fact, this sense of inviolability of the community's traditional values can easily be traced back to the presence of ethnocentric forms of communication highlighted by the analysis of the video-observations. As claimed before, this analysis, based on the reference to a generational or community 'us', seems to be in contrast with the general objective of promoting the participants' personal expression. The oscillation between personal expression and ethnocentric cohesion is perhaps the most interesting and controversial issue that has to be taken into account by CA and SC in dealing with non-western contexts.

Conclusions

The empirical observations carried out, thanks to the use of the video-observations, allowed us to identify the forms of communication that are more effective in promoting adolescents' social participation and expression of agency. The analysis of the extracts highlighted that the prevalence of affective expectations and the forms of interaction focused on the personal experience of the participants are some of the fundamental features needed in the communication in order to give it a promotional value. In spite of this, participation as well as capabilities can be considered to be effective when individuals really are in a position to choose and to have an impact on their life and social context. With regard to the promotion of children's participation, it is possible to observe frequent oscillations within educational and normative forms. In these cases, the ability of promotional interventions in making visible, supporting and promoting capabilities is limited to children's opportunities to learn. Therefore, participation risks becoming mere tokenism rather than citizenship (Hart, 1992).

Two further elements that have to be taken into account in promoting adolescents' agency turned out to be a) the context and b) the social system within which these initiatives take place. In the particular context of the Occupied Palestinian Territories the analysis pointed out the presence in the communication of forms of collective identity more than any individual one. The overlap between promotion of individual participation and ethnocentric orientation existing in Palestinian policy produces a paradox that is hard to solve. The forms of 'ethnocentric participation' or the 'lobby positions' entailed by some children during the workshops, far from being a solution, in fact amplify this paradox. It is a very common feature in Palestinian society, which is constituted of numerous clans and family groups, often in contrast to each other, thus producing complicated dynamics of participation.

Every interaction has to be considered within specific social systems that entail constraints, ways of action, objectives and functional operations. The promotion of agency, participation and capabilities is always accomplished inside specific social systems and for this reason has to be considered differently from a qualitative and quantitative point of view. Therefore, social systems, each of them endowed with a specific structure and semantic, have to be carefully considered when carrying out a capability or agency analysis. Taking this into consideration, the orientations, expectations, forms of contribution and forms of interaction can be used as methodological instruments to take into account these structural features.

Finally, opinions expressed by children during the two focus groups allowed us to observe the impact produced by the intervention on participants' daily routines. The activities carried out have been considered fundamental by the children, promoting their ability to act autonomously but also fostering the acquisition of awareness of their own rights and promoting the respect of children's rights in the community. Therefore, it is possible to say that the initiatives to promote participation have contributed to the expansion of children's capabilities sets. This impact is demonstrated both by the agency expressed by adolescents during the activities and by their perceptions of a change which occurred before and after the intervention.

References

Alanen, L., Olk, T., Qvortrup, J. & Wintersberger, H. (eds) (2007) *Childhood, Generational Order and the Welfare State: Exploring Children's Social and Economic Welfare*, Volume 1 of COST A19: Children's Welfare, Denmark: University Press of Southern Denmark.

Babic, B. (2011) Ohne intellektuelle Redlichkeit kein Fortschritt. Kritische Anmerkungen zum Umgang mit dem Capability Approach aus erziehungswissenschaftlicher Sicht, in: Sedmak, C., Babic, B., Bauer, R. & Posch, C. (eds) *Der Capability Approach in sozialwissenschaftlichen Kontexten. Überlegungen zur Anschlussfähigkeit eines entwicklungspolitischen Konzepts*, Wiesbaden: VS Verlag, pp. 75–89.

Ballet J., Biggeri M. & Comim F. (eds) (2011) *Children and the Capability Approach*, Basingstoke: Palgrave Macmillan

Bandura, A. (1989) Human agency in social cognitive theory, *American Psychologist*, 44, 1175–1184.

Baraldi, C. (2001) Il significato della promozione della partecipazione sociale di bambini e adolescenti, in: Baraldi, C. (a cura di) *I diritti dei bambini e dei preadolescenti, L'Aquilone. Saggi sull'infanzia e l'adolescenza*, Roma: Donzelli Editore.

Baraldi, C. & Iervese, V. (eds) (2012) *Participation, Facilitation, and Mediation: Children and Young People in Their Social Contexts*, Oxford: Routledge.

Baraldi, C. & Rossi, E. (2002) La prevenzione delle azioni giovanili a rischio. Angeli, Milano.

Biggeri, M., Libanora, R., Mariani, S. & Menchini, L., (2006) children conceptualizing their capabilities: results of the survey during the first Children's World Congress on Child Labour, *Journal of Human Development*, 7(1): March.

Bonvin, J-M. and Galster, D. (2010) Making them employable or capable: social integration policy at the crossroads, in Otto, H-U. & Ziegler, H. (eds) *Education, Welfare and the Capabilities Approach*, Opladen: Barbara Budrich Publishers, pp. 71–84.

Corsaro, W. (2005) *The Sociology of Childhood*, Thousand Oaks, CA: Pine Forge Press.

Goffman, E. (1981) *Forms of Talk*, Philadelphia, PA: University of Pennsylvania Press.

Giddens, A. (1984) *The Constitution of Society*, Cambridge: Polity Press.

Hart, R.A. (1992) *Children's Participation: From Tokenism to Citizenship*, Florence: UNICEF.

Holahan, C.J. & Moos, R.H. (1994) 'Life stressors and mental health: advances is conceptualising stress resistance', in Avison, W.R. & Gottlib, I.H. (eds) *Stress and Mental Health: Contemporary Issues and Prospects for the Future*, New York: Plenum.

Holland, S. & O'Neill, S. (2006) 'We had to be there to make sure it was what we wanted': enabling children's participation in family decision-making through the family group conference, *Childhood*, 13(1): 91–111.

Iervese, V. (2006) (a cura di) *La gestione dialogica del conflitto: analisi di una sperimentazione con bambini e preadolescenti*, Imola: La Mandragola Editrice.

James, A., Jenks C. & Prout A. (1998) *Theorizing Childhood*, Oxford: Polity Press.

Lazarus, R.S. & Folkman, S. (1984) *Stress, Appraisal and Coping*, New York: Springer.

Philbin, A. (1996) *Capacity Building in Social Justice*, Organizations Ford Foundation.

Robeyns, I. (2006) The capability approach in practice, *Journal of Political Philosophy*, 14(3): 351–376.

Sen, A.K. (1999) *Development as Freedom*, New York: Knopf.

Tisdall, M., Davis, J.M., Hill, M. & Prout, A. (2006) *Children, Young People and Social Inclusion: Participation for What?* Bristol: Policy Press.

Concluding Remarks

Caroline Sarojini Hart, Mario Biggeri and Bernhard Babic

This book has attempted to unravel the complex relationships between the nature of youth agency and participation, in education but also in wider political economic and social arenas, and the potential young people have to lead flourishing lives they have reason to value. In these concluding remarks it is argued that sustainable development is contingent on the nature of youth agency and participation in schooling and further afield.

The capability approach is per se a powerful framework for understanding children's well-being in terms of capabilities deprivation, since it forces us to think about the complexities that characterize their lives, ranging from opportunity freedom to agency and agency freedom. Therefore, we think that child and youth agency is critical for our societies in terms of human development. For children and youths this means being able, to a varying extent (according to the maturity and the age of the child), influence his/her life and/or general rules in the society. In other words, democratic societies should aim to produce capable agents and communities. Hence, the development of a democratic society passes through an education that promotes critical, creative and caring thinking in its citizens, so as to enhance children's and youths' autonomy and, at the same time, open their minds to confrontation and cooperation with different perspectives and points of view.

However, an authentic and meaningful participation requires first a radical shift in adult thinking and behaviour from an exclusionary to an inclusionary approach for children and their capabilities, from a world defined solely by adults to one in which children contribute to build the kind of world they want to live in. This means a change in decision-making processes, for example, using participatory, non-discriminatory, inclusive and empowering approaches, particularly with regard to children and young people. For instance, by developing inclusive and participatory communication tools and channels that support children and young people to actively participate in social action. This also implies that the ongoing discussion on the post-2015 global development agenda needs not only to ensure that children remain at the heart of that agenda but to make them part of these processes for institutional changes and thus create spaces for dialogue.

We have argued that it is necessary to look beyond schools themselves in order to understand the context of education within these institutions and its juxtaposition to wider social dynamics. Indeed it is impossible to fully understand a young person's agency and well-being in school without insights regarding their life experience as a whole. There will be times when a child's educational experiences support, and are supported by, family and community. However, there will also be times when complications, diversity and dissonance may interrupt the possibility of a harmonious relationship between schooling and the individual's life experience beyond the school gates. Through the continuing struggle to address the relationship of schooling to child and youth development emerges the critical importance of taking a holistic approach towards understanding the development of child and youth humanity and capabilities across societies.

The case studies presented in Part 2 of this book have foregrounded the importance of multi-agency working, international cooperation, continued advocacy for the most vulnerable and continued efforts to develop social protection policies. These endeavours will benefit from acknowledgement of, for example, the complexities of child labour (for example, where necessary to support low-income families) and the positive and negative factors underlying resistance to schooling by some children and their families (for example, where violence and intimidation are prevalent).

There are multiple major issues affecting children and young people worldwide that reduce individual capabilities and the opportunity to live a flourishing life. Some of these relate to access to schooling, child labour, housing, sanitation and poverty. Some particularly vulnerable children include those living a life on the streets, rural females in low-income households, disabled children and those living in conflict-affected states. The issues are not limited to the global south and issues of relative poverty, out of school children, neglect and child abuse are pervasive across all societies. Whilst it remains incumbent on adults of all nations to strive to support and protect children and young people it is also essential that the crucial work to develop the agency and full participation of young generations continues and expands. Indeed, in light of the number of countries where upwards of 50 per cent of the population are aged under 18 years this has never been so vital. Sadly, conflict continues to affect many countries around the world and it is often related to poor social, economic and environmental circumstances. Hence it is often the weakest and most vulnerable that are exposed to the greatest risk. The same is true in relation to some of the most serious health risks connected to HIV and AIDS, poor sanitation and lack of access to provision for basic health care needs.

The Millennium Development Goals, the Education for All agenda and many other international strategies and initiatives have targeted education as the source of great hope in the development of societies and their young people. Significant advances have been made in many areas, for example, to increase rates of school enrolment, completion of primary-level schooling and the provision of educational resources and trained teachers. However, the figures on out of school children, non-completion rates and staff absenteeism, among others, indicate that there is no time to lose in continuing to move the education agenda forward. The contributions in this book have sought to illuminate the highly complex relationship that schools have with their local communities and national contexts. It is clear that there are still widespread disparities in the young people's experiences of school-level and civic participation and their opportunities to exercise agency vary enormously within and between societies. There are certain social markers that make some individuals more likely to be vulnerable and to experience poorer opportunities than their peers. However, it is important to continue to look for the vulnerable individuals in sectors of the population who generally fare better than others. Thus although rural females from low-income families may appear to be among the most vulnerable, there may be males from high-income urban families who also lack agency and are at risk. For example, cyber-bullying is an increasing concern with regard to children of all walks of life who have access to the internet. The relatively new phenomenon of cyber-bullying brings further invidious threats to the well-being of new generations and in some cases has led to young people taking their own lives. Thus, constant vigilance is needed to understand the changing global environment in which we live and to strive to promote and protect the capabilities of all children to flourish.

We need to start from two premises. First, there is not a binary division between schooling and the wider community. Secondly, childhood experience cannot be bounded by institutional policies and practices. Rather, there is a deep and complex relationship between formal sites of learning in schools and the broader life experiences encountered by children and young people from all backgrounds. The notion of participation is helpful in understanding the relationships that young people have in these different environments and the extent to which participation in one environment may influence participation elsewhere. The new civic discourse suggests that civic education may be more likely to produce civic engagement and yet the nature of that engagement remains underwhelming, with many children and young people lacking autonomy in determining the social context and nature of their engagement in civic society. Similarly, education about participation rights, for example, cannot be equated with the capability to experience and effect those rights. This is a significant contribution of the capability approach in thinking about how children and young people's freedoms, or capabilities, are expanded.

Putting children at the centre stage and recognizing them as rights holders, as well as social actors, implicitly highlights the necessity of building their capacities to participate, promoting capable agents and enhancing critical, creative and caring thinking for active citizenship. At the same time, giving relevance to public education for creating active citizens and fostering democracy means recognizing governments as primary duty-bearers, accountable to children and youth and to the international community. This implies also: a) creating structures and mechanisms where rights-holders have continuous dialogue with duty-bearers, b) giving priority to the role of young people in decision-making processes, and c) creating child and youth friendly environments (including spaces for dialogue among children). This includes integration and participation, as well as civic engagement and citizenship education in school and informal education systems. It is thus central to establish a long-term goal, which clearly sets out international legal frameworks that are shared between governments, donors and civil society. This should include the quest to extend the reach of children's and young people's agency and effective participation in society.

The chapters in this book foreground the fact that valuable education may take place almost any time and anywhere. Schools are just one context offering opportunities, without any doubt a crucial one, for those who experience a school education. However, as some contributions have shown, in many parts of the world primary, secondary and tertiary education is often still a privilege, and for different kinds of reasons, inaccessible in the same way for everybody. Even in wealthy societies socially selective processes can be observed, which some-times seem to be quite resistant to attempts to overcome them. As a consequence, increasing efforts towards wider accessibility of educational systems is still a central challenge for policy-makers across the globe. One of the central messages of this book is that it would be inadequate just to ask how students can be adapted to fit existing educational systems. From a capability approach perspective, the more important questions relate to how a system can be adapted to the students and their values, and how school communities can be empowered to appreciate diversity instead of understanding it as an obstacle for efficient teaching. A first step in that direction would be to develop a dialogue with young people and their families and to take the outcomes of these dialogues into account concerning the further development of curricula and schools. Furthermore, when talking about education, the scope has to be expanded beyond school and the devaluation of informal education needs to be avoided.

Obama's claim for, 'a crucible moment'[1] and Cameron's call for a 'big society'[2] may remain political rhetoric that cannot be comprehensively fulfilled in the interests of children and young people in the US and the UK. Similarly, in many other nation states, the meaning of civic engagement and participation is under-specified and lacks tangible evidence of reaching young people from all walks of life. There is a continuing challenge, inside and outside of schools, to seek new ways of supporting children and young people in developing their capabilities to participate meaningfully in all facets of social and personal life. Critical reflection in the light of Amartya Sen's capability approach suggests that the roles of young people's agency and well-being freedoms in these processes are paramount.

Notes

1 See The National Task Force on Civic Learning and Democratic Engagement (2012) *A National Call to Action. A Crucible Moment – College Learning and Democracy's Future* (Washington, Association of American Colleges and Universities).

2 See www.gov.uk/govt/speeches/pms-speech-on-big-society.

Subject Index

abuse 237, 256, 261
access
  to education 3–5, 23, 51, 57, 146, 197
  to information 57, 64, 26–2
accessibility 68, 77, 84–8, 94–7, 107, 164, 261–3
activities and play 22, 55, 73, 112
adaptive preference 227
adequate resources (inadequate) 5, 45, 49, 106–7, 148, 168
adult perception 39, 152–4, 194, 199
agency 3–8, 17, 25, 28–31, 33–5, 37, 44–5, 47, 49–53, 55, 65, 67–9, 75–6, 88–9, 112, 114, 123–7, 129, 131–2, 146–7, 154–7, 168, 182–3, 186, 190, 200, 206, 219, 225–6, 233, 238, 243–6, 255–8, 260–3
  achievement 19–20, 29
  freedom 19–20, 29, 35–7, 47, 50–1, 84, 89, 156, 227, 246, 260
aspiration 17–9, 25, 29, 38, 45, 52, 57, 84, 89, 91, 95–8, 131, 148, 181–91, 193, 197, 200, 228
  dynamic multidimensional model of 189
  family related barriers to 38, 181, 191–3
  formation 97, 184
  school related barriers to 38, 181, 195
  set 183
attitude towards the child by parents/caregivers 131, 154
autonomy 11, 25, 28, 37, 45, 51–2, 69, 84, 86, 88, 90–1, 93, 95–8, 127, 146, 149, 153, 155, 165, 182, 225–7, 234–5, 245, 247, 260, 263

barriers 10, 146
basic needs 85, 262
basic needs approach 85
behaviour 26, 37, 50, 56–7, 105, 137, 167, 187–8, 191, 219, 233, 251, 253, 260
being a friend 127, 172, 200
being creative (creativity) 34–5, 51, 55, 124, 132, 135–6, 139, 226–7, 253, 260, 263
binding constraints 194–6
bonds 237
budget set 107
built environment 76
bullying 6, 262

capabilities 2, 17
  basic 21, 112, 146, 155, 157
  evaluating/evaluation of 140
  evolving 9, 46–9, 52, 54, 56–7, 139, 178, 226
  group 53, 164, 169–74
  and rights 18–19
capability
  approach 1–3, 6, 8–10, 17–9, 20–30, 36–9, 44–49, 51–2, 55, 63–8, 84–6, 101, 124, 139, 145, 155, 158–9, 163, 168, 181, 200, 207–8, 219, 226, 243, 246, 260–4
  collective 114, 158
  freedom from economic and non-economic exploitation 148–50
  identity (tradition, culture) 86, 147, 154, 248, 257
  individual 20, 38, 55, 69, 158, 207, 261
  leisure and leisure activities 65, 68, 74, 206

life and physical health 20, 25, 49, 107, 167, 182, 208
love and care 50, 208
meta- 20–1
to participate 1, 33–4, 44–5, 47, 51–3, 56–7, 65–7, 69, 75–7, 79, 87, 95, 109, 112, 125, 128, 133–4, 139, 153–4, 156–8, 178, 243–5, 249, 257–8, 263–4
personal autonomy (as agency) 11, 25, 28, 37, 45, 51–2, 69, 88–91, 93, 95–7, 149, 153, 155, 182, 225–8, 234–5, 245, 247
plan/imagine/think 53, 55, 57, 135, 155, 187–8, 193, 263
respect (dignity) 21, 25, 45, 47, 56, 114, 136, 145, 150, 155–6
selection 101, 112, 114
set 29, 47, 49, 55, 66, 108, 114, 158, 183, 226, 246
shelter and environment 146
social 250
to aspire 11, 20, 29, 49, 52, 154, 182–4, 201
to be educated 20, 49–50, 208
to bodily integrity and safety 25
understand/interpret 6, 53, 56–7, 135
capacity 47, 49–50, 55, 66–8, 77–9, 111, 126, 138, 148–9, 153–5, 226–8, 238, 245–6, 249, 256
capital
    cultural 68, 176
    human 1, 18, 24, 30, 46–7, 50, 68, 158, 206–7, 230
    social 68, 108, 225, 230, 236–7
caregivers 22, 163, 174, 177
Central Human Functional Capabilities 20–1, 25, 93
child
    active actor 6, 24, 34, 44–5, 51, 53, 56–7, 75, 78–9, 124–6, 133, 135, 139, 164, 166–9, 253, 255–6, 260, 263
    agent 244–5
    attitude towards 32, 154
    labour 8, 11, 94, 96, 107, 203–7, 211–8
    poverty 10, 101, 104, 106–7, 109, 113–5
    well-being 1–4, 11, 50, 88–9, 91, 93, 95, 109–10, 112–15, 146, 158, 164, 207–8, 211, 219, 244, 248, 260, 262, 264

child's choice 44, 49, 52–3, 66, 68–9, 86, 88, 93, 125, 146–9, 155–7, 167, 177, 193, 232, 245
childhood 6–7, 21–2
    culture of 244–5, 252
    sociology 124
children
    municipal council of 56, 248, 252, 254
    and research 28–36, 38
    well-being 1–4, 11, 18–20, 24, 27, 29, 35, 37, 47, 49, 50–1, 53, 69, 70 83, 87–89, 91, 93, 95, 107–10, 112–15, 127–8, 130, 146, 158, 164, 207–8, 211, 219, 225–6, 228, 230, 232, 238, 243–4, 246, 248, 260–2, 264
    rights 9, 11, 18–19, 22–3, 36–8, 45, 49, 51, 56, 63–79, 107, 110–14, 133, 135, 148, 150, 155–6, 159, 186, 212, 243, 248–52, 254–6, 258, 263
    self realisation 45
choice
    autonomy of 243
    freedom of 66, 101, 105, 108
    pathways 152, 182
    responsible 245
class 23, 51, 87, 93, 96–8, 129, 195, 231, 248
collective agency 127
conception of good 115, 208, 217, 251
conditions of life 95, 101, 104–8, 147, 154, 212–13, 248, 251, 255
connexions advisor 197
control 31, 95, 97–8, 110, 126–7, 147–8, 155, 165, 190–2, 200
control group 206
convention on the Rights of the Child (CRC) 18, 22–3, 28, 49, 63–9, 75, 77–8,
conversion factors 11, 23, 47, 55, 66, 69, 107–8, 114, 139, 181–5, 190, 200, 207, 246–7
CRC *see* convention on the Rights of the Child
    CRC Article 12 22, 36, 64, 68, 77–9, 81, 148
critical self-examination 25, 111
culture 21–2, 31, 47, 124, 132, 165, 195, 233–4, 244–5, 252
curriculum 129, 131–2, 134, 136, 139, 208
cyber-bullying 262

debate 3, 8, 21, 23, 27, 44, 57–8, 63, 65, 76, 78, 83, 88, 113, 155, 245
decision-making 8–9, 44–5, 50–1, 57, 66, 76, 123, 125–7, 134, 139, 148–50, 153, 176, 200, 249, 260
deliberative processes 49, 125
democracy 9, 37, 49, 52, 67, 124–8, 132–40, 263–4
democratic participation 8, 126
developing countries 225, 234
dimension / domain 1–2, 10, 23, 26–7, 55, 70–2, 76, 91, 93, 101, 106–7, 112, 114, 125–6, 130–9, 146, 181, 229–30, 233
disability 147, 150, 152–3, 159, 185, 211
disadvantage 88, 126, 149, 170, 204
discourse 7–8, 17–18, 21–2, 31, 51, 55, 75–8, 124, 136–8, 151, 182, 191, 263
discrimination 252

economic
    development 17
    growth 47, 135
education
    and the capability approach 24–6
    in schools 3–4
    instrumental role of 50
    intrinsic value of 51
    quality of 210, 219
    special educational needs/special education 10, 145, 150, 156, 159, 185–6
education for all programme EFA 204, 210
EFA *see* education for all programme
emotions 25, 53, 76, 111, 185, 192
employment 22, 95, 135, 154, 174, 189, 214–6, 218
empowerment 25, 44–5, 53, 200
entitlements 18, 21–2, 47, 66
equality 25, 28–9, 84–5, 128, 156
equivalence scales 10, 101–7
ethnicity 68
evaluation 1, 3, 10–11, 29, 46, 52, 72, 75, 77, 97, 108–9, 127, 155, 165–71, 177–8, 199
evaluative framework 9, 24
every child matters 18
evolving capacities 64, 69
exclusion 133–4, 153
expectations 6, 31, 37, 150–3, 164, 171–5, 183, 247, 250, 253–4, 257–8

facilities 103
family and friends 5, 47, 53, 69, 72–3, 87, 91, 94, 97, 127, 164, 172–3, 175–6, 181–3, 187, 191–5, 198–200, 205–6, 210–14, 217–18, 230–7, 251–2, 257, 261, 263
Focus Group Discussion (FGD) 70, 72, 163–4, 169–73, 177, 181, 248–9, 254, 256, 258
freedom 1–2, 18–19, 20, 25, 29, 35, 37, 44, 47, 49–52, 56, 63–9, 77, 79, 83–9, 93–5, 101, 105, 108–12, 114, 125, 127–8, 132, 134, 136–7, 146–7, 155–6, 159, 167–8, 183, 185, 200, 219, 226–7, 235, 246, 260, 263–4
functionings
    combination of 19, 108, 246
    list of 108, 113

gender 3–4, 10, 23, 25, 68, 74, 87, 89–93, 96, 214–15, 218–19,
gender equality 25
grade repetition 204

happiness 19, 83, 108, 130
HDCA *see* Human Development and Capability Association
HDCA's thematic group on children's capabilities 58
higher education 24–5, 28, 181–2, 186, 191, 194, 197, 199–200, 214
HIV *see* human immunodeficiency virus
human development 1, 17, 28, 44, 46–7, 52, 58, 63, 84, 86, 88, 94, 96, 123–5, 132, 134–8, 157, 187, 194, 243, 260
Human Development and Capability Association 58
human development report 194
human flourishing 25, 44, 47, 51–7, 88, 200
human immunodeficiency virus HIV 22, 262
human rights 18, 28, 67, 77, 110, 139, 149, 209, 230
humanity 24, 37, 88, 129, 145, 261

identity 30, 33, 76, 86, 147, 154, 248, 257
ILO *see* International Labour Organization
ILO Convention Minimum Age convention number 138, 212

ILO Convention Worst Forms of Child
　　Labour number 182, 212
International Labour Organization ILO
　　204–5, 212
inclusion 8, 56, 73, 94, 126, 132–4, 138–9,
　　150, 159, 166–7
income poverty 101–5
individualism 67
information 28, 57, 64–5, 73, 104, 127, 188,
　　192, 196, 213–14, 217
inter-subjectivity 55

justice 1–3, 7, 9, 17, 20–1, 26, 83–5, 128,
　　133–4, 152, 155, 165, 231

labour 8, 11, 51, 94, 96, 107, 203–18, 261
labour (jobs, working activity, work)
　　hazardous 211–12
learning 25, 30, 35–6, 38, 52, 53, 55, 57, 123,
　　131, 134, 137, 146, 150–1, 156, 174–7,
　　185, 207, 210, 247, 262
leisure 65, 68, 74, 77, 206
life good 47, 105, 115, 208
literacy 25, 210
loci of control 191
logical reasoning 53

mapping 189
marginalization 149
marriage 194, 211
method 3, 10–11, 22, 27–8, 30, 32, 38, 55,
　　63, 74, 90, 93, 103, 105, 109, 126–9,
　　163, 165–7, 169–70, 231, 236, 248
millennium development goals 7, 23, 262
model 28, 46–7, 55, 63, 70–1, 76, 84, 86–91,
　　93, 95–7, 114, 123, 127, 159, 173,
　　175–7, 183–8, 195, 214–17, 219
　　of change 187–8
　　of transition, see transition

national curriculum 209
navigation 190
needs life cycle and emerge 51, 164
normative framework 67
Nussbaum 's list 93, 112
nutrition 187

OECD 102–3, 164
operationalization 93, 106, 115

opportunity 1, 11, 29, 31–3, 37, 45, 47, 50,
　　52, 64, 78, 85–6, 91, 105, 110, 126–8,
　　131–4, 137–8, 140, 145, 147, 153–4,
　　156, 158, 164, 167, 169, 172–3, 176,
　　178, 185, 189, 205, 236–7, 244, 247,
　　249, 254, 260–1

participation
　　democratic 8, 126
　　social 11, 56–7, 131, 139, 157, 243, 248,
　　255–7
participatory methods 30, 176
paternalism 88–9, 105, 108
pedagogy 34, 53, 55, 135, 166
photography 169
planning 189–90
platforms 193
play 5–6, 22, 25, 38, 49, 55, 73–5, 78, 87–8,
　　112, 114, 123–4, 133, 145–6, 149, 156,
　　158, 190–2, 207, 226, 234, 236
policy 2, 4, 7, 17–18, 29, 38, 45–19, 53, 55,
　　57, 110, 126, 133, 148–9, 170, 178, 181,
　　208, 219, 257
policy implications 45, 53
poverty 1–2, 8, 10, 23, 101–9, 113–15,
　　163–4, 167–8, 205, 211, 214, 229, 261
poverty line 101–5
power 26, 28, 31, 37, 51, 77–9, 89, 97, 112,
　　124, 129, 131, 151, 169–70, 187, 225,
　　231, 234–5
preferences 72, 75, 83, 96–7, 127, 188, 199,
　　227
professionals 196
promotion 45, 51, 57, 242, 247–8, 254–7
protection (entitlement to) 63, 95, 148–9,
　　218, 243, 254, 261
public deliberation 9, 26, 49, 57, 127–8

qualitative analysis 10, 27, 67, 89, 97, 165–6,
　　169, 225, 228, 244, 248, 258
quality of life 147, 154, 208
quantitative analysis 27, 67, 89, 165–6, 244,
　　248, 258
questionnaire 94, 248

reason to value 1–2, 6, 18–19, 25, 37–8, 44,
　　52, 66, 83, 108, 113, 146–7, 150, 154,
　　159, 167, 181, 183, 185, 199–200, 227,
　　260

recognition 25, 57, 79, 111, 157, 167, 233
research 26–7
  and the capability approach 27–33
resilience 11, 176, 188, 190, 199, 227–8, 237
resources 1, 18, 26, 47, 55, 66, 85, 106–8, 114, 154–5, 158, 163–4, 167, 176, 181, 183–4, 200, 206, 208–9, 217–18, 229, 246, 254, 256, 262
responsibility 3, 45, 51, 53, 56, 94–8, 114, 137, 145, 148–9, 156–7, 186, 197
rights 9, 11, 18–24, 28–9, 31, 36, 38, 49, 51, 56, 63–9, 72, 74–9, 107, 110, 113–14, 133, 139, 146–9, 156, 186, 209, 212, 230, 243, 248–52, 254–5, 258, 263
Robeyns' procedure 25

satisfaction 95, 108
schooling 4–6
scoping 188
self-determination 45, 88, 125, 139, 154–5, 246
self-esteem 157, 202
SEMs *see* structural equation models 10, 84, 90–2
senses, imagination 25, 30, 52–3, 57, 111, 132, 137, 168
social arrangements 1, 49, 183
social justice 1–3, 7, 17, 21, 85, 155
social life 75, 139, 182, 247
social mobility 205
sorcery 225, 228–37
sports 73, 172, 193
standard of living 10, 83, 87, 102–5, 109
structural equation models 10, 84, 90–2
studies disability 185
support 10–1, 23, 25, 33–8, 70, 94, 132, 148, 150, 154, 157, 159, 173, 175–7, 187–8, 193–200, 210–11, 214, 219, 232, 251, 255–6, 260–1, 264
synchronicity 193

threshold 20–1, 29, 88, 106, 109
transition, 181–2, 185–201
  model 187–8

UN *see* United Nations
UNESCO *see* United Nations Educational, Scientific, and Cultural Organization
UNICEF *see* The United Nations Children's Fund
United Kingdom 5–7, 11, 18, 25, 30, 58, 181, 186, 191, 264
United Nations UN 3, 9, 18, 23, 36, 63, 113, 148, 209
United Nations Educational, Scientific, and Cultural Organization, UNESCO 3–5, 23, 46, 132
The United Nations Children's Fund, UNICEF 2, 56, 103, 107, 205, 212
utilitarianism 18, 46

value instrumental 29, 51, 94, 208
value intrinsic 1, 51, 94, 127, 146, 155, 168
valuing 137
victim 233–7
voice 8, 10, 25, 29, 31, 47, 52, 75, 77–8, 145–59, 176

WB *see* World Bank
welfare 1, 7, 51, 85, 148, 165
well-becoming 53, 208, 219
well-being achievement 19–20, 29
well-being freedom 19, 29, 50, 226, 246, 264
widening participation 181
witchcraft 225, 229, 231, 233, 237–8
work 2, 5–6, 8–9, 11, 18, 22, 24, 28, 30, 34, 36–8, 50, 68, 73, 76, 93–4, 96, 98, 112, 115, 123–4, 129–30, 132, 134, 137, 146–7, 153, 158, 163–4, 167, 169, 173–8, 182–3, 185–7, 198, 204–9, 211–2, 214, 219, 227–8, 251, 256, 261
World Bank , WB 209–10

Author Index

Addabbo, Tindara, 99
Agarwal, Bina 103
Aguilar Molina, Javier 230
Alanen, Leena 246
Alderson, Priscilla 28, 36
Alkire, Sabina 58, 66, 109, 112, 114, 127
Al-Rousan, Sataneeh 204, 206
Anand, Paul 93
Andresen, Sabine 88, 208
Anich, Rudolf 226
Antonio, Rachele 94
Apablaza, Mauricio 112, 114
Appadurai, Arun 182, 189, 201
Armstrong, Ann Cheryl 159
Armstrong, Derrick 159
Arnot, Madeleine 31, 151
Asogwa, Simon E. 205
Atkinson, Anthony Barnes 115

Babic, Bernhard 6, 58, 112,, 244, 246
Ballet, Jérôme 30, 47, 50, 124, 125, 158, 177,
    208, 221, 226, 233, 246
Bandura, Albert 224, 245
Banerjee, Sushmita R. 205
Baraldi, Claudio 45, 243, 244, 247, 253
Bartelheimer, Peter 114
Barton, Len 147
Basu, Kaushik 205, 219
Bates, Richard, 3
Bauer, Elaine 94
Becker, Gary S. 24
Bellanca, Nicolò 226-7
Berger, Peter Ludwig 67, 70, 77
Berges, Sandrine 23
Bernstein, Basil 151
Bhalotra, Sonia 205

Biaya, Tshikala K. 235
Biddulph, Chris 175
Biddulph, Fred 175
Biddulph, Jeanne 175
Biggeri, Mario 25, 27, 34, 39, 45-6, 48-9,
    50-3, 55-7, 66, 95, 109, 112, 114, 123,
    125-6, 133, 135, 139, 140, 154, 158,
    168, 206-8, 219, 226, 243-4, 246, 203
Bint-Talal, Basmah 209
Blumer, B. 70
Bolzan, Natalie 67
Bonnet, Michel 207
Bonvin, Jean-Michel 32, 46, 63, 66, 244, 246
Booth, Tony 153
Bornstein, Marc H. 168
Bourdieu, Pierre 23, 68, 185, 201
Boyden, Jo 45
Bradshaw, Jonathan, 2
Bridges, David 199
Bridges, William 187, 193, 195
Brighouse, Harry 3, 24, 26, 50-1, 113-14,
    148
Brown, Ann L. 53, 57, 137
Buhmann, Brigitte 103
Burchardt, Tania 28, 159
Buriel, Raymond 94
Burton, Linda 94

Cagatay, Nilufer 225
Calder, Gideon 134
Carter, Ian 99
Chau, Nancy H. 205
Chaubey, Jay 205
Christensen, Pia 21, 32
Cigno, Alessandro 207, 214
Clark, David, 114

Clark, Zoë 24, 80
Cohen, Gerald A. 109
Comaroff, Jean 2301 235
Comaroff, John L. 231, 234
Comim, Flavio 2, 49, 66, 93, 114, 125,
    168–9, 198
Cooke, Bill 127
Coram, Thomas 94
Corsaro, William A. 32, 124, 243
Crocker, David A. 124, 126–7

Dalbert, Claudia 95
Davis, John Bryan 113
De Boeck, Filip 229, 233–4, 236
De Herdt, Tom 229–30
De Villers, Gauthier 229
De Vos, Klaas 104
Dee, Lesley 186
Delanaye, Paul 235
De Ment, Terri 99
Deneulin, Severine 114, 125
Desjeux, Dominique 232
Deuchar, Ross 151
Devecchi, Cristina 31, 141, 146
Dewey, John 71, 128–30, 132, 135, 140
Di Masi, Diego 34, 123, 136, 139, 141
Di Tommaso, Maria Laura 34, 123, 136,
    139
Douglas, Mary 230
Dowding, Keith, 99
Downey, Jayne A. 176
Dowse, Leanne 151
Drèze, Jean 17, 125–6, 146
Drydyk, Jay 128
Dubois, Jean-Luc 52
Duflo, Esther 189
Dumbi, Claudine 229–30, 232
Duray-Soundron, C. 66
Durkheim, Émile 146
Dworkin, Ronald 106

Edmonds, Eric V. 207
Edwards, Michael 154, 234
Elias, Norbert 71, 75–6
Ellis, Carolyn 76
Elson, Diane 232
Engeström, Yrjö 123
Englund, Harri 231, 233
Esping-Andersen, Gøsta 207

Evans, Karen 49
Evans-Pritchard, Edward Evan 233

Facchinetti, Gisella, 99
Falangani, Mvondo Pashi 229
Farvaque, Nicolas 66
Faulkner, Dorothy 31
Faulstich, Orellana 94
Feeny, Thomas 45
Fegter, Susann 208
Fielding, Michael 151
Fisher, Robert . 33
Fisiy, Cyprian F. 231
Flaherty, Michael 76
Florian, Lani 147
Folkman, Susan 251
Freeman, Melissa 66, 139, 169
Freire, Paulo 23, 49, 166–7

Galster, Déborah 244, 246
Ganzeboom, Harry 93, 95
Gasper, Des 84, 86–8
Gassmann, Franziska 107
Geschiere, Peter 231, 237
Gharaibeh, Muntaha 204
Giavonola, Benedetta 113
Gibbard, Allan 106
Giddens, Antony 71, 77, 226–8, 238, 245
Giovannoni, Marco 225
Giri, Ananta Kumar 113
Goffman, Erving 75–6, 254
Graf, Gunter 112–13
Grasso, Marco 114
Grootaert, Christiaan 206
Guala, Francesco 99
Guba, Egon G. 27
Guske, Iris 94, 97

Habermas, Jurgen 31, 46, 138
Haddad, Lawrence J. 103
Hallett, Christine 45
Hand, Michael, 28
Hansen, Jim H. 159
Hart, Caroline Sarojini 17–20, 27–9, 39,
    45, 49, 52, 159, 181–3, 189, 201, 257,
    259
Hart, Roger A. 76, 92, 254, 257
Haveman, Robert 207
Hawamdeh, S. 212

Heady, Christopher 205
Heckman, James J. 46, 207
Hedge, Nikki, 8
Hennessey, Eilis 169
Hinchliffe, Geoff, 12
Hoare, Carol H. 175
Hodkinson, Alan 159
Hoeman, Shirley 204
Holahan, Charles J. 251
Holland, Sally 249
Hook, Sidney 128
Horgan, G. 152
Horna Pedron, Marisa 226
Hughes, Carolyn 232
Hulme, David 114
Hunter, Graham, 99
Hymer, Barry 33

Iervese, Vittorio 32, 49, 243–4

Jacoby, Hanan G. 206
James, Allison 6, 21–3, 30, 32, 45, 123–4,
    177, 244–5
Jurkovic, Gregory J. 94

Kabeer, Naila 232
Kanbur, Ravi 103, 206
Kellett, Mary 30, 34
Kellock, Anne 32
Kelly, Anthony 24
Kelsen, Hans 128
King, E.M. 219
Kittay, Eva Feder 155
Kline, Rex 90
Kline, Susan L. 90, 138
Kohler, Ulrich 217
Kothari, Uma 127
Kozulin, Alex 123
Kreuter, Frauke 217
Kruger, Diana 207

Lallau, Benoît 229–30, 232
Lalor, Kevin J. 232
Lame, Danielle de 233
Lansdown, Gerison 45, 107, 113–14, 148
Last, M. 232
Lavy, Victor C. 207
Lawson, Hazel 151
Lawthom, Rebecca 32

Lazarus, Richard S. 251
Legum, Harry L. 175
Leßmann, Ortrud 99, 109, 111, 113–14
Levine, Irene S. 169
Libanora, Renato 99, 126, 140
Lincoln, Yvonna S. 27
Lipman, Matthew 33–4, 46, 55, 129–30, 132,
    134–7
Littleton, Karen S. 170
Lloyd, Cynthia B. 206
Lopez-Calva, Louis F. 194
Lucchini, Riccardo 70
Lücker-Babel, Marie-Françoise 66, 77
Luckmann, Thomas 67, 70, 77
Lukes, Steven 67

MacConville, Ruth 151
Macleod, Colin M. 110, 113
Madungu Tumwaka. 232, 235
Malandi, K. 235
Marguerat, Yves 232
Mason, Jan 67
Mathison, Sandra 169
Matthews, Hugh 45, 52, 56
Mauthner, Melanie 169
Mayall, Berry 123
McBurney, Donald H. 75
McCall, Leslie 93
McLeod, Alison 167, 170
Mead, George Herbert 69, 71, 129
Meenakshi, N. Mehta 205
Mehrotra, Santosh 27
Miller, David 114
Mingat, Alain 207
Mithaug, Dennis 159
Molinari, Luisa 32
Monnier, P. 229
Monzenu, M. 232
Moos, Rudolf H. 250
Morrow, Virginia 36, 76
Munby, Stephen 151
Musenge, Mzanza, 236
Muta, Hiromitsu 209
Muwalawala, Kipanda 220
Mvuezolo Bazonzi, J. 234

Neill, Alexander S. 24
Nevo, Baruch 137
Nibell, L.N. 67

Nieuwenhuys, Olga 168
Nozick, Robert 110
Nussbaum, Martha 2, 20–1, 24–5, 29, 39, 46,
    51–3, 55, 66, 69, 80, 84–5, 89, 93, 95,
    98–9, 106, 109, 111–13, 128, 135, 141,
    146–7, 155–7, 201
Nzeza Bilakila, A. 230

O'Kane, Claire 32
O'Leary, Kevin 153
O'Neill, Onora 65, 165–6
O'Neill, Sean 249
Oliverio, Stefano 136
Ortiz, Isabel 163
Otto, Hans-Uwe 49

Paige-Smith, Alice 151
Palincsar, Annemarie Sullivan 137
Passeron, Jean-Claude 23
Patrinos, Harry Anthony 205–6, 218
Pavcnik, Nina 207
Perelman, Chaim 129
Philbin, Ann 256
Phipps, Shelley 112
Pirot, Bernard 230
Pring, Richard 27
Prochaska, James O. 187–8
Prout, Alan 27, 45, 52, 56
Psacharopoulos, George 205–6
Pufall, Peter 65, 70

Qizilbash, Mozaffar 113
Qvortrup, Jean 124

Radja, Katia 52
Ranjan, Priya 205
Rawls, John 84, 106, 110, 149
Raynor, JANET 23
Reay, Diane 31, 151
Reinecke, Jost 91
Resnick, Lauren B. 123
Reznitskaya, Alina 30
Riddell, Sheila 154
Rix, Jonathan 151
Roberts, Helen 32
Robeyns, Ingrid 18, 24–5, 29, 46, 107, 109,
    114, 158, 185, 208, 243
Roche, Josè Manuel 112
Roelen, Keetie 102, 107

Roggero, Paola 212
Rogoff, Barbara 45, 131
Rosati, Fulvio Camillo 207
Rose, Richard 141, 151, 159
Ross, Gail 32
Rossi, Elisa 49, 253
Rousseau, Sophie 228
Ruel, Malcolm 230
Runswick-Cole, Katherine 159

Sadlowski, Iris 3
Saito, Madoko 3, 84, 110
Salomon, Gavrieland 137
Santi, Marina 136–9
Sasaki, Ryo 210
Savaglio, Ernesto 106
Schischka, John A. 159, 169
Sen, Amartya Kumar 1–2, 17–21, 24, 29,
    34, 44, 47, 49, 51, 66, 69, 80, 84, 86,
    88–9, 102, 106–7, 109–12, 114, 125,
    134, 146, 149, 155, 167–8, 176–7, 181,
    200, 207, 225, 227, 246
Shahani, Lila 125
Shepherd, Jessica 200
Shevlin, Michael 141, 151
Siddiqi, Faraaz 205, 218
Simmel, Georg 67
Skoufias, Emmanuel 206
Soloaga, Isidro 194
Spencer, Nick 204, 212
Stewart, Frances 114
Stoecklin, Daniel 32, 63, 70–2
Sutcliffe, Roger 33
Swain, Peter 169

Tagore, Rabindranath 24
Tan, Jee-Peng 207
Terzi, Lorella 4, 12, 20, 24–5, 146, 186,
    246
Teschl, Miriam 113–14
Tilstone, Christine 159
Tisdall, E. Kay M. 243
Tollen, Eric 229
Toulmin, Stephen E. 129
Trabelsi, Milène 52
Trani, Jean-Francois 2, 48, 186
Trefon, Theodore 229–30
Treseder, Phil 76
Tzannatos, Zafiris 219

Unsworth, Richard P. 65, 70
Unterhalter, Elaine 3–4, 23–4, 26, 28, 40, 44,
    46, 50–2, 56, 58, 113, 146

Van Bueren, G. 66
Van Hees, Martin 93, 99
Van Ootegem, Luc 93
Venkatapuram, Sridhar 20, 39
Verhellen, Eugeen 66
Verhofstadt, Elsy 93
Vitello, Stanley J. 159
Vizard, Polly 66
Volkert, Jurgen 112, 114
Vorhaus, John 147
Vygotsky, Lev S. 123, 131

Walker, Melanie 1, 4, 12, 25, 46–7, 49, 56,
    113, 146
Wallace, Belle 34–6, 39

Wegerif, Rupert 138
Wehmeyer, Michael L. 151
Wenger, Etienne 23
Westcott, Helen L. 170
Wolfe, Barbara 207
Wood, David 137
Woodhead, Martin 31
Wright, Hazel, 1
Wüst, Kirsten 112, 114

Yacub, Shahin 168
Yalonetzky, Gaston 112, 114
Young, I. Marion 112, 126

Zaidi, Asghar M. 104
Zermatten, Jean 64
Ziegler, Holger 49
Zimmerman, Jane D. 169
Zinnecker, Jürgen 96

CPSIA information can be obtained at www.ICGtesting.com
Printed in the USA
LVOW04s1949211015

459193LV00004B/48/P